Challenge and Change in Language Teaching

Editors

Jane Willis & Dave Willis

Heinemann

Heinemann English Language Teaching
A division of Reed Educational and Professional Publishing Ltd
Halley Court, Jordan Hill, Oxford OX2 8EJ

OXFORD MADRID FLORENCE ATHENS PRAGUE SÃO PAULO
MEXICO CITY CHICAGO PORTSMOUTH (NH) TOKYO SINGAPORE
KUALA LUMPUR MELBOURNE AUCKLAND JOHANNESBURG
IBADAN GABORONE

ISBN 0 435 26606 3

Design by Hilary Norman
Layout by Newton Harris

Acknowledgements

We are grateful to HarperCollins*Publishers* for permission to
reproduce the extracts on pages 71-2 (Collins COBUILD English
Course Book 2), 73-4 (Collins COBUILD English Course Book 3)
and 98 (Collins COBUILD English Course Book 1).

The excerpts on pages 158-166 are reproduced by permission of the
University of Cambridge Local Examinations Syndicate.

The photographs on pages 161-2 are by Petrina Cliff.

Printed and bound in Great Britain
by the Bath Press, Bath

97 98 99   10 9 8 7 6 5 4 3 2

CONTENTS

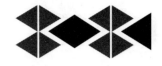

Introduction

Much of the language produced in language classrooms is language for display. Teachers offer students a model of the language forms which provide the focus of a particular lesson. They produce model sentences and ask learners to repeat. They ask questions designed to elicit specific responses which practise the target form for a particular lesson. In a lesson on *Likes and Dislikes,* for example, a teacher will ask questions designed to elicit responses such as *I like playing tennis; I don't like watching television* and so on. These activities are designed to ensure a precise focus on the forms under study. Teachers control the form of student responses by shaping them towards the desired form:

> T: Do you like watching television?
> S: Yes, I like.
> T: Yes, good. Listen to the question though. Do you like watching television?
> S: Yes, I like watching.
> T: I like watching television.
> S: I like watching television.

If you look at the sequence of utterances above you will see that it could only happen in a language classroom. Sequences like this are not intended to have any real communicative content. They are designed to focus on form.

Nowadays, however, there is a general acceptance that language learners need plenty of opportunities for language use. By language use we mean the production and comprehension of language to achieve some communicative objective. Carefully designed games and problem-solving activities are used to provide opportunities for this. Discussions are carefully organized to ensure real student participation. There is a range of techniques for encouraging learners to produce language in the context of reading and listening activities. Teachers employ sophisticated information gap and opinion gap techniques to promote interaction on a range of topics and issues. We have on the one hand a basic methodology which focuses clearly on language forms. We have on the other hand a range of established techniques which provide opportunities for communication in the classroom. The challenge is to propose a methodological framework which integrates formal and communicative activities.

In theory there is no difficulty in combining a focus on form and a focus on communication. One very widely used approach which aims to do just this is based on a three-part cycle:

Presentation

The teacher highlights a particular form for study. The form is contextualized in some way to make the meaning clear. Learners are encouraged to produce the target form under careful teacher control until they produce it with some consistency.

Practice

The teacher begins to relax control. Perhaps learners are encouraged to ask each other questions to elicit a response of the appropriate form or perhaps pictures are used to elicit the response.

Production

When the teacher feels reasonably confident that learners are able to produce the required form the lesson moves on to the production stage, sometimes called the free stage. This usually takes the form of a roleplay or discussion or problem-solving activity in which the target form has a high likelihood of occurrence. The important thing here is that learners are no longer working under close teacher control. The focus at this stage is said to be on language use. Learners are engaged in the negotiation of meaning in a context which requires the use of the target form.

This methodological cycle, often referred to by the acronym PPP, is so widely accepted that it now forms the basis of many teacher training courses. Indeed on some teacher training courses this is the *only* methodology offered to trainees. Yet all of the contributors to this collection of papers have some doubts about this dominant approach to English language teaching. Some accept the cycle as one way of teaching in certain circumstances, but believe that other teaching cycles and sequences should have a similar prominence. Other contributors have serious doubts about the principles which underlie the PPP sequence.

The dissatisfaction within the ELT profession with a PPP methodology is, I believe, well-founded and widespread. Skehan (Paper 3) goes so far as to say:

> The underlying theory for a PPP approach has now been discredited. The belief that a precise focus on a particular form leads to learning and automatization (that learners will learn what is taught in the order in which it is taught) no longer carries much credibility in linguistics or psychology.

Many teachers would reinforce these doubts on the basis of their experience in the classroom. We know all too well from bitter experience that what is 'taught' is not always learned.

We have all taught carefully prepared and apparently successful lessons only to discover later that what learners appeared to have learned they had not really learned at all. Question tags, for example, are notoriously resistant to teaching.

They play a large part in many English courses, but no matter how often they are presented it takes a long time before learners begin to use them consistently. But the PPP approach appears to be based on the assumption that what is taught is indeed learned. We believe that we are justified in focusing precisely on one particular item because this ensures that the item will be assimilated by learners in the presentation and practice stages of the lesson and will therefore be available for use in the production stage. The research into second language learning, however, suggests that this does not happen. However hard we may work at it, we cannot predict what learners are going to learn at a given time. Not only do they often fail to assimilate what has been explicitly taught: they often assimilate language which has not been 'taught' at all. Quite clearly the business of learning is much more complex than anything that can be accounted for within a presentation methodology.

Woodward (Paper 1) suggests that the profession is at a stage of 'paradigm shift'. There is dissatisfaction with the dominant paradigm, but there is no clear consensus as to the way forward. There is a fear, often openly expressed, that one rigid methodology will simply be replaced with another. This fear is understandable, but it should not prevent us from challenging existing practice. There is, of course, the danger of 'throwing out the baby with the bath water'. This very metaphor is often invoked in defence of the status quo. Again this danger should be recognized. But again it does not relieve us of the responsibility of searching for viable alternatives.

On the one hand we have a profession which is informed by established practice. On the other hand that practice is challenged by theory and also by the experience of many practitioners. We must take these challenges seriously. One thing is sure. If teachers are to be able to offer their learners a range of language learning activities, if they want to find out how best to meet the needs of their students, if they are to take full advantage of a range of teaching materials and to keep abreast of new teaching opportunities, then they need to adapt to new values, new approaches to language, to learning and to students. They need to assimilate a range of new techniques and procedures. They need to be prepared to experiment and innovate.

This collection of papers addresses the challenge of innovation. There are plenty of ideas around for what might be done to enrich teaching and teacher training. What we have tried to do here is draw together some of those ideas. In selecting and commissioning material for the book we have tried to anticipate the kind of concerns teachers have and the kind of questions they want answered. All of the papers are written by people who wish to explore and extend classroom practice in ways which they hope will be of use not only to themselves but to others as well.

As the title says, this book sets out to explore challenge and change in language teaching. Innovative proposals should be based on theory. That theory must be realized through an appropriate methodology. But theory and application should not be taken for granted, so research and evaluation have a place in any programme of change. Such programmes also need careful management if they are to be assimilated within an institution. Finally, if they are to have any lasting impact, the values and principles which lie behind any innovation must be transmitted to the profession through teacher training and education. All these aspects of change are covered in this volume. We hope that you will find it challenging, and that you will find the challenge relevant to your own teaching.

Dave Willis

Theoretical Perspectives

his section looks first at a particular theory of change and then at the theoretical basis for innovation in TEFL. In Paper 1 Woodward draws on Kuhn's theory of paradigm shift. This provides a background for the understanding of change. Woodward then goes on to look at change in the ELT profession, anticipating the ways we, as readers, may react to the papers in this book and the implications they carry.

Like other disciplines, English language teaching normally works within a dominant paradigm, a broadly defined set of values and procedures to which practitioners subscribe. This paradigm has powerful advantages. It provides a common framework for the transmission of knowledge and experience. It unites the participants in the process – learners, teachers, teacher trainers, academics – around a set of shared values. But, as Woodward points out, the benefits of the paradigm must be balanced against its drawbacks:

> One of the good things about having a shared paradigm in a professional community is that it helps members to talk to each other. One of the drawbacks is that it hinders discussion with people from other communities working inside different paradigms.

The paradigm is also a source of tension *within* a given community, particularly when a dominant paradigm is challenged. The dominant paradigm in ELT faces challenge. It is challenged by new views of language learning, by new language descriptions and by new values which emphasize the centrality of the learner. 'How,' asks Woodward, 'will we deal with this newness? Will we perceive it or deny it? Resist it or embrace it? Even if converted, will we use the new paradigms like foreigners in an unfamiliar land, or will we slowly cope with the new categories, new language, new materials, new theories?'

Woodward lists possible ways forward. We need to look carefully at current practice and to ask a number of critical questions. Do we accept the values and attitudes implicit in our practice in the classroom? How can we best evaluate the challenges to the existing paradigm? How can we maintain an open view of the possibilities in our own classrooms and exchange ideas with others? If we are to answer these questions we need to read and research:

> Whether we prefer to gain our information and ideas from colleagues or concordances, from books or from our own students, we need to keep deliberately seeking fresh views.

Papers 2 – 4 set out the theoretical basis for a shift in the currently dominant paradigm in ELT. They look at current research into language description and language learning. This research raises serious problems for those who see language as a set of discrete structures. It challenges those who believe it is possible to present these structures to learners in a predetermined order. The writers of these papers start from very different points but the recommendations they offer are strikingly similar.

Lewis is forthright in his dismissal of PPP. He argues that a grammatical description of language is inadequate as a model for teaching and learning. Although 'well-established grammar structures clearly provide some economizing frameworks' this is no more than a very small part of the learning task. Lewis's model of communicative language use emphasizes the lexical mode. Natural language use depends on a huge stock of lexical items and fixed phrases. Taking this as a starting point Lewis sees language learning as involving a constant cycle of *observation, hypothesis* and *experiment.* Learners observe and assimilate language forms in use, but the forms they assimilate are not abstract grammatical patterns but 'prefabricated chunks, often, perhaps usually, much larger than single words'. Learners draw conclusions from the language they observe. As they assimilate a range of patterns they begin to form hypotheses about the system which lies behind the patterning they observe. As they experiment with these hypotheses and compare their own output with authoritative input they begin to construct and reconstruct their own language system. They become less dependent on processing prefabricated chunks and more able to assemble language independently. This process feeds on exposure to language. Only wide exposure can provide learners with the information they need about the collocations and fixed phrases which are essential to natural language use. But it must be, for the most part, exposure to natural language, not to language designed to illustrate mistaken conformity to an idealized grammar. 'It is,' says Lewis, 'the quality and quantity of the input to which the learners are exposed which is the single most important factor in their progress.' This challenges the present generation of EFL coursebooks, and suggests much more extensive use of resource banks of tapes, texts and video, maximizing both the quality and, equally important, quantity of language to which learners are exposed.

Skehan takes note of the same developments in language description – the predominance of prefabricated chunks or lexical phrases. As his starting point, however, he offers a brief review of recent research into second language acquisition. This research shows clearly that there is no direct correspondence between 'teaching' and 'learning'. We can never be sure that what is presented to learners will be assimilated. Learning will proceed in a fashion determined by psychological processes beyond the conscious control of teachers and learners. Learners will assimilate features of the target system in their own good time, not at the time and in the order determined by a teacher. At first sight this seems to deny the value of language instruction. But Skehan asserts the value of instruction in that it obliges learners to focus on language form. Without this focus learners may rely on a lexicalized mode which stitches together prefabricated utterances. Without a language focus they will not be encouraged to attend to syntax. They will not, in Lewis's terms, be encouraged to hypothesize and experiment. But the instructional process can ensure that we draw learners' attention to certain features of the input. This does not ensure that these features will be mastered at once – but it does increase the chances that the learner will be aware of them and sensitive to them so that they will be processed more efficiently at some time in the future.

Skehan concludes that the findings of second language acquisition research are supportive of task-based approaches to language learning. But he is concerned that we should maintain a proper focus on language form: 'There needs to be a balance between a focus on form … and a focus on communication.' Learners need to develop a language system that will work in real time. Skehan, like Lewis, argues that the process of real-time language processing demands a 'lexicalized mode' in which patterns are holistic and can be rapidly called to mind and deployed in communication. The learner operates with lexicalized 'chunks' without being fully aware of the syntactic patterning which lies behind them. An appropriate focus on form prompts learners to re-examine and refine these lexicalized 'chunks' to bring them in line with the learners' growing awareness of the form of the target language. But these refinements will be real and lasting only if they can be incorporated into a real-time operating system, a lexical mode. We need therefore to prompt learners to move to increasing levels of grammatical awareness and, at each stage, to encourage them to make their increased awareness work in real time by refabricating units of language. In looking at ways of achieving this outcome in the classroom Skehan sees task design as central. His paper looks at ways of analysing and constructing task procedures which will ensure a balance between a focus on communication, using a lexicalized mode, and a focus on learning with an emphasis on highlighting and analysing language form.

In Paper 4, Shortall, like Skehan, asserts the importance of form-focused activities in the classroom. He begins by showing that learners already know a lot about language in general, and therefore about the target language as well as their first language. It seems reasonable to suppose that the main source of knowledge about language is the learner's first language. If this is indeed the case we might expect the learning process to be one of gradually replacing one set of realizations with another. Roughly speaking this is the process envisaged by contrastive analysis. According to contrastive analysis one would expect Japanese learners to have great problems with word order. But they do not seem to have these anticipated problems. Shortall shows how systematic similarities underlie some of the surface differences between one language and another. He goes on to consider the implications for language teaching of Chomsky's *Universal Grammar*, and to draw a distinction between *core* features of language, which are shared by many languages, and *peripheral* features, which are specific to a particular language. He argues that core features will be readily acquired by learners, and that our teaching effort should be directed towards peripheral features.

1 Paradigm shift and the language teaching profession

Tessa Woodward

Professional communities and shared paradigms

Teachers of EFL/ESOL come into the field from diverse routes. Some may have done one-to-one teaching for paying guests in their homes, or been substitute teachers at peak times in local holiday resorts. Others may have finished post-graduate teacher training courses or be refugee teachers from other subjects. Many, once they have found that TEFL is enjoyable or offers respite from unemployment, redundancy or sundry other hard knocks, take a preliminary qualification or certificate. On many preliminary teaching courses a model akin to PPP is a dominant paradigm. I take the word 'paradigm' from Kuhn (1970) and as meaning 'an accepted model or pattern or a coherent tradition'. It is the study of the dominant paradigm that prepares teachers in training for membership of their own TEFL teaching communities. If successful on the course and therefore allowed in, the trainee joins other people who learned the basis of their field and skill through the same paradigm. In subsequent teaching and discussion, therefore, there is seldom overt disagreement over fundamentals. There is a common professional language (we all know what 'drilling' is), a sharing of values (teacher talking time should be reduced), use of similar materials (tape recorders, coursebooks, flashcards) and a tendency to see the same things as significant (student oral production, the correction of errors). Since many of us have entered the field by this same route we tend to take all this for granted. We can thus talk to each other easily in staff rooms about students and books and levels. We can attend conferences and understand much of what is going on even though our teaching situations may vary tremendously. We take this so much for granted that it is only when we talk to someone from a different background, someone who does not share our paradigm, that we are jolted into recognizing difference. Here is Bernard Dufeu, who does not teach using our familiar PPP model, talking about a language class:

> Whole and blind half masks protect wearers from other participants, … the protagonist perceives his or her own voice and the voice of the animator in double, more clearly …
> (Dufeu 1994: 29)

Here we have a different professional language. We have new terms: 'double' and 'protagonist'; a new value: 'protection'; new materials: 'masks' and a new item of significance: 'perception of one's own voice'. We would need to take very different training courses to enter this language teaching community!

One of the good things, then, about having a shared paradigm in a professional community is that it helps members to talk to each other. One of the drawbacks is that it hinders discussion with people from other communities working inside different paradigms.

Paradigm debate within one community

Despite the fact that members of one professional community share a joint paradigm, it sometimes happens that problems start to become apparent with the accepted model. The community then enters a time of paradigm debate or paradigm shift and a new model tends to emerge. Precisely because the community has in the past adhered to a shared paradigm, new models tend to emerge with difficulty. Kuhn's work is on paradigm shift in scientific communities and he cites many examples of upheaval in astronomy, physics, mathematics, etc. In medicine he describes vividly the denunciation of x-rays as hoaxes. There are hosts of other examples too, such as the ridicule of Ignaz Semmelweiss for suggesting that doctors wash their hands before delivering babies, bitter debates over ideas which we now take for granted. A new idea often has tremendous difficulty fighting its way to acceptance.

Let's look at an example of paradigm clash in our own field. Imagine an assessor trained in and training with the PPP model, watching a lesson taught by a candidate who believes that language students learn best by participating in interesting activities in a relaxed, enjoyable atmosphere. One can imagine the trainer musing after the lesson. 'It was a nice lesson. The students were all involved. The activities were interesting. The visuals were great. But what was he actually setting out to teach? What language item had he isolated for the students to produce accurately by the end of the lesson? And he didn't correct anything! It's no good, I'll have to fail him!' Here we have an assessor working with an objectives/product paradigm assessing a candidate with a process-oriented view. The person enjoying most power will prevail for the time being and their paradigm will remain dominant, for a while. The incoming idea will be seen at first as aberrant.

Why is it so difficult for those of us working with an established paradigm to accept the new? Kuhn cites vivid examples of individuals grappling with newness:

> In a psychological experiment that deserves to be far better known outside the trade, Bruner and Postman asked experimental subjects to identify on short and controlled exposure a series of playing cards. Many of the cards were normal, but some were made anomalous, eg a red six of spades and a black four of hearts. Each experimental run was constituted by the display of a single card to a single subject in a series of gradually increased exposures. After each exposure the subject was asked what he had seen, and the run was terminated by two successive correct identifications.

> Even on the shortest exposures many subjects identified most of the cards, and after a small increase all the subjects identified them all. For the normal cards these identifications were usually correct, but the anomalous cards were almost always identified, without apparent hesitation or puzzlement, as normal. The black four of hearts might, for example, be identified as the four of either spades or hearts. Without any awareness of trouble, it was immediately fitted to one of the conceptual categories

prepared by prior experience. One would not even like to say that the subjects had seen something different from what they identified. With a further increase of exposure to the anomalous cards, subjects did begin to hesitate and to display awareness of anomaly. Exposed, for example, to the red six of spades, some would say: 'That's the six of spades, but there's something wrong with it – the black has a red border.' Further increase of exposure resulted in still more hesitation and confusion until finally, and sometimes quite suddenly, most subjects would produce the correct identification without hesitation. Moreover, after doing this with two or three of the anomalous cards, they would have little further difficulty with the others. A few subjects, however, were never able to make the requisite adjustment of their categories. Even at forty times the average exposure required to recognize normal cards for what they were, more than 10 per cent of the anomalous cards were not correctly identified. And the subjects who then failed often experienced acute personal distress. One of them exclaimed: 'I can't make the suit out, whatever it is. It didn't even look like a card that time. I don't know what colour it is now or whether it's a spade or a heart. I'm not even sure now what a spade looks like. My God!' In the next section we shall occasionally see scientists behaving this way too. (Kuhn 1976:62-64)

In our own field, inability to perceive newness or to allow it to exist shows up not just in an assessment by an established trainer but, for example, when a school manager decides to order some books and not others, hire and fire some teachers and not others.

Once it becomes clear to people that individuals in the same community are working from different paradigms, Kuhn suggests that there is often a period of re-examination of first principles. In the TEFL community this means questioning 'What is language? How does learning take place? What is good teaching?' In times of paradigm debate there are often quarrels over what is significant (Do errors matter?) and people tend to talk through each other because the meanings they attach to terms are so different.

The normality of paradigm debate

In the world of science examples of paradigm debate and paradigm shift abound. The scientific community has had to abandon problematic theories and take on new ones, form and shatter traditions again and again. From Copernicus to Newton, from Lavoisier to Einstein, science has seen the emergence of anomaly, competitive models, resistance, rejection and revolution.

In our own field we have seen changes from grammar translation to the direct method, from concern with reading and writing to a focus on listening and speaking, from the use of language labs to the use of jigsaw texts, changes in approach, method and technique. We are used to a degree of change. We are also used to resistance to change. We usually recognize it very clearly – in others! Whenever we have participants on our courses who say 'Yes, but ...' or 'I can't ...' or 'It won't work because ...' or 'I don't understand what you mean ...' it's tempting to put it down glibly to (their) resistance and keep at them in ever more subtly intrusive ways (using, for example, journal keeping and letter writing) to flush out and bend the resisters.

Managing our own change – two differences

But two things may be different this time. The first is that it is now *us*, the established teachers trained in the dominant paradigm, involved in paradigm debate and not us forcing paradigm debate onto others (in other countries, or lower down the career ladder than ourselves). I wonder how we will manage our own change. How will *we* perceive newness and break down resistance in ourselves as we hit perhaps the deepest fault-line yet in our own territory? As teacher training syllabuses are re-written to deliberately exclude any one methodological model (see Edwards, Paper 10), as new materials come through involving down-loaded corpora, as our familiar world of verb-phrase-based grammar is challenged in its importance, as process-writing and learner-based textbooks begin to appear, how will we deal with this newness? Will we perceive it or deny it? Resist it or embrace it? Even if converted, will we use the new paradigms hesitatingly, like foreigners in an unfamiliar land, or will we slowly cope with the new categories, new language, new materials, new theories? It will be interesting to find out!

The second difference is the depth of the change involved. Absorbing a new technique can take a while. Learning to use a word processor, learning how to get groups collaborating instead of competing by using new scoring systems, having several trial runs at interactive dialogue journals, can all be challenges to our ability to break up old teaching patterns and gain new skills. But these changes can be surface changes, and purely cosmetic if they are plastered on top of the same paradigm as before. In fact using a new way of teaching and learning to achieve old aims and fulfil old intentions can amount to 'pedagogical perversion' (Dufeu, private conversation). Let me give an example. Let's say we spend time at the start of a course eliciting from participants what they want to do on the course. An impression is given of learner-centredness or negotiation. But if the topics raised are then either ignored, forgotten, squeezed off the programme or are re-framed and re-named to fit under topics we had already planned to do all along, then the elicitation has done nothing except raise expectations falsely. 'Now, you said you wanted to do something on X. I think this will probably come up under P which we had thought of doing on Wednesday morning anyway. So that will take care of that.' If it does, OK. If it doesn't, you've got 'pedagogical perversion'.

Changing techniques on the surface does not involve paradigm shift. Paradigm shift is about changing our view of learning or language, teaching or training or all four. It's about changing categories, procedures and views of the world.

Ways forward

If we are no longer content with aspects of our dominant paradigm for teaching, learning and training then how can we best proceed? Here are some suggestions for ways forward.

1 Looking at what we already do in a new light
A relatively non-threatening way of working is to continue to do what we already do but to re-categorize it or describe it in a new way. By sitting and talking with a teacher from a different field about, for example, 'course planning' or 'review' I can learn new terms

for what I already do and new things to do under these same familiar terms.

Alternatively I can describe in detail what I already do but can re-categorize it or re-name it. Instead of P and P and P, I can re-name and re-chunk my practice according to A and R and C (see Scrivener, Paper 8).

By keeping on doing, for the moment, what I'm already doing but listening to the practice of others or re-describing my own, I become more aware of the paradigm within which I'm working and of other people's.

2 Doing what we think we're doing

Very often what we believe in and think we do (our espoused theory) is different from what we actually do (our theory-in-action). One way forward is thus to endeavour to bring the two closer together. Kerr, for example, (see Paper 9) asks trainers what they think is important for language teachers to learn and then examines whether these perceptions are actually matched by what happens before and on these trainers' pre-service courses. This involves working out what our beliefs are and then checking whether we're acting in accordance with them. The dominant paradigm can be refined in this way until it becomes more internally coherent and consistent.

3 Swapping one paradigm for another

If there is a great degree of dissatisfaction with a dominant paradigm (see Introduction, Lewis, Paper 2 and Skehan, Paper 3) then usually a new model gradually emerges accompanied by much resistance. There are many contenders available in TEFL: Total Physical Response, The Silent Way, Counselling Learning, Suggestopedia, Psychodramatic language learning, the Receptive Skills model, Stimulus-based teaching, the Bank Accounts model, the Natural Approach, the Options Approach, the Lexical Approach and Task-based Learning. (The final two are described in various papers in this volume; see references for reading on the others.)

They all have their own rationales, terms, materials, procedures, advantages and disadvantages. Theoretically then it should be possible for any of us to discard the PPP model, if we're unhappy with it, train in a new model and start teaching and training with that. Although such 'conversion' experiences are possible, in Kuhn's view they are rare. Kuhn points out that in the scientific community, at least, conversions are rarely based on logic or experimental evidence but more often on personal aesthetic appeal. A new model seems in some way simpler, more elegant, or more attractive than the old. But even if converted, Kuhn says we tend to use the new paradigm like a foreigner in an unfamiliar land, forever struggling with the new categories, new terms, materials, theories and shifts in significance. Just as we struggle with those trick pictures of duck/rabbits, old/young women, or profiles/candlesticks, at first we can usually just see one model. Then we begin to see the other but we keep losing it. Finally we learn to switch from one to the other more quickly but we can never see both at the same time! Following from this metaphor, using a true blend of several paradigms may be impossible. Most occurrences of change from one paradigm to another according to Kuhn happen more gradually over time as proponents of the old model simply die out or leave the profession! Of course we have an added problem in our own field which is the difficulty of truly testing the efficacy of *any* model.

4 Starting somewhere – the ripple effect

Rather than deciding to dismiss an old model in one foul swipe and attempt to force in a new one, a more natural way forward may be to start experimenting or applying insights a little at a time. This fits the current 'post-method' thinking and is in line with a current metaphor: the 'teacher as researcher' (see Özdeniz, Paper 11).

As a teacher or trainer you may have a hunch or insight about something in your job. The insight could come from SLA research or could simply be something that you feel strongly about. It could be about language, learning, teaching, lesson shapes, learners or teachers. It could be a tiny aspect of one of these or a more profound belief or principle. An example say, if you're a trainer, could be 'teacher assessment'. If you are no longer comfortable with the idea of presenting and practising small chunks of language in a forty-minute lesson, then you will not want an ability to do this to be a criterion in teacher assessment. Perhaps you would be happier drawing up a list with colleagues of thirty things you think every language teacher should be able to do. The list could include items such as 'relate in an unpatronizing, clear and helpful way to all students regardless of sex, age, colour, race and religion' or 'tell a story that weaves in new vocabulary and makes use of more than just teacher voice and written text'. You could make your list available to trainees and pass anyone who can do, say, twenty of the things on the list by the end of the course.

Whatever your insight or hunch, whether from SLA research or your own gut feeling, try applying the insight to a part of your course and see how it affects other parts of the course. You may start with an apparently tiny change and find that the ripple effect is considerable and beneficial throughout the rest of the course.

Whilst wrestling with change

Whether we instigate change in small or large amounts or whether it simply starts lapping at our feet without warning, it is likely to make us feel, at times, de-skilled, frustrated, ill at ease or bad tempered. According to Kuhn this is quite normal! There do seem to be a few common sense measures, however, that may help us all to feel more comfortable with ourselves and each other. Reading about change and paradigm shift will help us to understand its inevitability and its patterns. Recording the effects of our own experiments and sharing them with others (as Bygate, Foster, and Özdeniz do in this volume) will keep us all in touch and informed. There is now a large and growing literature on alternatives to PPP for us to share.

Practice in meeting novelty and monitoring our own reactions to it, is possibly the most useful measure of all. Whether we prefer to gain our information and ideas from colleagues or concordances, from books or from our own students, we need to keep deliberately seeking fresh views. For change will come again, and then again. We cannot always meet it with incomprehension. We can choose whether to try to keep an open mind, or whether to block on regardless. In our own school, in our own staffroom, what will our style be from now on? When we meet new books, new colleagues, when we observe and give feedback, when we hire and fire, … will we see the anomalous card for what it is? Or will we deny its very existence?

Tessa Woodward is a teacher and teacher trainer at Hilderstone College, Broadstairs and edits *The Teacher Trainer* for Pilgrims, Canterbury. Among her publications are *Models and Metaphors in Teacher Training* (CUP) and *Ways of Training* (Longman). Her main area of professional interest is how adults learn.

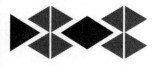

2 Implications of a lexical view of language

Michael Lewis

I n *The Lexical Approach* (1993), I argued that language consisted not of vocabulary and structures, but essentially of different kinds of lexical item – socially sanctioned independent units of meaning, many of these being multi-word items, which were un- or mis-identified in earlier language study. Four major categories of lexical item provide a framework for analysis:

1 a *words* (eg push, exit, fruit)
  b *polywords* (eg by the way, on the other hand)
2 (relatively fixed) *collocations* or *word partnerships* (eg an initial reaction, to assess the situation)
3 *institutionalized utterances* or *fixed expressions* (eg I'll see what I can do; It's not the sort of thing you think will ever happen to you)
4 *sentence frames* or *heads* (eg Considerable research has been done in recent years on the questions of ...; At present, however, expert opinion remains divided; some experts believe ... etc.)

The fundamental idea is exceptionally simple – much of our supposedly 'original' language use is, in fact, made of prefabricated chunks, often, perhaps usually, much larger than single words. Although opinion remains divided on the best way to identify, analyse and codify these chunks, the basic perception of language consisting of chunks is now standard among those working in lexicography and related fields. Such a view is, of course, independent of any views on language teaching methodology. The analysis does, however, lend support to the view that the mature native speaker has a stock of many tens of thousands of separate items stored and readily accessible for both receptive and productive use. Large numbers of lexical items – both single words and multi-word items – are used exclusively or almost exclusively in either the spoken or written mode. This view, long held intuitively, is clearly endorsed by recent work on spoken corpora. It suggests that we carry separate but overlapping resources, thus further emphasizing the sheer size of the competent language user's store of individual items.

Well-established grammar structures clearly provide some economizing frameworks, but many grammatically possible sentences such as *I desire the salmon*, or *It's forty past five* are dismissed by native speakers as, if not impossible, at least highly unlikely. (Well, you could say that – but you wouldn't.) The acceptability of many collocations is unpredictable (*in deep trouble*, but not *in shallow trouble*) and they need social endorsement. The probable or highly frequent sentences of the language form only a small subset of the possible sentences.

All these factors suggest a vastly greater role for memory in language learning, and a greatly reduced role for (implicit or explicit) understanding of 'grammar rules', however that term is understood.

Accepting the fact that the language contains many thousands of separate lexical items has embarrassing implications for methodology. If learners need thousands of discrete items, each of which needs to be 'taught', classroom language learning appears impossible. 20,000 items taking two minutes each to 'teach' would take up a typical student's entire learning programme over eight years of English in school. This is patently absurd, and self-evidently it is not the case that every item which is learned needs to be formally taught. Indeed, the majority of language acquired by the learner must come from sources other than formal teaching.

In the area of grammar, it is by no means clear within a lexical framework that the most generative structures are those of the traditional language course. Studies of real language use suggest rather differently – much 'agreeing' is done by one speaker using a close synonym of a lexical item used by the other, rather than the more 'obvious' *I agree completely/I don't (really) agree* more likely to be found in the coursebook unit on agreeing and disagreeing politely; fixed expressions belong on a spectrum of idiomaticity, where the meaning of the whole is anything from transparent to opaque by reference to the constituent words and structure. (Why are you asking *me*! I wouldn't know.) Many such expressions have not appeared in traditional language courses, and it is by no means clear where they can, or should, be put in any modern syllabus.

A further question arises – is the so-called generative grammar rule a generalization based on proto-typical fixed expressions, or does the fixed expression somehow 'follow' the rule? Even more confusingly, perhaps the two processes are in some way parallel and overlapping? Two things are clear:

- There are many more – tens of thousands more – individual items to be learned than language teaching has ever recognized.

- In direct contrast, within what is traditionally thought of as 'grammar', the structures are not discrete and sequenceable, but intersecting and inter-related domains of meaning, where the study of one feature, for example the present perfect, necessarily involves the simultaneous understanding of the meaning relations behind other patterns – for example the present, past simple, present perfect continuous. The meaning of each is partly determined by the system of contrasts between it and one, or, more frequently, several others. Any attempt to isolate one structure for the purpose of study inevitably distorts the language.

One methodological conclusion is inevitable – any paradigm based on, or remotely resembling, Present – Practise – Produce (PPP) is wholly unsatisfactory, failing as it does to reflect either the nature of language or the nature of learning. It is not sufficient to suggest that such a paradigm represents one of a number of ways in which language is learned; the fact is the PPP paradigm is, and always was, nonsense. The element of the language which may be susceptible to PPP teaching is not more than a tiny and peripheral part of the language needed for communicative language use.

Recent commentators have suggested alternative paradigms, including my own Observe – Hypothesize – Experiment. This paradigm is a methodological possibility for short-term teaching sequences such as individual lessons; it is essential to any long-term teaching strategy because it is neither more nor less than a summary of how learning actually occurs. These new suggestions share certain features:

- They typically involve three elements.
- They are learning paradigms, concerned with learner, not teacher, activity.
- None makes any claim about its applicability to short-term teaching sequences such as individual lessons or phases of the lesson. It seems likely that short-term sequences which reflect the long-term paradigm should form an important and regular part of any teaching programme but the illusion of 'knowing that the students have learned that' is avoided.

These factors deserve further examination.

Three elements

- Language is essentially social – the language I use is always and inevitably acquired from outside. What I refer to as 'my' language, however intimately it may be 'mine', always came first from outside, so language is acquired exclusively by exposure of some kind. All the language skills, including productive skills, are acquired from listening and reading. Any learning paradigm must contain an element which reflects this incontrovertible aspect of the nature of language.
- Not all language to which learners are exposed produces measurable acquisition. Not even things formally 'learned' can in any way be guaranteed to be available for later spontaneous use. Dispute continues about whether only unconscious implicit decision making aids long-term acquisition (in Krashen's restricted sense), or whether this is also helped by conscious, and explicitly articulated, decision making. Everyone agrees, however, that some mental processing – decision making about the language – is a second essential element of the learning process. This cognitive decision-making process must also be represented within any learning paradigm.
- Finally, language is successfully acquired only when it is available for spontaneous, original personal use with other people. We do not simply use language according to prescriptive rules. We manipulate language, creating new forms to meet our needs. I referred earlier in this paper to *the spectrum of idiomaticity*. It is perhaps an unusual phrase, and not one which I can recall having seen before. It is not a phrase which is sanctioned by usage, but it expresses the meaning I was looking for and I had no hesitation in 'creating' it. The learner too must discover whether or not he or she can function as an effective member of the linguistic community in the same way, contributing to the social stock of language, rather than simply acquiring elements from that stock.

However the elements of a learning paradigm are labelled, the three-part nature of the paradigm appears to be intrinsic to the nature of language and learning.

Learning not teaching

We know a great deal about what teachers do in the classroom – based on observation and interview – but very little about the relationship between teacher-activity and learning. A fundamental flaw in the PPP paradigm is that the first element is exclusively about teacher-activity, and only the latter two (including the frequently omitted, and even more frequently unsatisfactory, Produce phase) refer to learner-activity. All modern learning paradigms, overtly or covertly, exclude reference to the teacher. This, perhaps inevitably, makes them more difficult to promote on teacher training courses.

Short-term teaching sequences

One of the main attractions of the PPP paradigm is that it allows teacher training courses to introduce trainees to the idea of a neat lesson plan, with neat and distinct phases to the lesson. But language and 'the good lesson' are both organic, holistic concepts, where the success of the whole is much more than the success of the apparent component parts. Teacher training has over-valued PPP precisely because it allows teaching to focus on discrete, and apparently manageable, language items; the teacher has control over what is being 'taught'. But this control is illusory. All forms of procedural or skill-based learning are, in fact, not subject to the kind of linear sequencing intrinsic to any assertion that we know exactly what is being learned at any given moment.

The Observe – Hypothesize – Experiment paradigm

Most importantly, this does not replace PPP as a teaching paradigm. My claim is that learning involves a constant cycle of O–H–E elements, but a cycle in which …

- … much of what is happening is entirely internal to the individual student's personal cognitive activity, so that no external observation can judge the effectiveness or otherwise of particular phases of the lesson.

- … there is no suggestion that these three elements occur in linear sequence, only that all three occur, perhaps in parallel, or in different orders on different occasions, and with many areas of overlap. Experimenting on some language feature may involve observation of another. I explicitly reject the idea that procedural learning can be segmented and sequenced for the convenience of a supposed understanding of what is 'being taught'; real learning is essentially a long-term process.

Methodological innovation within the Lexical Approach

The Lexical Approach has less to say about innovative methods than might be expected. This is because it is explicitly an approach, not a syllabus or method. It advocates a total re-evaluation of the language which is offered to students, and how that language is analysed. It also suggests that many traditional classroom activities and attitudes are counter-productive and should be abandoned, or at least greatly de-emphasized. Most notable among these suggestions, for most teachers, are the uselessness of almost all 'grammar rules' other than those wholly devised by the learners themselves, on the basis of observation of text, and an insistence that reformulation is the only method of 'correction' which is helpful to long-term language acquisition (although I would tolerate some more formal correction in the short term if its abandonment simply produces learner resistance).

The belief in grammar rules and the importance of avoiding mistakes both go very deep into both teacher and learner expectations. To question their value and decrease their importance is, in itself, a radical methodological innovation for many teachers. But a lexical perspective implies methods based more on questions than answers. It also encourages in both learners and teachers an acceptance of the ambiguity and uncertainty which underlies language. Students need a certain security in the classroom, but a major element of learner training is to gradually move students away from the (usually false) security of learned rules and formally 'accurate' sentences, towards a willingness to use even inadequate linguistic resources to attempt to communicate real meaning. The importance of helping learners to live with the insecurity intrinsic to 'trying to say what you really mean' cannot be overestimated.

In addition to the two major negative suggestions above, approaches which take seriously the lexical nature of language need to introduce, or give much greater emphasis than in the past to, a number of activities.

Observe

Teachers on training courses – particularly initial training courses such as CTEFLA – need to engage in language observation tasks to greatly increase their awareness of the component elements of a text. Once teachers have been introduced – explicitly or by default – to the idea that language consists of words and structures ('the tenses'), it is difficult for them to rid themselves of this over-simplified and misleading analysis. Teacher training courses must actively encourage teachers to see the multi-word chunks of which much text is made up. This awareness involves a clear understanding of collocation, including the non-reciprocal nature of many collocations, and the cline from fixed to free. Modern EFL materials increasingly make reference to collocation but usually only to pairs of adjacent or nearly adjacent words – *to catch the bus, a big (*not *large) disappointment*. Many important collocations are not realized in naturally occurring text in this simple way. The grammar may mean the partnership words are widely separated, eg *The opportunity to implement the changes with a minimum of disruption was lost as the decision was delayed repeatedly as a result of political squabbling.* Here the word partnership *to lose an opportunity* is buried. One element of a collocation, typically the nominal, is often only realized pronominally, eg 'What did you think of Lord of the Flies?' – 'I haven't finished it yet.' Here the partnership *to finish a book* is doubly obscured, until one has learned to observe the language in such a way as to see the structure of many multi-word items. Unless teachers learn to observe accurately in this way, they cannot be expected to help students to observe the language to which they are exposed in ways which are maximally useful for them. The Observe element of the paradigm is not synonymous with exposure – it is exposure subject to critical examination. Accurate perception of the linguistic form, and in some cases the underlying categories exemplified by the particular example, are essential if Observation is to encourage the process of Hypothesis formation.

Chunking of written text principally involves words, word partnerships and, for those learning to write in a particular genre such as academic English, developing an awareness of the sentence heads and frames typical of the genre. For spoken English, it frequently means identifying the (pragmatic) meaning of whole utterances, many of which are far from transparent. The importance of these utterances is a major new emphasis within a lexical perspective. Traditionally such language has usually been thought of as either picturesque (and correspondingly advanced) idioms, or useful but rather marginal – a few 'politeness phrases'. It is now clear that students can usefully employ a repertoire of at least several hundred, if not many thousand, institutionalized expressions. Such expressions are central to effective spoken communication, both receptive and productive. These highly probable sentences, as well as forming part of dialogues for explicit study, should feature frequently in all language practice materials, where the emphasis should be moved decisively from the possible sentences beloved of traditional grammar, to the probable sentences central to a lexical perspective.

Hypothesize and experiment

These phases so frequently overlap that to deal with them as linearly sequenced would be misleading. The teacher's primary role is the selection of materials and tasks and the creation of an appropriate atmosphere. Patience, a teaching style which values questions, and the ability to endorse curiosity, experiment and creativity are essential. From a more formally linguistic perspective, the teacher helps students make explicit their perceptions of similarity and difference, and then, by selecting the further input materials or providing the learners with good questions about the input, helps them to correct, clarify and deepen those perceptions. Methodologically it implies activities which involve sorting, matching, identifying and describing. These may be for self-study, resembling language puzzles (but with very carefully selected language input), or class-based, involving, for example, collocation dominoes, dictations where students write down only utterances of a particular kind, or collocates they hear of words given on a worksheet. The emphasis is not on radically new methods, but on applying a wide range of familiar activities to input selected according to lexical criteria, and with no expectation that any of the new language will be 'learned' in a particular lesson.

Mastering written sentence heads and frames such as the Type 4 examples given at the beginning of this paper involves comparing well and badly written versions of the same material, leading students to produce similar texts themselves in ways which emphasize the process of writing. This means group writing tasks, peer correction and modification, and several re-writes of the same text rather than many separate and disconnected writing tasks. The teacher acts as editor and adviser rather than providing correction and evaluation.

If teachers are to be competent and confident in helping students in the ways just described, they themselves need a deep and clear understanding of the language. This suggests teacher training courses need to pay much greater attention to the subject matter and less to methods.

For a long time language teaching has gone in diametrically the wrong direction – the PPP paradigm was a travesty, for philosophical, psychological, ideological and methodological reasons. It suggested that languages were best learned by limiting the language to which learners were exposed and practising it intensively. In fact, the direct opposite is probably the truth – it is the quality and quantity of the input to which learners are exposed which is the single most important factor in their progress. This challenges the present generation of EFL coursebooks, and suggests much more extensive use of resource banks of tapes, texts and video, maximizing both the quality and, equally importantly, quantity of language to which learners are exposed.

Complex socio-political processes are at work. While the 'applied' linguist may indulge in a degree of idealization about how the language works, the teacher trainer and teacher are often, at least in their own perceptions, seriously constrained by outside factors – the commercial necessity to keep students happy in private language schools, or the necessity to ensure good grades in external examinations, however much these may militate against best practice from the stand-point of long-term effective language learning. Change and using materials and methods which run counter to (perceived or real) student expectations are often seen as commercially dangerous. It may be, however, that schools and teachers who understand, fund and implement approaches which reflect the real nature of language and learning may achieve the best possible advertising, namely successful learners. I would certainly like to hope so.

Michael Lewis is co-author of *Source Book for Teaching English* (Heinemann 1994), *Practical Techniques for Language Teaching* (1985), *The English Verb* (1986) and *The Lexical Approach* (1993). The last three are all published by LTP, the independent publishing company he founded and runs with Jimmie Hill.

Second language acquisition research and task-based instruction

3

Peter Skehan

Contrasting notions of learning

The traditional approach to language teaching is PPP: presentation, practice and production. A focused presentation stage is followed by practice activities. These practice activities are designed to enable learners to produce rapidly and easily the material which has been presented. In the production stage opportunities are provided to use language freely and flexibly in the expectation that this will consolidate what is being learned and extend its range of applicability.

Such an approach has a number of advantages. First of all, it is very comforting for the teacher. The teacher is in charge of proceedings, and has a clear professional role which, in general, it is relatively easy to organize, since it requires the teacher to take the 'structure of the day' and do whatever is necessary to ensure that that structure is learned. The PPP approach comes 'bundled' with a range of techniques (Rivers 1968). These techniques enable the teacher to orchestrate classroom behaviour, ie to use a defensible methodology thought to promote learning, while at the same time maintaining authority, ie by using the bundled techniques to show to students exactly who is in charge. And these techniques are eminently trainable, with the result that the teachers have the reassurance of being able to apply what was the main part of their training while, as Hubbard et al (1983) point out, generations of trainers are simultaneously provided with gainful employment.

Second, the approach lends itself to accountability, since there will be clear and tangible lesson goals, which can then be evaluated. There is a belief that learners will learn what is taught in the order in which it is taught. The units used and the ordering of those units are therefore open to the teacher or syllabus writer to control (White 1988). The emphasis is on product, with the result that testing is generally straightforward, assessments of adequate syllabus coverage are non-problematic, and there is an easy route to the current buzzwords of 'quality assurance'.

Finally, there is the possibility of clear connection with underlying theory. Learning is focused on rules which are then automatized as a set of habits. This viewpoint seems to accord with a great deal of learning theory as described in Hilgard and Bower (1975) that was particularly influential in North America.

With the passage of time, however, these arguments have become less and less powerful. Two major reasons account for this. First of all, the evidence in support of such an approach is unimpressive. Levels of attainment in conventional foreign language learning are poor, and students commonly leave school with very little in the way of usable language (Carroll 1975; Stern 1983). In other words, most language learning is associated with relative failure. Only the gifted learners achieve impressive levels of proficiency (Skehan 1989). Comparative studies, similarly, suggest that up to now methodological factors have had relatively little impact on general levels of success (Stern 1983). For example, one of the most influential 'comparative' studies suggested that instruction has no effect on language learning. A comparison was made between a group of instructed learners (in an ESL context) and a group of uninstructed learners, matched for length of time in the target language country. The two groups did not differ in level of achievement (Fathman 1976). This led to the claim that it would be wiser, if one is going to the country where the target language is spoken, to spend one's money having a good time and interacting, rather than on language course fees!

But the second reason why PPP approaches are inadequate is equally powerful. The underlying theory for a PPP approach has now been discredited. The belief that a precise focus on a particular form leads to learning and automatization (that learners will learn what is taught in the order in which it is taught) no longer carries much credibility in linguistics or psychology (Brumfit and Johnson 1979; Ellis 1985). Instead, the contemporary view of language development is that learning is constrained by internal processes. Learners do not simply acquire the language to which they are exposed, however carefully that exposure may be orchestrated by the teacher. It is not simply a matter of converting input into output.

Learners do, however, use the language they experience to make inferences, hypotheses and generalizations about the language system as a whole. In other words, we can be sure that learners will make use of the language they experience, but we cannot be sure *how* they will make use of it. These processes are hidden. They are not amenable to teacher control. But the teacher cannot ignore the impact of such processes or of the learner's contribution to learning, as we will see in the following paragraphs.

But the point must be made now that it is curious to see how resistant to change the PPP approach has been. Given that there is little *evidence* in its favour, or *theory*, it is surprising that it has been so enduring in its influence. To account for this, we must return to the points which were made regarding its convenience for the teaching profession. It has served to perpetuate a comfortable position for teachers and for teacher trainers. The attraction has been that to implement a PPP approach is simultaneously satisfactory for:

- the professional techniques a teacher is seen to command
- the power relations which operate within the classroom
- the role that teacher trainers have in perpetuating familiar, but outmoded, methodologies
- the accountability mechanisms which can be seen to operate.

Clearly these institutional reasons for continuing with such a teacher-focused approach have proved more influential than the approach's lack of success, its lack of theory and its lack of explicit concern with the learner.

However, a contrasting approach to language learning has emerged in recent years. This approach emphasizes the fact that language input, however provided, simply offers raw material on the basis of which learners may review their picture of the target language system. Second language acquisition (SLA) research (Ellis 1985, 1994) has established that teaching does not and cannot determine the way the learner's language will develop. The processes by which the learner operates are 'natural' processes. Teachers and learners cannot simply 'choose' what is to be learned. To a large extent the syllabus is 'built in' to the learner.

This applies to learner error also. Learners often go through a developmental sequence which does not go directly to the target form, but involves a number of errors on the way. And these errors are not simply the result of first language interference. They are often common to learners from a wide variety of L1 backgrounds. Finally there is variability in language performance (Lightbown 1985). Learners seem to have control of a particular system under some circumstances, perhaps when they have time for conscious processing, yet not under other circumstances. The notion of learning is, then, a very complex one. It is certainly not a smooth progression – the elements of the target language do not simply slot into place in a predictable order.

A major concern for SLA research has therefore been to take account of such changed views on language and to explore their implications for language teaching. Early accounts stressed that input was the key factor. The important thing for teachers was to provide high quality and 'tuned' language input. Learners should be exposed to language which was varied in form and which was at the edge of their comprehension – comprehensible, but only with careful processing. Given this, the learner's language system would automatically develop without language-focused instruction (Krashen 1985). This account, and in particular the implication that instruction is irrelevant, has been severely criticized (Swain 1985; Gregg 1984), and later researchers have emphasized the roles of instruction and interaction. Long (1983, 1988), for example, has demonstrated that instruction does have an effect (in spite of the findings of Fathman 1976, cited above) but that this effect is indirect and non-immediate. He argues it is important for learners to pay careful attention to language form in general. But this does not mean that we need to focus on a particular form in a particular lesson. So it *is* of importance to provide instruction for learners, but one should not expect to see the immediate and specific impact of any particular 'bit' of instruction on any particular 'bit' of language. Instructed learners, that is, make faster progress than uninstructed learners and reach higher levels of ultimate attainment. But they do this in their own way, following their own developmental sequence, not a sequence imposed by a teacher (Long 1988).

Findings such as these are two-edged. They respond to the critique (Fathman 1976) mentioned earlier in that they do demonstrate that instruction is, globally, a good thing. But what they do not do is clarify how instruction can be most effectively managed. This first phase of SLA research, which took us up to something like 1985, demonstrated clearly that a PPP approach is misguided, but did not give a very clear idea about what should be done instead. From around the mid-1980s, however, this situation was corrected somewhat. Researchers began to look at what kind of classroom interaction would promote learning most rapidly and efficiently (Duff 1986; Doughty and Pica 1986). As teachers began to develop communicative activities in the classroom so researchers began to evaluate the effectiveness of those activities and towards the end of the 1980s a consensus began to emerge.

The teachers' concern for meaning-based activities and the researchers' investigation of patterns of interaction suggested a task-based approach to foreign language instruction. Tasks, in this viewpoint, are activities which have meaning as their primary focus. Success in the task is evaluated in terms of achievement of an outcome, and tasks generally bear some resemblance to real-life language use. So task-based instruction takes a fairly strong view of communicative language teaching. It is the task which drives the learner's system forward by engaging acquisitional processes (Long and Crookes 1993). It is the task which is the unit of syllabus design (Long and Crookes 1991). A PPP approach looks on the learning process as learning a series of discrete items and then bringing these items together in communication to provide further practice and consolidation. A task-based approach sees the learning process as one of learning through doing – it is by primarily engaging in meaning that the learner's system is encouraged to develop.

But if we regard these moves towards task-based learning as beneficial, in that they support an approach to teaching which avoids the problems of PPP, several problems nonetheless remain. To some extent, these problems are unavoidable, as the details of operating a relatively new approach to language instruction are worked out. But some of the problems are more deep-seated, and need to be addressed with care. The present chapter will examine the following questions relating to task-based approaches:

- What dangers are there in taking such a perspective?
- What goals should underlie the use of task-based approaches?
- How can tasks be sequenced?
- How can tasks be implemented …
  … to minimize dangers?
  … to achieve goals?
  … to be adaptable to different contexts and different learners?

Dangers in task-based instruction

L1 speakers have developed a range of strategies to make meaning primary in their communication. These strategies can be for production or for comprehension (Skehan 1992). In each case, the language user is able to draw upon knowledge of the world, or of the immediate context, or of preceding discourse. This enables users to predict meanings, and therefore to reduce the need to focus on form, on grammar and lexis, without compromising the capacity to express or comprehend meanings. In production, incomplete utterances may be sufficient to keep the interaction moving along successfully, providing that the participants can draw upon other knowledge sources to fill in the gaps, so to speak. When we deal with L2 learners, the situation is not terribly different with respect to their capacity to express meanings contextually and resourcefully – the difference is largely that they have a lower level of language proficiency, and so, when faced with tasks to transact, may rely even more on strategic competence (Bachman and Palmer, in press) to express meanings. Examples of task transaction of this sort are commonplace, with words and gestures substituting for language in, for example, the transaction of information gap tasks (Bygate 1988). Speakers may know that they have not produced impressive language, either for complexity or accuracy, but if they expect that their interlocutors will understand anyway, then to fumble with form would be disruptive for the meanings which underlie a developing conversation. In comprehension, similarly, inferencing skills are required all the time (Wilson 1994) to work out what has not been explicitly stated: in the case of limited form, the inferencing skills simply have to work a little bit harder (Anderson and Lynch 1988).

But there is another factor which has importance in such communicative encounters. Although much of language teaching has operated under the assumption that language is essentially structural, with vocabulary elements slotting in to fill structural patterns, many linguists and psycholinguists have argued that native language speech processing is very frequently lexical in nature (see Lewis, Paper 2). This means that speech processing is based on the production and reception of whole phrases, units larger than the word (although analysable by linguists into words) which do not require any internal processing when they are 'reeled off'. Pressure comes from the need to produce and comprehend language in real time. The central issue is how to plan (or decode) the linguistic and the conceptual content of messages while time is passing, and while other members of an interaction might take the floor, steal turns, leave rooms empty, etc.

The claims that have been made in this area (Bolinger 1975; Pawley and Syder 1983; Widdowson 1989) are that to cope with the complex mental procedures that real-time language use requires, we use lexicalized modes of processing. We make use of prefabricated phrases and manipulate these in minimal ways to meet the demands of real-time communication. Using lexical units in this way requires less in the way of mental resources and so leaves us free to deal with other aspects of communication. The claim, in other words, is that we are able to store in our memories many chunks, such that the same lexical element may appear in several chunks (making for an inefficiently organized but rapidly usable memory system). In this way, the several chunks can, when required, be processed and produced faster and with greater ease.

Now, as native speakers, we engage in such lexicalized language processing continually, relying on phrases such as 'if you see what I mean', 'the thing is'. We can, if we choose, express our meanings with great precision. On the other hand we can operate to some extent by stringing together prefabricated phrases incorporating prefabricated meanings. We operate a sort of dual-mode system (Skehan, in press), in which we can shift from one mode to the other, as appropriate to communicative pressures, to the need to be precise, etc. When analysis and precision are important, we indulge them: when real-time communication is pre-eminent, we resort to more lexicalized forms.

We can now put these points together, and relate them to task-based approaches to instruction. Native speakers have a dual-mode system available to them. They can move with great flexibility between what Widdowson (1989) has termed accessibility and analysability. On the one hand under pressure of time language users rely on considerable background knowledge and shared assumptions. In these circumstances they can deploy a readily available and effective lexicalized system. On the other hand native speakers do have recourse, when necessary, to language structure, to a rule-governed system, and to the capacity to generate creative language. Given sufficient time and processing capacity they can use the system to tailor meanings more precisely.

The central problem for the foreign language learner, taught by task-based means, is that learners operate under pressure of time and under the need to get meanings across. This approach places a premium on communication strategies linked to lexicalized communication. These strategies provide an effective incentive for learners to make best use of the language they already have. But they do not encourage a focus on form. They do not provide an incentive for structural change towards an interlanguage system with greater complexity. The advantages of such an approach are greater fluency and the capacity to solve communication problems. But these advantages may be bought at too high a price if it compromises continued language growth and inter-language development. Such learners, in other words, may rely on prefabricated chunks to solve their communication problems. But such solutions do not lead them to longer-term progress, even though they do lead to resourcefulness in solving such problems.

Three pedagogic goals for task-based approaches

The central point we are dealing with here is that the information processing systems available to language learners have limited capacity. Learners do not have the resources to attend to many things at the same time. We can distinguish between three goals and, as we will see later, achieving an effective compromise between these three goals is more likely to lead not only to the capacity to be an effective communicative problem solver but also to longer-term linguistic development. The three goals are accuracy, complexity/restructuring and fluency:

- Accuracy, fairly obviously, concerns how well language is produced in relation to the rule system of the target language.
- Complexity concerns the elaboration or ambition of the language which is produced. How far do learners rely on prefabricated phrases and established routines, and how far do they need to expand their language resources to meet the communicative challenge? The process which enables the learner to produce progressively more complex language is restructuring, ie a willingness and capacity, on the part of the learner, to reorganize their own underlying and developing language system, to frame and try out new hypotheses and then to act upon the feedback which is received from such experimentation.
- Fluency concerns the learner's capacity to produce language in real time without undue pausing or hesitation. It is likely to rely upon more lexicalized modes of communication, as the pressures of real-time speech production are met only by avoiding excessive rule-based computation (Skehan 1994).

It is fundamental for the designer of task-based instruction to engineer situations which maximize the chances that there will be a balance between these different goals when attentional resources are limited.

It is assumed here that these three goals are in some degree of mutual tension. We cannot give our full attention to each of these goals. This means that the pursuit of one of these goals can easily be at the expense of the others. To put this another way, it is assumed that it is desirable that the learner should not emphasize one of the goals for any extended period of time at the expense of the others, and that it is desirable, from a pedagogic point of view, to ensure that attention is divided between them as effectively as possible. In other words, it is important to arrange situations such that a balance is struck between syntactic and lexical modes of communication, on the one hand, and between conservative and ambitious syntactic use on the other. The first of these tensions balances restructuring and accuracy against fluency. The second tension balances restructuring against accuracy.

Sequencing tasks

These considerations now enable us to address, in a more principled way, the question of how tasks can and should be sequenced. The aim of effective sequencing is to ensure that the demands on language are of the right level. On the one hand excessive task difficulty should not lead the learner to rely on lexicalized communication. Such a reliance carries the danger of fossilization and may produce only routine solutions to communication problems, rather than tailor-made solutions. On the other hand, tasks should not be so easy that no extension of interlanguage development or consolidation is achieved. So it is of importance that some means is found for analysing the difficulty of tasks to enable a reasonable balance between the different goals.

Given that tasks, by definition, make meaning primary, but require language to enable meanings to be communicated, Skehan (1992, 1994) proposes that the difficulty of tasks can be analysed using the two general categories of language factors and cognitive factors. In detail, they can be broken down, in turn, into:

Language factors
- syntactic complexity and range
- lexical complexity and range

Cognitive factors
- *familiarity of material in the task,* ie does the task simply require learners to produce well-organized language from memory, in ready-organized chunks, or does it require new or less-organized material to be drawn on?
- *nature of material: abstract vs. concrete,* ie are real-world referents involved, or does the learner have to deal with generalizations, abstractions, etc, eg working with LEGO models compared to making judgements, or giving advice (Brown et al 1984)?
- *reasoning operations required,* ie does the task require a number of mental operations for its completion, with material involved needing to be transformed or manipulated in some way, eg collaborative solving of some sort of mental riddle (Prabhu 1987; Brown et al 1984)?
- *degree of structuring contained,* ie is there inherent structure because of the requirements of a task, eg a narrative in which beginning, middle and end are reasonably clear, or a description based on some clear underlying schema, eg a tour of a house?

In a study illustrating the operation of such factors with L2 speakers, Foster and Skehan (1994), for example, report that the three tasks of Personal Information Exchange, Narrative, and Decision Making/Choice lead to different levels of complexity in the language which is produced, and also have an effect on the level of accuracy attained. Similarly, Brown et al (1984) show that a range of different tasks, when analysed by categories such as those given above, produce a general ranking in terms of difficulty. Research studies such as these enable more principled decisions to be made as to which tasks to use with given groups of students to achieve the right level of challenge.

Implementing tasks

To approach task selection in this way is really to take on the familiar syllabus problem of sequencing, but with different sorts of units. The central goal is to have some idea of task difficulty so that the particular task which is chosen is appropriate for a given group of learners and pitched correctly at their level of competence. But simply to analyse and select tasks does not automatically determine task difficulty, although it does constrain it. There are also a number of influences which may modify the difficulty that the task produces, and which may also lead to more productive language use. How a task is implemented can have a strong effect on task value. In this respect, it is worth noting, in passing, that we have moved on to consider issues of methodology. As it happens, some proponents of task-based approaches to instruction, eg Nunan (1989), regard the distinction between syllabus and methodology as no longer relevant since they regard tasks as containing their own methodology, ie a communicative approach to language teaching. The present section, by demonstrating how important implementational decisions are, will attempt to show that there may be life in this distinction yet!

We can distinguish between three stages in task implementation: pre-, during and post.

Table 1: Stages in task implementation

	Purpose of phase	*Examples*
Pre-task	Cognitive: ease subsequent processing load	*foregrounding, eg introduction to topic of task* *observing* *doing similar tasks* *planning*
	Linguistic: introduce new forms into attention	*explicit teaching* *implicit teaching* *consciousness-raising*
During task	Manipulate pressure: influence processing balance	*speed, deadlines* *stakes* *number of participants*
	Calibrate: influence processing balance	*provide visual support* *introduce surprise elements*
Post-task	Retrospect: remind learners of importance of form	*public performance* *analyse* *consciousness-raise*

At the pre-task stage, two broad alternatives are possible: an emphasis on the general cognitive demands of the task, and/or an emphasis on linguistic factors. Attention is limited in capacity, and it is needed to respond to both linguistic and cognitive demands. If one looks at attention in this way, then engaging in activities which reduce cognitive load will release attentional capacity for the learner to concentrate more on linguistic factors. There is then a greater possibility of learners using strategies which are likely to extend the language system. Table 1 suggests that the cognitive activities which reduce cognitive load in this way are foregrounding; observing similar tasks; doing similar tasks; and planning.

All of these activities serve to prepare the learner for handling the cognitive demands that a task contains and enable the channelling of attentional resources towards language form. Foregrounding directs attention to the task topic and simply activates relevant knowledge that the learner already possesses, in the same way that this operates as a pre-reading or pre-listening stage (Grellet 1981). The learner, as a result, does not have to devote so much energy to the retrieval of information from long-term memory 'on-line' during task completion and, in addition, the task is likely to contain greater naturalness and authenticity. Observing and doing similar tasks allows the learner to draw more, during the actual completion of a task, on planned discourse (Ellis 1987), such that less time is spent wondering what task requirements are or how the task may need to be structured. As a result, attention can be directed to the more micro-activity of the detail of the language which is being used.

Finally, planning has considerable potential for easing the task of using attentional resources during task completion, ie of releasing people from having to think of too many things at a time when both composing thoughts and producing speech. Crookes (1989) reported that planning time was associated with greater complexity of syntax and a wider variety of lexis. Developing this line of research, Foster and Skehan (1994) confirmed the strong effects of planning time on complexity of syntax; variety of syntax; breadth of vocabulary; and, very strongly, the fluency and naturalness with which tasks were done. Skehan and Foster (1994) also report that, in contrast with Crookes' results, planning was associated with greater accuracy. However, this was a complex relationship (see Foster, Paper 12).

The second pre-task category from Table 1, linguistic preparation, refers to the amount of language work that takes place. This may involve an explicit focus on specific language forms believed to be useful in the coming task. It may be more indirect – involving, for example, a consciousness-raising activity dealing with communication problems which may occur in the task. Whatever the language focus may be, two things must be borne in mind. First, there is no guarantee that the language worked on in the pre-task phase will be used in the task. Second, there can certainly be no guarantee that the language focus will lead to learning in the short term. One should regard any pre-task focus on language as a useful stage, but one which may not reliably lead to learning – only create the conditions under which it *may* occur. The intention is that this focus on language should come to fruition at some stage in the future. The impact of working with attention in this way, hoping that conditions have been set up which make the use of a particular form more likely, may take time to show itself.

So we see that there is a considerable range of useful things that can be done at the pre-task stage (which will come as no surprise to teachers). But there are also choices which can be made during task completion. The most important of these, probably, is simply to get the level of the task right, (as was discussed in the earlier section of task sequencing and difficulty assessment). But beyond this, Table 1 makes it clear that there are other ways in which the attentional demands of a task can be manipulated. This will probably have an effect on issues such as accuracy and complexity and on the extent to which attention is devoted to these goals as opposed to simply achieving task completion.

First of all, there are methods of influencing the communicative pressure for task completion. Let us look briefly at three factors which will affect language production:

- Pressure of time will force learners to make use of language that can be readily accessed rather than to attempt to create language in real time. There will be a minimal concern with accuracy and no incentive for learners to extend their existing language system.

- A pre-task focus on specific language forms may induce a particular mind set in learners. The more pressure is put upon learners (a) to conform to the use of certain structures (Willis 1993) and (b) to use these accurately, the less likely it is that learners will achieve acceptable levels of fluency and use 'cutting edge' and riskier language structures.

- The greater the number of participants there are in a task (Brown et al 1984), the greater the pressure on those transacting a task, and the greater the likelihood that fluency will predominate as a goal over accuracy and complexity/restructuring.

There are also methods of adjusting task difficulty during task completion. To make tasks easier, one can try to provide visual support to ease the processing load that is required. Many tasks have a potential visual component, and it is easier while doing such tasks to have access to some visual representation so that less information needs to be kept in working memory, and more shared assumptions can be presumed. In this way, more attentional resources can be used elsewhere. On the other hand, to make tasks *more* difficult, one can introduce surprise elements. Learners may think they have clear expectations about what will happen in a task, (and may have prepared accordingly), but unforeseen elements may emerge because they have been 'designed in' by the (Machiavellian) author of the task. In some ways, one could regard the approach to listening tasks taken by Anderson and Lynch (1988) as fitting in to this viewpoint, in that learners are provided with materials which contain deliberate discrepancies which are meant to provoke a more active approach to listening. In such cases, ie surprise elements or deliberate discrepancies, the intention is to avoid learners (of presumably reasonable proficiency) being able to take a comfortable strategy to tasks which are well within their capacity. The task designer believes that learners need to be stretched through the communicational demands of the task itself, and to have their communicational problem-solving competence extended.

Finally, one can consider how post-task activities can be used to promote pedagogic goals. The methodological cycle may incorporate a post-task public performance. This requires one of the groups or pairs who have transacted a task to repeat the task, or to engage in a similar task which is a development of the original. This extension of the initial task would be carried out not in the security of a small group, but publicly, in front of an audience (Willis and Willis 1988). For example, if the different members of a group produced several narratives, the post-task could be a justification of the best narrative which was produced. The 'audience' may consist of other students; the teacher; a video camera; or even, the other students while watching the video recording! In this way, learners doing tasks know that they may be called upon to do the same thing in less private circumstances, and that when such a public performance is required, members of the audiences concerned may well focus on correctness and the complexity of the speech used. So, if, when actually doing a task, learners think ahead to the later possible public performance, they will not prioritize task-completion to the exclusion of other goals. In other words, without having to resort to explicit monitoring and correction, (which would defeat the object of using a task-based approach), the teacher can insinuate a concern for form into the way the task is being done.

When we examined the danger of approaching a task with the exclusive goal of completion we saw that a consequence could be that fluency is prioritized at the expense of accuracy and complexity. Obviously, pre-task activities (as discussed earlier) can reduce the chances of this happening. In the pressure to get a job done, one cannot control how learners will use their attentional capacities. If task focus predominates, (as, in a sense, it is very likely to, given that tasks, by their nature, emphasize meaning), problems may develop. Accuracy may suffer, and the language used may be restricted so that it is well within the learners' established repertoire. But if post-task activities are used regularly, and if learners know that they are to come, this may change the way that a task is actually transacted. It may lead learners to switch attention repeatedly between accuracy and restructuring and fluency. So post-task activities provide another means of inducing effective use of attentional resources during tasks, and of balancing the various goals that are desirable. These activities all have the goal of focusing attention more clearly on language itself, so that when subsequent tasks are done, the knowledge of what is to come, and the connection that has been made with such activities in the past, will alert learners to the need to attend to form during tasks.

We also need to consider what sort of actual operations will take place as part of the public performance. Students themselves, as when they were doing the main task, are likely to make meaning primary, with the result that careful procedures are necessary to bring the focus back to language. The first such procedure to consider is that of analysis. Clearly, a range of possibilities present themselves here. For example, teacher and students may consider the initial performance of a task and analyse it from the point of view of:

- accuracy
- complexity
- use of particular structures
- accuracy of particular structures

In each case, attention is directed to a targeted area, whose importance should therefore be raised for the learner. The value of the exercise is to demonstrate to learners that what they were doing in a task is susceptible to analysis. They will soon learn that in future they should give some attention to linguistic considerations. They need to be well prepared so that if their group is chosen for public performance that performance will stand up well to the process of analysis! So a focused post-task activity of this sort should linger in memory and have an impact on how future tasks are done.

But if post-task analysis is the high-profile method of directing attention, one can also consider less painful, and possibly, in the longer term, more enduring and self-directed methods. One might, that is, try to induce individuals to reflect on the nature of their performance on a routine basis. In other words, one would like to raise consciousness *after* a task is done just as much as before it. To do this, the individual learner has to be encouraged to reflect upon the language which has been used, to relate this language to the goals which have been established, and to consider the alternative ways of expressing meanings which have been used. At one level this requires the development of metacognitive skills on the part of the learner (O'Malley and Chamot 1990). At another, it requires a willingness to become involved with language itself, and to direct attention to this area so that emerging structures can be internalized more effectively (Hulstijn and De Graaf 1994).

Specific structures, individual learners and the role of teachers

We can now turn to two of the issues in task-based instruction that are most difficult to resolve: the extent to which one can target individual structures, and the extent to which instruction can be adapted to individual learners. In the first case we are dealing with the problem teachers face in deciding what impact instruction might have. In the second, we have the issue of how far teaching plans can be designed for learners in general, or, on the other hand, how far they need to be specific in order to take account of learner differences.

Earlier, we saw that the evidence on second language acquisition is not encouraging to the proposition that one can target and teach individual structures in whatever order a pedagogic or syllabus plan may decree. Teachers are constrained by the power of internal learner processes. Equally, it seems to be the case that an unremitting diet of task-based instruction may not pressure effectively for underlying language change or language accuracy, since lexicalized language and strategy use may be proceduralized. This creates something of a problem, since neither focused instruction nor acquisition-oriented activities can be guaranteed to produce results. Yet teachers have to act, and to have a principled basis for how they plan their teaching. So it is unrealistic to expect predicted learning of specific items to occur. It may, however, be possible to arrange conditions to produce *probable* learning of a range of structures. It is possible for the language teacher to direct learners' attention to particular forms, and noticing forms is an important preliminary to their internalization. The three-phase approach to task implementation presented in Table 1 is intended to maximize the chances of achieving two goals: some degree of control of the quantity of pressure on attentional resources (cf calibrating task difficulty, planning effectively beforehand); and the manipulation of attentional focus (assuming that some degree of *spare* attentional capacity has been achieved) so that there is a focus on both accuracy and complexity of language (Van

Patten 1994). If the approach is successful in these respects, then what one is doing, through instruction, is pushing certain aspects of language into prominence before the task, (pre-teaching, consciousness-raising), so that they will be more available during the task, (given the assumption of attentional capacity and disposition to focus on form). There is no guarantee that specific targeted language will be incorporated into actual language use, but these conditions make it more likely. This greater probability is magnified by the post-task activity which is almost totally directed towards a focus on form.

Whatever the focus on form, it does not follow that the language that is targeted will become part of the learner's repertoire as the result of a particular lesson. It is, however, more likely that over a block of time, targeted forms will be incorporated into a developing interlanguage system. The teacher, in other words, can be more forceful regarding his or her aims of what learners will notice, but cannot be certain that what is brought into attention and noticed is then internalized (Schmidt 1990, 1994) and becomes part of the learner's repertoire. But this approach does allow the teacher to design instruction such that there is a plan of what should be noticed within blocks of time, allowing pedagogic goals to be set, but in looser terms than used to be considered feasible with structural syllabuses.

Finally, we need to consider how the individual learner can be accommodated to this approach to task-based instruction. We have seen that in organizing task-based approaches to instruction, there needs to be a balance between a focus on form (with this dividing, in turn, into accuracy and complexity), and a focus on communication (prioritizing real-time processing, lexicalized language and fluency). The goal of instruction is to contrive a better balance between these different forces. But what is relevant in this regard is that it has been argued that learners, too, can be regarded as oriented towards analysis or synthesis (Skehan 1986, 1989). Some learners are drawn to language-as-pattern, while others are more concerned with achieving the expression of meaning. Some learners, other things being equal, are likely to focus their attention on form, on 'cracking the code' because they enjoy analysing verbal material and finding patterns. Others are more inclined to treat the task of language learning as one of memory, with the need to assimilate a wide repertoire of functional expressions which can then be used as ready-made chunks. Then, in an ideal world, analytic learners would need to synthesize and integrate language, while the memory-oriented learners would benefit from analysing their wide repertoire of memorized language.

But now we need to consider the relationship between learner orientation and type of instruction. An optimistic perspective would suggest that matching learners and instruction, (eg analytic learners with an analytic methodology), will result in happy learners who will feel in tune with the instruction they are receiving since they are being asked to do what they are naturally good at. A pessimistic interpretation, though, would suggest that matching learner and instructional orientation in this way, rather than playing to strengths, simply consolidates weaknesses. Analytic learners will be allowed to concentrate on what they are good at, and, as a result, not have to deal effectively with areas of weakness, ie communication, and a fluency-orientation to language. Memory-oriented learners, similarly, will be confirmed in their attitude to language. They will achieve communication, but will not be required to explore areas which do not come naturally. They will not be obliged to focus on more complex forms to achieve a given communication, or on the need for accuracy. Similarly, one could regard 'mismatches' between learner orientation and type of instruction as good and bad: good, since they force learners to deal with areas of weakness, thus preventing the narrow perspectives on language and learning which would otherwise occur; bad, since learners might be alienated by the unfamiliarity of the methodological approach.

This account simply places even more responsibility upon the teacher in task-based approaches to instruction. What it means is that in addition to the processing constraints on balancing the goals of accuracy, complexity and fluency that have been covered already, the teacher has to try to engineer some degree of self-awareness on the learner's part so that there is avoidance of the danger of only playing to one's strengths and never addressing one's weaknesses. There is also the need, when designing, sequencing and implementing tasks, to take account of learner factors in deciding what emphases to place on the different aspects of instruction.

One can generalize here and say that the teacher, in a task-based approach, needs to command a significantly wider range of skills than in more structural approaches. These include:

- an ability to select and sequence tasks for supplementary activities
- the competence to organize, appropriately, pre- and post-task activities
- a willingness to adapt task difficulty during the actual task phase
- a sensitivity to individual differences and the capacity to adapt tasks to take account of differences in learner orientation.

Above all, though, what the teacher has to try to achieve is to channel the attentional focus of his or her learners, in such a way that it is more likely that they will balance the three goals of accuracy, complexity and fluency. In other words, the teacher has to contrive a situation in which learners are simultaneously alert to language-as-form and language-as-meaning. The teacher has also to switch attention between these two areas rapidly to ensure that the one does not lead to development at the expense of the other. An excessive focus on meaning during task completion runs the risk of learners becoming confined to the strategic solutions they develop without sufficient focus for structural change or accuracy. An excessive focus on form will not push learners to integrate language structure into effective on-going communication. So, if one is using a task-based approach to instruction, it is necessary to design into the materials ways in which attention is directed to form, to capitalize on learners' own ability to internalize new language when it is brought into the focus of their attention.

Peter Skehan
teaches on the MA and MPhil/PhD programmes at Thames Valley University, London. His main interests are in individual differences, language testing and second language acquisition. His most recent publication is *Language Learners and Language Learning* (OUP 1996).

What learners know and what they need to learn

4

Terry Shortall

From the 50s through to the late 70s, the Audiolingual method (ALM) dominated the world of language teaching. Languages were dissected into lists of isolated grammatical structures (usually based around verb tenses) and these were taught to learners in piecemeal fashion using the PPP approach (see Willis, D., Paper 5 and Skehan, Paper 3), the idea being that learners acquire whatever structure is presented to them and then move on to the next one. Loosely speaking, there was seen to be a connection between ALM and Behaviourist theory, the idea being that learners could be programmed to acquire the structures we teachers chose to present in class.

During ALM's heyday, Contrastive Analysis (CA) was also in vogue: this was the idea that you could contrast any first language (L1) with any target second language (L2) and, from the list of structural differences, predict the errors that learners would make. This belief is still widely held today.

In 1959, Chomsky demolished Behaviourism as an explanation of (first) language acquisition. His ideas began to filter through to the world of language teaching, and by the late 70s, both ALM and CA had, in theory, been consigned to the rubbish heap. With them went certainty and security for the language teacher. No more could carefully measured dollops of carefully analysed structures be meted out to rooms full of monolinguals desperate to share in our bilingual vision of the world.

Since then, we have seen the coming (and going?) of numerous approaches and methods, such as The Silent Way, Suggestopedia, the (still with us?) notional-functional approach, and latterly, the advent of a variety of eclectic approaches loosely gathered under the banner of Communicative Language Teaching (CLT), many of which reject the explicit teaching of grammatical structure (see, for example, Brown 1994 for a review of these approaches).

Developments away from the rigidity of ALM are undoubtedly a healthy source of renewal in the profession. But there is a danger that we can develop such a fixation with the teaching of communication skills that knowledge of linguistic structure is regarded as somehow irrelevant or unnecessary. We cannot afford such rejection of the teaching of grammar: 'There is growing evidence that a lack of concern for form … can lead to fossilization and an excessive dependence on communication strategies' (Skehan, Paper 3).

But this certainly does not imply the retention of a focus on grammar along the lines established by ALM. It suggests that we should look more closely at the kind of grammar we are teaching and how we are teaching it. We need, as Kerr (Paper 9) points out, to 'take greater stock of recent developments in SLA [Second Language Acquisition] theory and models of language description'. The comments of people like Skehan and Kerr suggest that there is a need for a return to some kind of classroom focus on linguistic structure. In this paper, I will be looking at how both traditional and recent theories of SLA can inform such a focus.

I will attempt to examine some recent developments in SLA (specifically, theories of Universal Grammar) and show how these, when combined with a more traditional Contrastive Analysis perspective, can inform the ways we teach grammar and allow us to develop an understanding of the vast amount of knowledge which L2 learners bring with them to the acquisition task. Eventually this may allow us to make principled decisions about what areas of structure need to be focused on and what areas are likely to be acquired without overt instruction.

Traditional Contrastive Analysis

Every teacher and learner of foreign languages (FL) knows that L1 grammars influence the state of L2 grammars. That this has influenced the way we teach FL is common knowledge. This idea of contrasting languages in order to produce teaching materials was formalized half a century ago:

> … the most efficient materials are those based on a scientific description of the language to be learned, carefully compared with a parallel description of the native language. (Fries 1945)

The notions of language transfer and L1 interference have also been around for some time. Lado suggested that

> … individuals tend to transfer the forms and meanings and the distribution of forms and meanings of their native language and culture to the foreign language and culture. (Lado 1957:2)

The basic ambitions of the kind of Contrastive Analysis implied by Fries and Lado have been defined by Van Els et al (1984:38) as being threefold:

- providing insights into similarities and differences between languages
- explaining and predicting problems in L2 learning
- developing course materials for language teaching

Larsen-Freeman and Long (1991:53) describe the contrastive analysis hypothesis as having the following tenets: 'where two languages were similar, positive transfer would occur; where they were different, negative transfer, or interference, would result'.

In its strongest formulation, CA predicted that all structural differences between an L1 and L2 would be the source of learner errors. If this were the case, Japanese learners of English would have considerable problems with word order. While English has an SVO order (Subject – Verb – Object), Japanese has SOV. Where English has *I saw John,*

Japanese has *Watashi wa John o mimashita* (literally *I John saw.*) Also, while English prepositions come before the noun (*in the garden*), Japanese has *niwa de* (*garden in*). So the English *I saw John in the garden* is rendered in Japanese as *Watashi wa niwa de John o mimashita.* These differences are shown in Example 1a – d, where the error predicted by CA is marked with an asterisk:

(1a) Watashi wa   niwa   de   John o   mimashita.

(1b) I (subj.)   garden   in   John (obj.)   saw.

(1c) 'I saw John in the garden.'

(1d) *I garden in John saw.

According to CA, therefore, Japanese should have considerable initial difficulties with English word order and these difficulties would be revealed in a rash of errors. The problem for CA theorists is that there is little evidence of Japanese learners producing such errors, even at early stages in the acquisition process. Japanese children start to study English in junior high school at the age of 12; although they are given examples of English sentences with appropriate word order, they are exposed to a limited number of pedagogic activities which focus on the contrasting word orders. Despite this lack of overt instruction in word order, there is strong evidence that these features of L2 English are acquired at an early stage and without any great incidence of error (survey of eight Japanese high school teachers of English).

Another error predicted for Japanese learners relates to the definite and indefinite article. In Japanese, there is no direct equivalent to the definite or indefinite article, so a contrastive analysis would suggest that these would be omitted by Japanese learners of English; if we ignore word order predictions, this would produce the error shown in Example 2d:

(2a) Kuruma o   fuite   kudasai.

(2b) Car (obj.)   clean   please.

(2c) 'Please clean the car.'

(2d) *Please clean car.

This time, the prediction is (at least partly) true. Japanese learners have been known to omit articles where these are essential but, at the same time, include them when they should be omitted, as in Example 3 (not predicted by standard CA theory):

(3) *The history was a difficult subject for me.

The problem with CA predictions is simply that they are often gross over-simplifications. As we have just seen, not all contrasts lead to error. In addition, errors not predicted by CA often occur.

CA fails to consider, among other factors, individual variation in learners, the effects of affective factors, educational background, the individual communicative requirements of learners, and so on. And it also fails to systematically account for cross-linguistic differences in terms of a multilingual context, what we now know as Universal Grammar (UG).

In 1980, in one of the definitive CA publications, Carl James suggested that

> … without [reference to universals], CA can be no more than a listing of language idiosyncrasies and a random itemization at best. The existence of some universal set of basic categories will allow the pairing of the respective idiosyncrasies of L1 and L2, since they can be matched by reference to the same underlying category. (James 1980:66)

What James was saying was that side-by-side comparisons of pairs of languages in isolation was ineffective in predicting learner behaviour, and that what was needed was a frame of reference that would encompass the universal properties of all languages. What James was predicting is now known as the UG Principles and Parameters Theory, which I will refer to in the next section. But by then it was too late to save CA, at least in its original form. Because of its inaccuracies, CA had already lost credibility among second language acquisition researchers and many language teachers. And as a result, a powerful (and often useful) tool was virtually abandoned.

In the next section, I will attempt to show that a theory of Universal Grammar can to some extent explain the inaccurate predictions made by CA and in this respect help to rehabilitate the concept and re-establish its relevance to current SLA theories.

Universal Grammar and second language acquisition

There is much debate about whether or not there are similarities between the way we acquire our first languages as children and any subsequent languages as adults. Theories of language acquisition arising from Chomsky's (1981 and ff.) theory of Universal Grammar have attempted to address this question. Chomsky proposed something quite startling. He suggested that in spite of these surface differences all languages have basic similarities in terms of design features. As part of our human inheritance we are born with knowledge of these features which, in UG theory, are known as universal principles. In effect UG suggests that children are born with an innate capacity to learn languages, which we will call the UG faculty. The UG faculty consists of, or contains, the basic properties of the grammars of all natural languages.

But if all children are programmed in the same way for learning language, how is it that a child exposed to Japanese ends up speaking Japanese, whereas a child exposed to English ends up speaking English? UG offers an explanation for this.

A simple example might be related to prepositions. For example, it is a universal principle that all languages have words which perform the function of prepositions, like *in, on, under,* etc in English; in UG theory, we would say that the child is born with knowledge of this principle. Let's then say that one half of the world's languages place prepositions before nouns (as in English)and the other half place prepositions after nouns (as in Japanese). In UG terms, this would be called a parameter, and is seen to work like a switch: if you grow up listening to Japanese, you'll set the switch to 'prepositions-last' position, while if you grow up listening to English, you'll set the switch to 'prepositions-first' position.

In its crudest form, this is how UG sees language: a collection of universal principles which the child is born with and a set of parameters waiting to be switched one way or another depending on the language of the environment. Once the parameters have been set, the basic properties of the language (in UG this is called core grammar) have been learned.

Taken to the extreme, this suggests that all languages are pretty much the same. And in fact, in one of his more outrageous statements, Chomsky has suggested that 'there is only one human language, apart from the lexicon, and language acquisition is in essence a matter of determining lexical idiosyncrasies' (Chomsky 1989:44).

While this may seem an extremely crude generalization to most language teachers, it does begin to suggest that there is a wealth of language knowledge which the (L1 and L2) learner possesses about universal grammar which is perhaps not being taken into account, at least in L2 classrooms.

Next we will look at the structure of one of the UG parameters and consider what light this can shed on the CA predictions outlined above. (Accessible accounts of UG and its relevance to L2 acquisition can be found in Cook 1988 and White 1989.)

The Head Parameter

The so-called Head Parameter describes how lexical heads behave in relation to their complements. To illustrate how this works, I will reanalyse the sentence from Example 1, which I repeat here:

(1a) Watashi wa   niwa   de   John o   mimashita.

(1b) I (subj.)   garden   in   John (obj.)   saw.

(1c) I saw John in the garden.

(1d) *I garden in John saw.

First of all, I will divide the English sentence (1c) into phrases using square brackets:

(1c) I [saw John] [in the garden].

The first phrase, *saw John*, is a verb phrase (VP): the key word (often called the lexical head) is the verb *saw* which is followed by its complement, the noun *John*. This can be represented diagrammatically (fig. 1).

Figure 1: English verb phrase

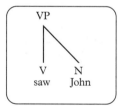

The second phrase, *in the garden*, is a prepositional phrase (PP); again, the lexical head, the preposition *in*, precedes its complement, *the garden* (fig. 2).

Figure 2: English prepositional phrase

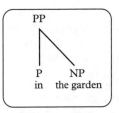

In UG parlance, English is said to be head-initial in that the lexical heads of each phrase always come first in their respective phrases (ie the heads precede their complements).

If we now look at the equivalent Japanese sentence at (1a), we can see that Japanese lexical heads always follow their complements. The verb *mimashita* follows its complement, *John o* (fig. 3).

Figure 3: Japanese verb phrase

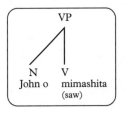

while the preposition (in Japanese, a post-position) *ni* follows its complement *niwa*: (fig. 4).

Figure 4: Japanese prepositional phrase

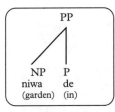

A side-by-side visualization of the head-complement structures of English and Japanese (I have included an example of a noun and its complement) creates a striking image of symmetric variation (fig. 5).

Figure 5: English and Japanese head-complement structures

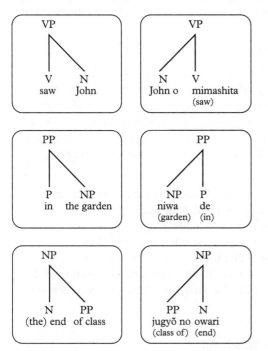

A superficial analysis of English and Japanese reveals that there is a difference in word order. Our more detailed analysis shows that the differences are not random – they are highly systematic. In English the head comes before the complement, while in Japanese the complement precedes the head; and this generalization (ie English is head-initial while Japanese is head-final) holds for all phrase types (ie adjective, noun and adverb phrases as well as verb and preposition phrases).

A number of important consequences arise from the above analysis. I have already suggested that there is an important generalization underlying the superficial differences between English and Japanese. But even more important is the fact that this systematic similarity and variation applies not only to English and Japanese, but to almost all languages. Practically all of the world's languages can be analysed as either head-initial or head-final; and this is a much more powerful contrast than those reached through the traditional CA system of contrasting pairs of L1s and L2s. Finally, and of considerable importance to acquisition studies, is the fact that, despite the complexities of head-complement structures and how they apply across all phrase types, children learn head-complement directions at a relatively early age.

Japanese children recognize from the very earliest stages that all phrases (VP, PP, AdvP, etc) are head-final, and this obviously *cannot* result from any conscious language learning. Children are simply unequipped to make conscious generalizations across such a wide range of phrase types. Child language acquisition can only be accounted for if we accept that the child possesses a specific innate mental (UG) faculty for this purpose. The notion that specific parameters are set to a +/– setting, in particular, is a convenient way of explaining how children, at an early stage in life, and after only limited exposure to language, perform complex linguistic operations at a phrasal level.

The Head Parameter and L2 learners

This innate understanding of grammatical variables applies not only to children learning a first language, but also to L2 learners. Adult Japanese learners of English produce sentences to accord with the head-initial nature of English at an early stage, and with minimal overt rule-teaching, suggesting that L2 learners also have access to something resembling the UG faculty (for a discussion of whether the UG faculty is still active in adults or whether it is only available via L1 knowledge, see, for example, Eubank 1991).

The idea that adult learners can reset parameters is in itself an important finding. It shows us quite clearly that learners are learning aspects of grammar that we are not teaching them, and that they have unconscious knowledge of grammar systems which we, as teachers, are often unaware of. Learners possess huge amounts of apparently flexible linguistic knowledge, as well as the ability to 'discover' (consciously or otherwise) grammar rules from the input received in the classroom; recognition of this has to be factored into teacher decisions about what structures to teach and when and how to teach them.

Out on the periphery: territory for teaching

What are the final implications of all this? Obviously there are research implications. So far we know relatively little about Universal Grammar and can make only isolated statements which are of immediate value to teachers. Meanwhile what are the implications for the teacher?

As we have seen, Core Grammar is constructed by setting values for fundamental linguistic structures (ie parameters). Core grammar, might, for example, establish that any language has a set of determiners – in English these are words like *the, a(n), some, this, her,* which are found at the beginning of the noun phrase. On the basis of their innate knowledge of Universal Grammar, learners will expect to find a system of determiners in any language they encounter. What these determiners consist of, however, will not be established, and will be very much a language-specific phenomenon (ie peripheral to the core). Compare, for example, the set of determiners available in English with those available in Japanese (Table 1).

Table 1: Determiners in Japanese and English

Determiners	English	Japanese
articles:	the, a	–
demonstratives:	this, that, etc	kore, sore, etc
quantifiers:	some (a little), every	sukoshi, zenbu
possessives:	my, your	watashi-no, anata-no
Wh- determiners:	whose, what, which	dare-no, nan-no, dochira-no

Presumably, the L2 learner will quickly establish that a set of determiners exists, but he/she will have problems determining the exact nature and distribution of these. This would explain the errors predicted by CA at (2) and (3), repeated here:

(2a) Kuruma o   fuite   kudasai.

(2b) Car (obj.)   clean   please.

(2c) 'Please clean the car.'

(2d) ★ Please clean car.

(3) ★ The history was a difficult subject for me.

Interestingly, Skehan (Paper 3) suggests that errors such as that in (2) are common in learners who haven't received instruction, while the overgeneralization error in (3) is more likely to be committed by learners who have received instruction.

This shows quite clearly that if we take the category *determiner* as a starting point then Japanese and English have a great deal in common. If, however, as most courses do, we take the definite and indefinite articles as our starting point, then Japanese and English have relatively little in common.

This suggests that a description which starts from universal categories, such as determiner, may well provide learners with a surer foundation than a description which starts from language-specific categories like articles.

By rooting the (English) language-specific notion of article in the greater context of a determiner system, we can show Japanese learners how English articles perform functions which in Japanese are performed by demonstrative determiners and context clues. This means that, rather than introduce articles to Japanese learners as something which has no counterpart in their L1, we can perform this introduction in a meaningful and identifiable context.

Core grammar and peripheral grammar

We have suggested that languages share universal design features – built-in principles at birth and parameter 'switches' waiting to be set. Together, principles and 'set' parameters make up the fundamental, core features of a language. Beyond these core features, it is clear that languages differ from one another in important ways. Obviously the lexicon is fundamentally language-specific: there is no systematic way to describe differences between the English *dog*, the French *chien*, the Portuguese *cão* and the Japanese *inu*. Words have to be learned.

But while words differ from language to language, we have seen that, in terms of their structural relationship with any complements they take, they behave systematically and in universally predictable ways. At the same time, we must recognize that words behave non-systematically and in highly language-specific ways, for example, in the way they combine non-structurally with other words. It makes sense in English to talk about *leading a dog's life* but *mener la vie d'un chien* makes no sense in French. The word *lead* in English collocates with *life*, and *a dog's life* is a fixed expression in English. In French although *mener* collocates with *vie*, the phrase *la vie d'un chien* does not have the status of a fixed expression in French. These collocations and fixed phrases are not core (universal) features, but (language-specific) peripheral features.

The notion of core and peripheral aspects of grammar (fig. 6) allows us to rehabilitate to some extent the Contrastive Analysis Hypothesis: the core is acquired with ease, while language-specific peripheral aspects may lead to L1 interference, and it is these areas which may need some kind of focused instruction.

Figure 6: Core and periphery in grammar: some examples

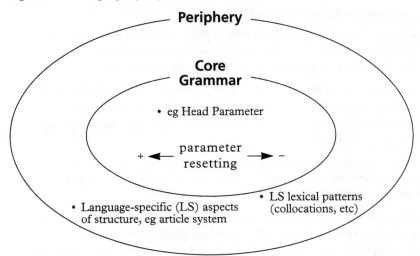

Obviously, there are other problems with a strong CA approach: allowances have to be made for individual variation, overgeneralization, inappropriate input and so on. At the same time, it must be remembered that structure (especially language-specific structures) is highly dependent on lexis; the teaching of language-specific structure through a focus on lexical patterns, as advocated by Willis, D. (1990), may provide the kind of insights learners need to negotiate the periphery.

In the final analysis, there does seem to be a reasonably strong case for once again trying to examine the effects of L1 on L2 (arguably through a universalist prism). Most language learners make L1 vs L2 comparisons. It may be time teachers and applied linguists started doing so again.

After all, there does seem to be strong evidence that L2 learners

- have considerable knowledge (possibly unconscious) about the universally common features of language and use this in acquiring an L2;

- bring their L1 knowledge to bear on the process of acquisition and, while this may lead to error, it will almost certainly accelerate the acquisition process.

In recognizing the sophistication of these processes used by learners, and in sharing this recognition with learners, teachers can show learners that while the path to L2 linguistic competence may be slow and arduous, the knowledge that learners bring with them will certainly make the journey easier.

Finally, the positions outlined here also have implications (even if somewhat limited) for syllabus design. It is now generally accepted that the arbitrarily established lists of verb-based structures used in audiolingual syllabi are inadequate and often ignorant of real acquisition processes. What we can now say is that those structures which relate to core grammar need not be explicitly taught, and it is only those at the periphery which may require enhanced input (instruction of one kind or another). In a way, this amounts to an anti-syllabus syllabus. Rather than imposing unreliable lists of structures on students and teachers, we may be more profitably employed in suggesting lists of those structures which probably do not need coverage.

There is a long way to go before we can reach that point. At present, only a small number of core linguistic features have been identified. We have looked briefly at the head parameter. Another fruitful area of investigation concerns the 'pro-drop parameter'. Some languages, like English for example, always have a grammatical subject. Often this subject is a pronoun referring to a person, as in *I speak English*. Even where there is no person to refer to, languages like English will insist on the presence of a 'dummy' subject as in *It's raining*. Other languages, like Portuguese, referred to as 'pro-drop languages', can drop personal pronouns, thereby producing *Falo portugues*, literally, **Speak* [first person] *Portuguese*. Such languages have no way of including a dummy pronoun when it is not personal, so that *It's raining* becomes *Está chovendo*, literally, **Is* [3rd person] *raining*. Another feature of pro-drop languages is that they allow post-verbal subjects, as in the Portuguese *Chegou o tren*, literally **Arrived the train*. The English (non-pro-drop) equivalent, *The train (has) arrived*, would not, of course, allow the subject to come after the verb. For a discussion of the prop-drop parameter, see White (1989).

The striking fact here is that all languages can apparently be seen as +/– pro-drop. In other words, languages are either pro-drop languages, or not pro-drop languages. And again, as with the Head Parameter, this symmetry along a universal feature is another example of the way languages display a consistent pattern of behaviour rather than random idiosyncrasies.

Once we know that languages differ in one way we can predict that they differ in other ways as well. The same applies to similarities. This opens up the possibility of a typology of languages. If the differences and similarities between languages are systematic we can begin to describe the systems in operation and make powerful general statements about different languages.

As I have said, there is much to be done before we reach that point. Still, these are exciting times, and there is much reason for optimism. In years to come, if and when we have sorted the universal from the language-specific, we may look back and agree with Chomsky that 'there is only one human language, apart from the lexicon'. (I wonder what language teachers will be doing then.)

Terry Shortall teaches on the MA in TEFL at the University of Birmingham. He has taught EFL in Japan, Brazil and Portugal. His main interests are innate abilities in second language acquisition, grammar and learner attitudes.

2 Some classroom implications

ave Willis offers a critique of PPP based on the way language is used in the classroom. The *presentation* and *practice* stages of a lesson are normally seen as focusing on accuracy. Willis challenges this and argues that the real focus at these stages is on conformity. Conformity 'is designed to ensure that learners produce language in line with the form or forms required by the teacher'. Accuracy on the other hand is concerned with 'the relationship between what is intended and what is achieved in communication'.

Willis echoes Skehan and Lewis in rejecting the assumption implicit in PPP that conformity leads directly to mastery. He then goes on to argue that even the production stage of a lesson often puts a heavy premium on conformity because learners believe that at this stage they are required to produce the target forms irrespective of whether or not they are appropriate to the task in hand. If this is true, then there is little concern for language use in the PPP cycle, and an overwhelming concern for conformity.

Willis does not, however, dismiss conformity activities. He argues that they have a place, though a limited place, in the methodological cycle. He sees an effective cycle as having components which focus not only on *conformity,* but also on:

Fluency   'opportunities to process language for communicative purposes as receivers and producers'.

Accuracy   achieved when learners have time to consider the communicative demands they are about to face so that they can make the best possible use of their existing language system.

Analysis   conscious searching for patterns and regularities in language.

If we are to achieve an effective methodology we must find a way of balancing these demands on the learner.

Jane Willis proposes a task-based methodology which attempts to achieve this balance. Central to the methodology are language tasks carried out spontaneously in pairs and groups which provide opportunities for real-time language use (fluency). Learners are then asked to reflect on these tasks and, after some preparation, to report the outcome of their work to the class as a whole. This report stage involves planning time and therefore allows for a focus on accuracy as well as fluency. In Skehan's terms, the report stage offers learners a linguistic challenge which will help to drive their interlanguage development forward. At the final stage of the task cycle (analysis), learners are asked to look critically at elements of the language involved in the task, highlighting certain forms and noting the ways in which they are used.

This task framework is contextualized within a good deal of language exposure. There is an introduction to the topic and task in which the teacher explains to students what is expected of them. There is discussion of the outcome of the task. Willis argues that the task cycle and this contextualizing exposure meet the four essential conditions for language learning. They provide rich *exposure* to real language. They provide opportunities for real *language use*. They provide *motivation* in that they provide a challenging context for language use; and they provide for a *focus on language form* in the analysis stage.

Willis also argues that all the components of this methodology are in regular use in our classrooms even where the relations between the components are not carefully thought out. There is nothing here to frighten even the novice teacher. Indeed Willis describes an informal experiment which introduced novice trainees to the idea of task-based teaching. They were quickly able to offer a shrewd analysis of what was happening in the task-based classroom.

In Paper 7 Willis and Willis look in detail at language work in the task-based classroom. They recommend a consciousness-raising (C-R) approach to language study and go on to define this. They then list aspects of grammar and language study which need to be focused on in C-R activities. They show how language data can be made available for language study and they offer a classification of C-R activities. They go on to discuss starting points which make language study accessible to students and they finish by working with two texts, one written and one spoken, to show how a series of C-R activities can be generated.

5 Accuracy, fluency and conformity

Dave Willis

Outline

I would like to do four things in this article.

- I would like to characterize the teacher-controlled classroom activities which form the basis of the first two stages – presentation and practice – of a PPP methodology. These activities are usually seen as providing a focus on accuracy. I will suggest that this is a mistaken view. What they really focus on is conformity. The theory of learning which underpins them is basically behaviourist, shaping the language produced by learners so that it conforms to that demanded by the teacher.

- Secondly, I will look at the third stage of the PPP cycle – the production or free stage – and see if it offers activity of a genuinely different kind, see if it is indeed the communicative activity it is often claimed to be.

- Thirdly, I would like to go back to reassess controlled activities. I will argue that these do not promote the learning of grammar in the way they are believed to do. They may, however, contribute to learning other aspects of language. They may also contribute strongly to student motivation.

- Finally, I will make recommendations for lesson planning and the provision of an effective learning environment. In doing this I will attempt to retain the benefits of the PPP approach, while replacing it with something which rests on more secure foundations.

A methodology which is based on presentation, practice and production appears at first sight to allow for three important elements contributing to language learning. It allows for a precise focus on specific target forms of the language. It encourages learners to produce language with a proper concern for form, and it provides opportunities for language use in a communicative context. I will argue that this appearance is illusory. PPP does offer a precise focus on specific target forms but in doing so it shows a serious misunderstanding of the learning process. The concern for form is achieved by encouraging students to produce language unthinkingly in accordance with stimuli provided by the teacher. There is no real communicative language use. The production stage of the lesson is a further exercise in producing language expected by the teacher rather than using language for communication.

Accuracy, fluency and conformity

One way of contrasting a presentation methodology with a task-based approach to learning is to say that the one sets a premium on accuracy and the other sets a premium on fluency (see Brumfit 1984a). A presentation methodology entails a good deal of language control on the part of the teacher in the interests of accuracy. It is based on the assumption that out of accuracy comes fluency. A task-based approach, on the other hand, is normally realized through a deep-end strategy whereby learners do their best to achieve some kind of resolution to a communicative problem through the deployment of their existing language resources. Those resources may be supplemented as necessary, but the main focus is not on accuracy but on fluency. An approach of this kind is based on the assumption that out of fluency comes accuracy. I would like to look briefly at the notions of accuracy and fluency and to suggest that if we are to describe the kinds of activity that are typical of many classrooms we need at the very least a third element – conformity.

It seems to me that to be meaningful a focus on accuracy must take account of meaning. Accuracy should describe the relationship between what is intended and what is achieved in communication. Controlled practice in the classroom is not concerned with accuracy in this sense. It is designed to ensure that learners produce language in line with the form or forms required by the teacher. This sort of extract from the classroom is very familiar:

> T: Virginia, ask erm Sokoop, Sokoop, being erm a father. Can you ask him? Being a father.
> V: Er yes, er yes. Do you like being a father?
> T: Mm hm.
> S: Yes, I am … I am er father of four children.
> T: Yes. Listen to her question though. Say it again. Say it again.
> V: Do you like being a father?
> S: Yes I like being … to be …
> T: Mm hm. Yes.
> S: Yes I do.
> T: Yes I do. I like being a father.
>
> (Data taken from Willis, J. 1992:73)

When the teacher says *Yes. Listen to her question though* what she means is *Yes, your answer is acceptable, but the form is not acceptable. Listen to the question. That will give you a clue as to the form of the answer.* Sokoop, however, is somewhat confused at this stage. The teacher finally rescues him from this confusion by providing the appropriate answer in the appropriate form: *Yes I do. I like being a father.* But Sokoop's original answer is accurate. It is accurate in the sense that it is an acceptable sentence of English. It is also accurate in the sense that it achieves the response Sokoop wants to achieve, emphasizing his pride in his family of four children. It is interactively appropriate in that Sokoop happily nominates his family as the next topic of conversation. But the answer is not accurate in the teacher's terms. The teacher requires a response of a particular form. She is looking not simply for accuracy, but for conformity. Sokoop might have elicited the teacher's approval by saying: *No, I don't like being a father* or possibly by saying *I love being a father,* but a host of other possibilities such as *Yeah, it's great now the kids are older* or *It depends what you mean,* are ruled out.

The practice stage of the lesson continues the focus on conformity. Again students are expected to produce utterances of the form identified by the teacher. There may be an appearance of meaningful language use but the language produced is meaningful in only the most restricted sense. Meaning entails choice and there is no real choice here – it is a question of the teacher orchestrating predicted student responses.

The production stage – fluency or conformity?

A focus on fluency comes, it is claimed, in the production stage or free stage. Here learners are supposed to be free to use to communicative effect whatever language they have at their disposal. But there are, I think, serious problems with the notion of a production stage. The belief that lies behind the PPP sequence seems to be that if an item is presented to learners and if they have time to practise this under teacher control they will then go on to incorporate it in a production stage – that *conformity* leads directly to mastery. The production stage is to be taken as evidence that the target item has become an active part of the learner's linguistic repertoire. But evidence from our own classroom experience, from observation and transcripts of language lessons, and overwhelmingly from second language acquisition research, suggests that this does not in fact happen. It is quite unrealistic to expect students to make acquaintance with a 'new' language form and, within the space of a single lesson, incorporate it into their working grammar of the language.

Although there is a good deal of controversy among second language acquisition researchers, there is almost unanimous agreement on one point: we cannot isolate a particular language form and 'present' it to learners in such a way that it becomes a part of their communicative performance. Long and Crookes put this strongly:

> Where syntax is concerned, research shows that learners rarely if ever move from zero to target-like mastery of new items in one step. Both naturalistic and classroom learners pass through fixed developmental stages in word order, negation, questions, relative clauses, and so on – sequences which have to include often quite lengthy stages of *non*-target-like use of forms as well as use of non-target-like forms. (Long and Crookes 1992:31)

Long and Crookes go on to quote a wide range of sources in support of this view. Ellis expresses the same view more informally but equally forcefully in a recent interview:

> It seems to me that there's plenty of evidence that we can do PPP until we're blue in the face, but it doesn't necessarily result in what PPP was designed to do. And yet there is still, within language teaching, a commitment to trying to control not only the input but actually what is learned. (Ellis 1993:4-5)

Indeed one could cite research going back at least to Corder (1967) and continuing to this day (see, for example, Skehan, Paper 3). There is abundant evidence that the PPP paradigm does not work in the way it is supposed to work. Learners do not and cannot proceed smoothly from first acquaintance with a target form to the production of that target form as a part of their communicative repertoire.

If learners do incorporate the new target form in the language they use in the production stage there are three possible reasons for this. The first is that the learners were familiar with the form before the presentation and practice stages. It was already part of their linguistic repertoire. They would have been quite capable of producing the required form even without the presentation and practice.

The second possibility is that the target form is, as it happens, about to make 'the shift from careful to extemporaneous use' (Foster, Paper 12). In other words the structure that has been 'presented' is actually not new at all. It is already part of the learners' system, but is not yet a part of their spontaneous production, although it is near to becoming so. This is an ideal scenario. The PPP cycle would be reinforcing the learners' natural language development. The chances of teacher intervention being so timely are, however, pretty remote.

The final possibility is that learners do not treat the third stage of the lesson as an opportunity for fluent communication. They regard it as an opportunity to display the target form. If learners perceive that the aim of the production stage is to provide some evidence that they are aware of the target form which has been identified in the earlier stages of the lesson, then they will be at pains to provide this evidence. Learners are, after all, generally compliant and co-operative. But if learners do take this co-operative line this nullifies the very purpose of the production phase. It is no longer a stage in which learners seek to achieve some communicative purpose as best they can – a process which may *incidentally* involve the use of the target form. Instead it becomes a stage in which they are at pains to display the target form and *incidentally* to go through the appearance of using language to achieve a communicative outcome. In other words what we have from the learners' point of view is a continuing concern with *conformity* rather than an attempt to deploy their growing language competence in the process of communication. Although they do display the target form, production is far from fluent. It is faltering and inconsistent, requiring constant correction and reformulation.

This faltering production is not to be taken as evidence that learners have achieved a communicative command of the target form. As soon as they switch to circumstances in which the focus *is* on communication rather than conformity learners will 'regress'. They will no longer produce the target form, even when its use may be required by the communicative demands of the situation in which they find themselves. This situation is distressingly familiar to all teachers. We may go through a lesson with every appearance of success. Learners may appear to have produced the target form successfully. They give an appearance of mastery of the first conditional or the interrupted past or whatever the target may be. But next time the occasion arises to put the form to communicative use they fail to do so. The mastery is illusory. It is there as long as there is a focus on conformity, but as soon as there is a demand for communicative fluency the mastery evaporates.

There is, it seems, little evidence to suggest that the PPP paradigm works in the way it is supposed to work. It does not, as is claimed, lead in easy stages from presentation to mastery. At the same time, as a paradigm which focuses throughout on conformity it leaves little room for communicative language use. Finally, because it 'presents' language and requires little intellectual involvement on the part of the learner it does not provide for a critical focus on language form.

The value of conformity activities

But many teachers would claim that the PPP paradigm does work, that it does provide an environment in which learners move gradually towards mastery of the target system. We should think carefully before abandoning activities which have such a following. Brumfit (1984b) makes precisely this point:

> Many language learners have testified to the usefulness of [such traditional learning activities as exercises and drills], and an authoritative rejection of such procedures needs to be based on firmer evidence than has been forthcoming. Much more useful would be to explore the role that such traditional practices have had for learners who have found them helpful. (Brumfit 1984b:320)

Even while denying that conformity-based activities contribute to the learning of grammar I would accept that controlled repetition can serve three important functions in the classroom:

- It allows students, particularly in the early stages of learning, to pay careful attention to the acquisition of the complex motor skills involved in the pronunciation of a new language. It may well be that behaviourist techniques are particularly effective in this endeavour.

- It helps students identify some of the fixed phrases which make up a large part of language and the mastery of which is a large part of language learning, and it helps them consolidate these units (see Sinclair 1988; Widdowson 1989; Lewis, Paper 2).

- It helps motivate learners in two ways. First it highlights a clear and specific learning goal. It makes learning appear achievable. Secondly successful repetition creates the comforting illusion that learning has actually taken place.

The first of these purposes is not affected by what I have argued so far. The fallacy I am attacking is that controlled repetition leads to a mastery of the grammar of the language. I have not sought to deny that controlled repetition may play an important part in teaching and learning pronunciation. The second purpose also has little to do with the teaching of the grammatical system. Just as learners may be encouraged by their teacher to get their tongues round new lexical items so they may be encouraged to commit to memory fixed phrases which are seen as extended lexical items. These phrases may later provide input to help the grammar develop, but initially the aim is to focus on a phrase as a lexical item rather than on a phrase as an illustration or exemplar of a particular grammatical generalization.

The third purpose may involve the repetition of pattern sentences very similar to those presented in the first stage of a PPP lesson. But the purpose as defined above sees the activity as contributing to motivation rather than contributing directly to learning. Certainly motivation is a powerful factor in making learning activities more effective. A teacher who smiles and encourages students is likely to achieve better results than a teacher who does not. But the confidence and well-being generated by those smiles and encouragement are not learning activities. Smiles and encouragement are part of the effective packaging of learning which is an essential part of the good teacher's repertoire. They contribute to learning indirectly. In the same way the definition of learning goals and the appearance of achievement do not lead directly to learning. Like the teacher's smile they contribute indirectly by making learning activities more acceptable and more effective.

The shortcomings of conformity activities

Once we begin to view presentation and practice as focusing on conformity rather than accuracy we are able to see that the approach underlying PPP is behaviourist in nature. It sets a premium on automatic response to stimulus rather than on creative thought. It does not encourage learners to think for themselves about the target language. It encourages them to see the target language as a set of isolated patterns which can be accumulated by obediently following the lead given by their teacher. Rutherford (1987) neatly labels this the 'accumulated entities' view of language.

In fact the most powerful element in the learning process is the learner's intelligence and creativity. If we are to take advantage of these faculties we need to confront learners with language problems which demand an intelligent and creative response. Problem-based activities of this kind, under the name of consciousness-raising activities, are becoming an important part of the thinking of some language teaching theorists and practitioners (see Rutherford 1987 and Papers 3 and 7 of this volume). It is this kind of language work which should be central to a dynamic approach to learning.

Another problem with PPP is that it necessarily limits exposure to language. In the interests of clearly defined and limited lesson aims teachers deliberately restrict the language to which learners are exposed. But if we are to encourage learners to apply their creative intelligence to find regularities in language and to make generalizations about the relationship between form and meaning then we must provide them with plenty of language data to work on. They need exposure to as much language as they can reasonably handle.

Finally learners need to consolidate and refine their language system in use. They need opportunities to use the language for communication. These opportunities should promote genuine communication rather than the appearance of communication which is actually subordinate to the need to display required forms.

Towards an integrated methodology

We may argue for the inclusion of controlled repetition as part of the teacher's repertoire directed towards limited learning goals and as providing useful motivation for students. But it should not be seen as central to a methodology. If we are to see conformity activities primarily as motivating rather than contributing directly to learning two things seem to follow from this. First, controlled repetition should take up a good deal less class time than it does under the PPP paradigm. Learning will be prompted not through activities which promote conformity, but by activities which encourage learners to think critically about language.

Secondly, if it is to reinforce consciousness-raising activities, controlled repetition should come late in the methodological cycle. A natural progression would be to move from communicative use to consciousness-raising and finally to controlled repetition. The purpose of controlled repetition would be to provide a summary of the lesson and a retrospective definition of goals (for a detailed discussion of this see Paper 7).

The major components of a new paradigm should be communicative activities and consciousness-raising activities. Learning is best achieved by first processing language for meaning and, having done this, by examining critically the language that has been processed. Anything, including controlled repetition, which is likely to assist this process should be incorporated, but nothing should usurp the central place of language use and critical language study.

Let me summarize, then, by proposing a methodology with components focusing on four outcomes:

- Fluency: Learners need opportunities to process language for communicative purposes as receivers and producers. These opportunities should be unfettered by the perceived need to conform to teacher expectations in terms of the production of specific language forms. Activities which provide for this focus on fluency are already found in most classrooms as the basis of 'skills lessons'. They are found in some classrooms as the basis of language learning tasks.

- Accuracy: Whenever learners are involved in communication they are concerned with accuracy in that they are making the best use of their language system to meet the communicative demands placed upon it. In spontaneous communication learners have little time to reflect on the language they produce. If, however, they are given time to prepare what they have to produce then there will be a concern for formal accuracy within a communicative context (see Foster, Paper 12; Skehan, Paper 3; Bygate, Paper 13).

- Analysis: Successful learners constantly try to work out for themselves the relationship between form and meaning. They look for patterns and regularities in language. They refer to their knowledge of their own language and the way it is used and apply this knowledge to the learning of the target language. We should encourage all learners to do this.

- Conformity: We need activities which have firm teacher control. It may be argued that these activities contribute strongly to pronunciation and intonation. They may also help familiarize students with the fixed phrases which make up a large part of language. Perhaps more important, these teacher-controlled activities may be used to package learning in a way which makes it more acceptable to many learners. They can be used to provide a precise language focus at the end of a cycle to summarize the lesson by saying 'These are some of the items we have focused on. These are some of the possible learning outcomes of this sequence.'

Many experienced teachers and teacher trainers will claim that this is what they do anyway. They play down the importance of conformity-based activities and try to provide activities which challenge students to use language effectively and to think critically about the language they produce and the language they read and hear. Teachers who have reached this position have already abandoned PPP as a basic paradigm. But PPP still forms the basis of most coursebooks and of many teacher training courses. Some forty years ago a behaviourist methodology, in line with thinking on learning and language description current at that time, dominated classrooms. It is still with us.

We are well aware nowadays of the importance of the learner's contribution. We recognize language learning as a creative process. We know that language is a complex system which cannot be 'presented' to learners in a series of neat packages. Yet many teachers are launched on a career with a methodology based on teacher control which stifles learner initiative and grotesquely simplifies language. Many coursebooks are rooted in a presentation methodology. It is possible for teachers to transcend this limited approach but it takes time, experience and ingenuity.

I am reminded of the old joke about the aged local who was asked the way to Tipperary. After many hesitations and false starts he finally said, 'Well, I know the way all right. But if I wanted to go to Tipperary, I wouldn't want to start from here.' If we are to introduce real independence and creativity into language teaching for both teachers and learners we badly need a new starting point.

Dave Willis
teaches on MA programmes in TEFL and Applied Linguistics in the Centre for English Language Studies at Birmingham University. He is interested in pedagogic language description. He is the author of *The Lexical Syllabus* (Collins Cobuild 1990).

6 A flexible framework for task-based learning

Jane Willis

An overview of a task-based framework

We began to experiment with task-based learning in the early eighties, frustrated by the limitations of the PPP model, even when backed up by 'skills' lessons. We were encouraged by the success of Prabhu's Communicational Teaching Project in primary and secondary schools in Bangalore (Prabhu 1987), and felt supported by recent research findings in the field of SLA such as those summarized by Ellis (1993) and referred to by Skehan earlier in this volume.

The framework that I describe in this chapter was developed over a period of time, working with students aged 14 and upwards in both multi-lingual and mono-lingual classes in a number of teaching environments.

This task-based framework differs from a PPP cycle because the focus on language form comes at the end. The communication task itself is central to the framework. Such a task may involve student production of language and/or may be linked to a spoken or written text. A single task would normally involve both productive skills, eg speaking and note-taking, and receptive skills, eg listening and often reading.

Learners begin by carrying out a communication task, using the language they have learnt from previous lessons or from other sources. They then talk or write about how they did the task and compare findings. At some point they might listen to recordings of other people doing the same task, or read something related to the theme of the task, again relating this to their own experience of doing the task. Only after that is their attention directed towards specific features of language form – features that occur naturally in the recordings they have heard or the texts they have read.

In other words, learners begin with a holistic experience of language in use. They end with a closer look at some of the features naturally occurring in that language. By that point, the learners will have worked with the language and processed it for meaning. It is then that the focus turns to the surface forms that have carried the meanings.

One of the main problems we have in the classroom is providing a context for grammar teaching. In this procedure the context is already established. The framework can be summarized thus:

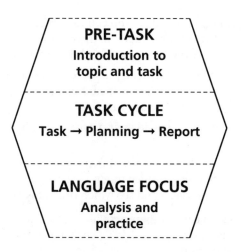

PRE-TASK
**Introduction to
topic and task**

TASK CYCLE
Task → Planning → Report

LANGUAGE FOCUS
**Analysis and
practice**

No new teaching techniques are needed for a task-based approach, although it does demand a different weighting and sequencing. Most of the activities will be the kind of activities that Scrivener classifies as 'Authentic' (see Paper 8). At the end of the cycle, learners may benefit from some 'Restricted' and 'Clarification' activities which focus on specific language forms.

Before illustrating the framework in more detail, I want to define the term 'task'.

What is meant by 'task'?

By 'task' I mean a goal-oriented activity in which learners use language to achieve a real outcome. In other words, learners use whatever target language resources they have in order to solve a problem, do a puzzle, play a game, or share and compare experiences. Some examples follow. The first would be suitable for beginners learning English (instructions could be given in L1), since most of the words are internationally known:

- All these are English words. How many ways can you classify them?
  *hotel   football   taxi   disco   jeans   sandwich   tennis   music   hamburger   video
  goal   museum   Pepsi   dollar   basketball   TV   radio   computer*

- Think of a teacher from your early schooldays whom you remember well. Write down three things you remember about him or her. Then, in pairs, tell each other about them. Try to find two things your teachers had in common.

- Look at the headlines and the first three lines of the following news story. Now together think of and write down seven questions that you both think will be answered in the full story. Give those questions to another pair. Finally read the whole story and see how many of those questions were actually answered.

One topic can give rise to a number of different tasks, and these might be linked in order to provide a thematic 'unit' of study. For example, the topic 'Families' could, depending on the level of your students, give rise to:

- Draw a family tree for your partner's family.
- Family survey: find out if there are more males than females in your partner's family.

- Tell each other all the family birthdays you can remember. Which is the most common month/time of year for birthdays in their family? Make groups of six and see if any one of your family members has a birthday on the same day.
- Memory challenge. Show your partner a photograph of your family. Tell them the names of five or six people in your family including those in the photograph. Turn the photo over. How many names can your partner remember?
- Find out what kinds of work people in your partner's family do or hope to do. Compare with people in your family.
- Decide what you think are the three most difficult problems a single-parent family with two children aged five and thirteen might face. What solutions can you suggest? Then listen to this radio interview and see which problems are mentioned.

It is important to note that in each of these activities there is an identifiable outcome – a family tree is drawn up, a question is resolved, a challenge is met, a list is drawn up, comparisons are made and so on.

Tasks can have a variety of starting points. They may draw on learners' own input, eg personal experience, general/world knowledge, or intellectual challenge; they may be based on written text, recordings of spoken data, or visual data; they could be activities like games, demonstrations or interviews; they could be a combination of several of these, like the last example above.

The important thing is that while doing the tasks, learners are meaning what they say, and focusing on meaning. They are using language to exchange meanings for a real purpose. They are free to use whatever language forms they want. The games they play, the problems they solve, the experiences they share may or may not be things that they will do in real life, but their use of language, because it is purposeful and real, will replicate features of language use outside the classroom.

I would like to clarify here what tasks are not. Tasks (as defined above) do not include activities which involve language used for practice or display, such as 'Describe the picture using the words and phrases from the list below' or 'Ask your partner if he likes the food listed here using the forms *Do you like …? Yes, I do/No, I don't*' where there is no outcome or purpose other than practice of pre-specified language.

Neither would most roleplay activities count as tasks. Very often in roleplay situations there is no actual outcome for students to achieve, other than to enact their roles. Students have to think of suitable things to say to each other, but they are unlikely to be exchanging real meanings.

Certain types of roleplay, however, become games or problem-solving activities in their own right. For example, in 'The Shopping Game', where students take the roles of shoppers and shop keepers; the shoppers have to bargain to 'buy' items as cheaply as possible while shop keepers try to sell out before the others – all keeping within a set budget. In business simulations students might take on roles of company personnel in order to solve a problem and reach a decision that is acceptable to all. Both these activity types would count as tasks because there are outcomes to be achieved.

To summarize briefly, if we believe that learners learn better through taking part in meaning-oriented interactions, then we ought to be thinking in terms of providing such opportunities for interaction. It is these that I am calling 'tasks'.

Are tasks sufficient on their own?

It would of course be possible to fill our language lessons with nothing but tasks. Learners, talking to each other in pairs and small groups, would get plenty of opportunities to interact, to express themselves freely and gain confidence in using the target language.

But, as Skehan stresses in Paper 3, there is a danger in this. Learners tend to gain fluency at the expense of accuracy. Also, some learners become adept at task completion strategies and manage to get by on a very limited use of the target language.

A variety of topics and range of task types will broaden their language experience, extend their vocabulary and prevent boredom. But will this prevent learners from evolving a type of classroom 'pidgin' or from fossilizing early? Skehan suggests that learners need to be kept on their toes, that they need a constant linguistic challenge and it is this that helps to drive their interlanguage development forward.

Here the studies carried out by Labov (1972) are relevant. Labov collected samples of people talking in a range of social settings. He found that people who made common use of vernacular forms in some settings would change to a more prestige version when speaking in a more formal setting. In the same way, even in our mother tongue, we are always aware of when we need to be on our best linguistic behaviour. If we have to speak in public, or present a case in a business meeting, we often plan beforehand what we want to say. We tend to speak more carefully and use different types of words; we may even change our accent. The same applies when writing. We will dash off a quick, personal letter to a friend, but take far more care when drafting a letter to be published in a newspaper or a report to be made public.

The variety of language we use, then, depends on the circumstances of communication. We can summarize these and relate them to classroom language use as follows:

Private use	**Public use**
in pairs or small groups	*talking to whole class*
• spontaneous	• planned
• exploratory	• rehearsed
• ephemeral	• permanent (eg recorded)
Focus on fluency and getting meanings across somehow.	Focus on fluency, accuracy, clarity and organization as befits a public presentation.
Correction rarely requested or acted upon.	Correction and advice welcomed.

The task framework

The Pre-task phase and the Task cycle proposed below take advantage of the socio-linguistic norms described above, and ensure a smooth and natural transition from private to more public interaction. The complete framework aims to create in the classroom the essential conditions for language learning.

1 PRE-TASK

Introduction to topic and task

- T helps Ss to understand the theme and objectives of the task, eg brainstorming ideas with the class, using pictures, mime or personal experience to introduce the topic.
- Ss may do a pre-task, eg topic-based odd-word-out games.
- T may highlight useful words and phrases, but would not pre-teach new structures.
- Ss can be given preparation time to think how to do the task.
- Ss can hear a recording of a parallel task being done (so long as this does not give away the solution to the problem).
- Or, if the task is based on a text, Ss read part of it.

This initial phase gives useful exposure which helps students to recall relevant words and phrases and to recognize new ones. The preparation time helps them to think of the kinds of things they can say, and seems to result in better quality language use at the task stage (Foster, Paper 12).

2 THE TASK CYCLE

Task

- The task is done by Ss (in pairs or groups) and gives Ss a chance to use whatever language they have already to express themselves and say what they want to say. This may be in response to reading a text or hearing a recording.
- T walks round and monitors, encouraging in a supportive way everyone's attempts at communication in the target language.
- T helps Ss to formulate what they want to say, but will not intervene to correct errors of form.
- The emphasis is on spontaneous, exploratory talk and confidence-building, within the privacy of the small group.
- Success in achieving the goals of the task helps Ss' motivation.

- -

Planning

- Planning prepares for the next stage, when Ss are asked to report briefly to the whole class how they did the task and what the outcome was.
- Ss draft and rehearse what they want to say or write.
- T goes round to advise students on language, suggesting phrases and helping Ss to polish and correct their language.
- If the reports are in writing, T can encourage peer-editing and use of dictionaries.

- The emphasis is on clarity, organization and accuracy, as appropriate for a public presentation.
- Individual students often take this chance to ask questions about specific language items.

Report

- T asks some pairs to report briefly to the whole class so everyone can compare findings, or begin a survey. (NB there must be a purpose for others to listen.) Sometimes only one or two groups report in full; others comment and add extra points. The class may take notes.
- T chairs, comments on the content of their reports, rephrases perhaps but gives no overt public correction.

This component gives learners practice in public, prestige use of language and increases other students' exposure to spoken or written language.

Post-task listening

- Ss listen to a recording of fluent speakers doing the same task, and compare the ways in which they did the task themselves.

This component gives additional exposure to topic-related material and increases students' experience of the target language in use.

3   LANGUAGE FOCUS

Analysis

- T sets some language-focused tasks, based on the texts students have read or on the transcripts of the recordings they have heard.
- Examples include:
  - Find words and phrases related to the title or topic of the text.
  - Read the transcript, find words ending in *s* or *'s* and say what the *s* means.
  - Find all the verbs in the simple past form. Say which refer to past time and which do not.
  - Underline and classify the questions in the transcript. (For more suggestions see Paper 7.)
- T starts Ss off, then Ss continue, often in pairs.
- T goes round to help; Ss can ask individual questions.
- In plenary, T then reviews the analysis, possibly writing relevant language up on the board in list form; Ss may make notes.

The aim is to help students to explore language, to develop an awareness of aspects of syntax, collocation and lexis, to help them systematize what they have observed about certain features of language, to clarify concepts and to notice new things.

Practice

- T conducts practice activities as needed, based on the language analysis work already on the board, or using examples from the text or transcript.
- Practice activities can include:
  - choral repetition of the phrases identified and classified
  - memory challenge games based on partially-erased examples or using lists already on blackboard for progressive deletion
  - sentence completion (set by one team for another)
  - matching the past tense verbs (jumbled) with the subjects or objects they had in the text
  - Kim's game (in teams) with new words and phrases
  - dictionary reference work on new words from text or transcript

---

Note that I am not suggesting that learners will necessarily gain instant command of any of these features. We are helping them to notice salient features, in the hopes they will recognize them when they meet them again in other texts and recordings. See Conformity activities, Paper 5.

Optional follow-up

- At the end of the task-based framework, students could:
  - Repeat the same or a similar oral task but with different partners.
  - Go back through the task materials or earlier texts and write down in their language notebooks useful words, phrases and patterns that they have noticed.
  - Discuss how they felt about the task and the task cycle and what they might like to do next or some time later (and/or note this down in their diaries for their teacher to read later).

Flexibility within the framework

How flexible can this framework be?

Some lessons – especially those based on reading texts or listening – may be planned with two or three mini-task cycles, each task supplying a different reading goal, and having a very brief report after each mini-task.

Some tasks will not need a formal reporting phase, because the subsequent task grows directly out of the first. Other tasks, such as story telling, where each pair or group has something quite different, may naturally produce a lengthy reporting phase. With problem-solving tasks, it is sufficient to hear only the groups that can offer different solutions. After the report, a vote can be taken for the best story or solution.

Depending on the needs and backgrounds of students, the components of the framework can be weighted differently. Students who are already quite fluent, such as those working as 'au pairs' in Britain, may need a greater emphasis on accuracy and analysis work, ie less task time and more planning and formal report time, with more tasks requiring written outcomes. Recording their reports on audio or video would give them a greater desire for clarity and accuracy. Students from a grammar-oriented background, used to writing and reading, may need a diet of tasks, initially with no reporting stage, to give them confidence in speaking.

With beginners, the actual task itself may be a 'listen and do' type of task, requiring only recognition of meaning, with only the teacher summing up at a Report stage. With ESP/LSP students who require a reading-only knowledge, the tasks set would be based on a text in the target language, and could be discussed and reported in L1.

There can also be flexibility in the way students are grouped. With a task-based approach, students of different levels can work together more easily; the weaker ones can learn from the others, and gain confidence from the support of the small group. Sometimes, though, shy students feel less intimidated and contribute more if asked to work together.

How does this TBL framework fulfil the conditions for learning implied by SLA research findings?

Although the learning styles of individuals may differ, the overwhelming evidence is that, in order for anyone to learn a language effectively in a classroom, there are four key conditions to be met. In this section, I will outline these conditions and relate them to components in the task framework.

Key conditions for language learning

- ***Exposure*** *to a rich but comprehensible input of real language, ie the kind of language that learners will be needing or wishing to understand and use themselves*
  Exposure and input come from teacher talk (especially during the pre-task phase and when reviewing language analysis), students listening to each other, reading the texts or listening to recordings of others doing the task. This input is not confined to sentence level examples, but consists of real, often spontaneous, language use.

- *Opportunities for real **use of language** – chances for learners to experiment and test hypotheses, to mean what they say and express what they mean in a variety of circumstances*
  This TBL framework gives students opportunities to use language to express what they want to say, to gain practice in turn-taking, controlling the interaction, interacting spontaneously in pairs. The Report phase then offers them the challenge of drafting and perfecting their report for a wider audience. The Planning stage gives students the confidence and support they need before they actually perform in public.

- *Motivation to listen and read, ie to process the exposure for meaning; and also to use the language, to speak and write*

  The goals of the task provide the main motivation; students generally want to achieve the task outcomes which involve them in playing the game or solving a problem. Success in completing the task is in itself a motivating factor. Then, because they have done or will do the task themselves, they are keen to listen to a related recording and read the transcript or a related text.

- *Focus on language – in order to prevent fossilization, and to challenge learners to strive for individual improvement, they need chances to reflect on language and to try to systematize what they know*

  In the task framework, there is a natural focus on language form as students prepare to 'go public' for the Report, and therefore strive for accuracy. The Analysis activities cast students into the role of 'text investigators'; during the consciousness-raising activities they are free to work as individuals at their own pace; free to make their own discoveries which they will be able to apply at some later time, when they are ready to. They are not being forced to work in lock-step, or concentrate on one single structure pre-selected by the book or the teacher, as in a PPP approach.

We can now usefully expand the summary diagram as follows:

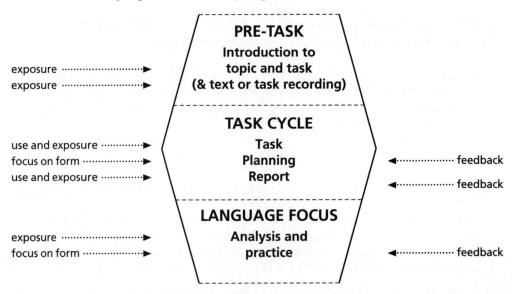

Once students are used to a task-based approach and become aware of the learning opportunities it offers, they develop both as learners and language users, achieving greater fluency and confidence. It is, however, vitally important that both learners and teachers alike understand the principles behind the approach, and the rationale behind each component of the framework.

Task-based learning for novice trainees?

The biggest challenge for the teacher used to a teacher-led PPP approach is to stand back, have faith and let learners get on with their learning. Untrained teachers find the cycle a very natural one to follow, since it progresses naturally from private to public use of language, with a planning stage in between. There is no need to make up examples to fit patterns, or invent contexts for isolated language items. Neither do teachers need to try to teach complicated rules of sentence grammar that they may not feel confident with themselves.

In 1992, a colleague in Turkey decided to experiment by introducing TBL on a Certificate Course for novice trainees. All sessions were video-recorded on a single camera in a back corner. After experiencing PPP and reading about the TBL framework as described above, trainees were asked to identify similarities and differences between the two approaches. This is what they said:

The trainees' initial comments (written after the reading)

Similarities
'TBL is like a sort of PPP upside down – the steps are there but in a different order.'

'Most of the teaching techniques are similar.'

'There is attention to both accuracy and fluency.'

'They both include a focus on language form and meaning.'

Differences
'TBL doesn't teach isolated chunks of language then attempt to put them back into the "whole body" of language.'

'TBL starts with the "whole body" of language – language comes out of what learners know/can do/want to do, and out of the task.'

'The skills are really integrated and include what other methods call "micro-skills" as well as "the four skills"'.

'There is a real need to communicate and to listen.'

'TBL distinguishes between private communication (fluency-based) and public communication (accuracy with fluency together).'

Trainees then experienced some TBL cycles for themselves – one based on comparing pictures, one based on a short newspaper story. Finally for Teaching Practice they planned and shared the teaching of their own task-based lessons with their TP class of basic elementary adult students.

Trainees' subsequent comments (after experiencing and teaching TBL)

'Tasks are intrinsically interesting.'

'You can do a lot with this approach.'

'You never know what the students have in their heads – it's amazing what comes out, and you find they have a lot they can build on.'

'Recordings of spontaneous spoken English – of people doing the same task – a radical departure from most coursebook tapes because they are genuinely authentic; easy to understand because of natural repetition; students are motivated to listen because they have just done the same task and they want to compare how they did it.'

'The language-focused work was a bit too analytical for beginners – a focus on key phrases might have been better for them.'

'You're using what learners know and can do; much more learner-centred in a genuine way.'

'The students really talked a lot … and were very responsive and involved throughout.' (despite trainees' initial doubts)

The trainer said …

'It went better than a PPP lesson would have gone at this stage.' (Perhaps because TBL rests on natural communicative behaviour, rather than the tightly controlled teaching behaviour of PPP.)

'Trainees found the language analysis component hardest and were not always sure when to correct and feed in new language – but this was their first time.'

'In spite of the hitches, which seemed largely due to trainees having to "unlearn" PPP, the lesson flowed and the students loved it.'

'The question now is – can we do without PPP altogether?'

It is abundantly clear that we can. Many schools have succeeded in making the switch and many learners of all ages have benefited. But, as Woodward points out in Paper 1, any such major change involves a paradigm shift. Less successful are the classes where teachers have not truly grasped the rationale for TBL, where teachers and/or students adhere to the security of a teacher-led presentation of grammar and language form and pattern practice before the task, and those who believe that learners 'must be taught the right forms first, otherwise how can they do the task?'.

So is TBL like PPP upside down?

I hope I have illustrated that a TBL framework is more flexible and offers students far richer learning opportunities than just 'PPP upside down'. It requires no radical new techniques, but the techniques it does use, and the order in which the components are sequenced, are chosen on the basis of sound theoretical principles, unlike PPP. And since it gives learners experience of language in use before studying language in detail, it might even be better to think of it as 'PPP the right way up'.

Note
An earlier and shorter version of this paper appeared in *The Teacher Trainer,* March 1994.

Acknowledgement
I am most grateful to Barbara Garside for conducting the experiment described on page 61 with her novice trainees. Our joint thanks to British Council, Turkey, the trainees and students at the British Council Centre in Izmir and video camera-man Yusuf Özkaya who video-recorded the whole experiment for us to present at IATEFL Swansea,1993.

Jane Willis
teaches on the MSc in Teaching English/ESP programmes (Distance Learning) at Aston University, Birmingham, UK. Her main areas of interest are task-based learning, classroom interaction and lexis. Her most recent publication is *A Framework for Task-based Learning* (Longman, 1996).

Consciousness-raising activities

7

Dave Willis and Jane Willis

Introduction

anguage is so vast and varied that we can never provide learners with a viable and comprehensive description of the language as a whole. We can, however, provide them with guidelines and, more important, we can provide them with activities which encourage them to think about samples of language and to draw their own conclusions about how the language works. The general term for activities of this kind is consciousness-raising (C-R). C-R activities have been a part of language teaching for a very long time. Indeed the grammar-translation approach to language teaching certainly embodied C-R. Learners worked from language data to formulate rules for language production. Under grammar-translation, however, there was generally a very restricted range of C-R techniques and the methodology paid a very high price in other ways – by restricting exposure to the target language, for example.

In the 1970s and 1980s a good deal of the research into language learning suggested that, given exposure to the language, learners could be left to work out the grammar for themselves. Formal instruction was seen as contributing very little to learning. Such views are associated particularly with Krashen (Krashen and Terell 1983). Current concern with C-R, however, is largely a reaction against approaches to language learning which played down the contribution of instruction. One of the early attempts to define C-R (Sharwood-Smith 1981) specifically addresses Krashen's work. Rutherford's (1987) *Second Language Grammar: Learning and Teaching* is a landmark in the development of C-R and there are many recent contributions; some (eg James 1994) taking universal grammar (see Shortall, Paper 4) as a starting point, others (eg Ellis 1992) taking a more general approach. A highly accessible introduction to the notion of C-R is to be found in Ellis (1993).

For the rationale which lies behind C-R we would refer you to the sources cited above. This article is intended more as a do-it-yourself manual for the analysis and construction of C-R activities than as a discussion of the nature and value of C-R. We will offer a brief definition of C-R and will then move on to look at what aspects of language it can help us to study and how we can organize that study for our learners.

What is C-R?

Ellis (1993) contrasts C-R with practice activities. Among the characteristics of C-R he lists:

- The 'attempt to *isolate* a specific linguistic feature for focused attention'. From the wealth of language data to which learners are exposed we identify particular features and draw the learner's attention specifically to these.

- The provision of '*data* which illustrate the targeted feature'. It is our contention that this data should as far as possible be drawn from texts, both spoken and written, which learners have already processed for meaning, and that as far as possible those texts should have been produced for a communicative purpose, not simply to illustrate features of the language.

- The requirement that learners 'utilize *intellectual effort*' to understand the targeted feature. There is a deliberate attempt to involve the learner in hypothesizing about the data and to encourage hypothesis testing.

If we believe that the successful learner is actively involved in looking for regularities in language data and in drawing conclusions from those regularities then we have an obligation to encourage this process. If we are successful in this we will not only succeed in making specific generalizations about language available to learners, we will also succeed in inculcating learning habits which will pay valuable dividends whenever and wherever the learner encounters language. C-R, then, can be seen as guided problem solving. Learners are encouraged to notice particular features of the language, to draw conclusions from what they notice and to organize their view of language in the light of the conclusions they have drawn. This relates closely to the three-part process *Observe – Hypothesize – Experiment* described by Lewis (Paper 2).

What should learners notice about grammar?

Most pedagogic grammars are very unbalanced. A look at the list of contents in most coursebooks or students' grammars will show that there is a preoccupation with the grammar of the verb phrase, particularly tense. Other important elements of the grammar, such as the structure of the noun phrase, are often overlooked. In particular we need to look more closely at the behaviour of individual words and classes of words. We need perspectives on grammar which take account of the interface between grammar and lexis.

Willis (1993) identifies a number of perspectives on grammar. Some aspects of the grammar can be efficiently described by a system of rules. Other aspects defy description of this kind. They need to be noted and learned rather than generated by base rules. Here is a brief summary of five perspectives on language:

The grammar of structure
It is possible to offer very powerful rules describing the structure of the English clause. It contains a subject and a verb, nearly always in that order. Very often the verb is followed by some sort of necessary completion – an object, a complement or a

prepositional phrase of some sort. Almost always these elements come after the verb. However, in terms of order, adverbials in English are problematical. Temporal adverbs, for example, may come more or less anywhere in the clause. Some adverbs, adverbs of degree, for example, have particular restrictions on their position in the clause:

> *I enjoyed the party very much.*
> not **I enjoyed very much the party.*

In general, however, it is possible to provide very powerful guidelines for the structure of the English clause. The same is true of the structure of the elements which make up the clause, the noun group, for example:

> *That big black cat over there.*
> not **Black big cat that over there.*

The order of elements within the English clause is very fixed. This may be comforting for learners. Less comforting is the fact that in order to maintain this order and at the same time allow for flexibility in the way information is presented and highlighted English has some complex devices like clefting, involving the use of a dummy subject *it*:

> *I thought it was someone playing a joke.*
> *It's always the money that gets reported, isn't it?*

These devices present a learning problem. They need to be drawn to the attention of learners and treated systematically. This can only be done by looking at clauses within texts. Since the structure of a given clause is determined by its place in discourse we need to look at clauses and sentences in context, not in abstract.

The grammar of orientation

Language learning materials always spend a good deal of time on the tense system, on the articles and on other determiners such as *some* and *any*. These systems are central to the language because they relate what is being spoken or written about to the real world and to other elements in the text. Given the elements in a clause *wife–work–garden–weekend* we know what the clause is about but we are unable to find any 'orientation' – we cannot identify who the message is about or whether it refers to past or present time, to a particular wife and garden or to wives and gardens in general. But given the clause *My wife works in the garden most weekends* you can identify the wife as the wife of the speaker, and the garden as their garden. The tense of the verb tells you that the statement is a general statement relevant to present time. This is reinforced by the use of the general determiner *most*. The function of the tense system and the system of determiners is exactly this, to enable us to orient ourselves to the elements in the proposition. The past tense, for example, is used to refer to something which occurred at a specific time in the past. The use of the present perfect tense asserts that the action of the verb has some relevance to the present or future. The definite article tells hearers/readers that the entity referred to is readily identifiable from the text or context. These grammatical devices, then, act as 'pointers' showing how items relate to one another in terms of time, place and identity. Like the grammar of structure these elements of the grammar are highly systematic. We can make useful generalizations about them. Again they need to be studied in context, since their function is necessarily related to context.

The grammar of class

Teachers are used to allocating nouns to two classes – countable and uncountable. This is an important distinction to make since the patterns in which these items occur are quite different. The class of double object verbs (*give, ask, send, etc*) is another which is often identified and highlighted for learners. We are, therefore, used to classifying words according to their grammatical behaviour. This is a valuable procedure which can usefully be taken a good deal further.

There is, for example, a very important class of nouns which are often postmodified by a clause with *that* :

*Please don't get **the <u>idea</u> that** I am a supporter of women's liberation.*
*There was **this <u>theory</u> that** women always pass first time.*
*I got **the <u>impression</u> that** it was trying to get in.*

These words play an important part in highlighting ideas in discourse. They play an important part in all kinds of English from everyday conversation to abstruse academic discourse. It is important to make learners aware of words like this.

It is not clear in how many ways words might usefully be classified. The grammar of class is much more open-ended than the grammar of structure and orientation. The learner faces two problems. What classes of word are there in English and how are the words of the language allocated to these classes? Learners are obliged to work on these questions simultaneously whenever they meet new linguistic items or become aware of new patterns of behaviour.

Lexical phrase

The importance of fixed phrases in language is receiving increasing attention (see Lewis, Paper 2). There are fixed phrases like *as a matter of fact*, which behave like lexical items. There are frames like *as (adverb) as possible*; *would you mind _____ ing*. A fluent speaker of a language has a vast stock of these prefabricated phrases. Some of them are closely related to particular word classes. The nouns postmodified by *that*, illustrated above, for example, are often found in frames like:

> *fact*
> *The problem is that …*
> *danger*

We can offer learners hints like this which may help them assimilate these fixed phrases, but the learning task is still very open-ended. Some scholars (eg Pawley and Syder 1983) have estimated that there are tens of thousands of such phrases.

Collocation

We can think of collocation in terms of word association. For an English speaker the word *hard* calls up words like *work* and *luck* because it often occurs in their company. It also calls up words like *cold*, again because the two often go together. Words often collocate with their antonyms – *hard* and *soft*. Sometimes several words build up as we have seen into lexical phrases. Sets of words and the lexical relations which hold between them contribute to lexical cohesion, for example. An illustration of this can be seen in the C-R activity on page 71, where words to do with aircraft and flight contribute to the cohesion of a text.

What other aspects of language should be highlighted?

Frequent words

It is important to provide good coverage of the most frequent words of the language – prepositions and modal verbs, for example. These words need to be highlighted for the learner thoroughly and systematically, simply because they are so common. They are covered in other perspectives on grammar. Many of their uses are covered under *Lexical phrases*. Prepositions contribute heavily to the structure of the noun group. But these words are of such frequent occurrence, and so central to the meaning and structure of the language, that they need to be constantly recycled.

Text structure

Work on cohesion and coherence (see for example Hoey 1991) and genre analysis (Swales 1990) helps us to identify macro-structures in text.

Metaphor

Metaphors such as those described in Lakoff and Johnson (1980)('Time is money' – you can *spend, save, etc* both; 'Discourse is a journey' – you can *go back to a point, come to the end, reach an agreement, take another approach*) give the learner the power to generate a whole set of new meanings using familiar words.

Skills

There are two aspects of the teaching of skills. Students need to practise in the classroom the things they will need to do with the language outside the classroom. They need to practise processing written text quickly and efficiently. The challenge here is methodological. How do we design activities which reproduce in the classroom the demands students will face outside? But skills are based on language. To put it crudely, the best way to improve your language skills is to learn more language. When, for example, readers scan a text for specific information they look for key words. Their knowledge of word association and lexical sets comes into play. There are two ways C-R can help. The first is by making them conscious of what knowledge is invoked in carrying out a given task. The second is by helping them to organize their language in a way which will help them tap this knowledge.

Where does language data come from?

It is useful to think of the language to which the learner is exposed as a *pedagogic corpus* (Willis 1993). We try to offer learners exposure to a body of text, written and spoken, which will illustrate for them the important things they need to know about the language – about the way it is structured, about the way particular words behave, about the common words and phrases and so on. Once we have drawn up a set of texts which meets these requirements we need to design a series of communicative tasks which will oblige learners to process the texts for meaning, so that the texts become a part of the learners' experience of English. (See Paper 6 on Task-based learning.) Secondly we need to analyse the texts to see what aspects of the language they can exemplify for us, what can be learned from them to provide the learner with insights into the language as a whole. These aspects can then form the focus for C-R activities.

Ideally a single text would provide the basis for a self-contained lesson. First it would contain within itself enough important features of the language to provide a stimulus to learning. Secondly these features would be well enough exemplified within a single text and would require no supplementation. Most, indeed almost all, naturally occurring texts fulfil the first of these requirements. There is normally a wealth of possibilities to exploit. The difficult judgement is what to include and what to leave out. Relatively few texts, however, fulfil the second requirement to any great degree. It is usually necessary to supplement a given text from other sources in order to find enough appropriate illustrative examples of a particular language item. Where then does this supplementation come from?

The first additional source to be tapped is other texts with which learners are familiar. Let us say, for example, a text under study contains two isolated, but well contextualized, examples of a particular use of the modal *would*. Almost certainly there will be other examples of this in previous texts the learners have studied. There will also be other uses of *would* which may be recycled to build up a general picture of the word and its use. The exemplification of the word will be firmly based in text the learners have already experienced.

A second valuable source may be found in texts that learners are about to experience. Texts that are designated as part of their future study will yield useful examples of important features of language. The study process is inevitably cyclical and examples taken from texts to be studied later will provide learners with a source which will jog their memories when those texts are studied in detail, and which will provide examples of the target item in use, not in isolation.

Thirdly, illustrative examples may be taken from a supplementary corpus of real language. It is, I think, important to work with real language as far as possible. There is, after all, plenty of it about. I am not arguing that authenticity in itself is a virtue. What is required is a citation which is typical of the use of the language feature under study. More and more dictionaries and grammars offer corpus-based illustrations of the language. Usually these examples are carefully chosen to provide an illustration of the typical pattern and use of the feature under discussion. They are true to the language in a way in which decontextualized examples concocted specifically for the purpose of illustration may not be.

I would not argue that concocted examples should never be used, but they should be used as a last resort. They should also be checked for typicality of grammatical and lexical environment, ie compared to corpus-based examples from a dictionary or grammar. This helps us to avoid using examples such as *Prince Charles is now a husband* (see Sinclair 1988) or *Do you like being a father?* that are possible but untypical, and unlikely to be useful to learners.

What C-R activities can we use?

We aim, then, to provide learners with language data either in the form of a single text or a set of examples from familiar sources. They will then perform certain operations on these samples of language. The outcome of these operations will be an increased awareness of and sensitivity to language. We will list here the kinds of operation that students might be asked to perform and will go on to exemplify these in the next section.

Identify/consolidate

Students are asked to search a set of data to identify a particular pattern or usage and the language forms associated with it.

Classify (semantic; structural)

Students are required to work with a set of data and sort it according to similarities and differences based on formal or semantic criteria.

Hypothesis building/checking

Students are given (or asked to make) a generalization about language and asked to check this against more language data.

Cross-language exploration

Students are encouraged to find similarities and differences between patternings in their own language and patternings in English.

Reconstruction/deconstruction

Students are required to manipulate language in ways which reveal underlying patterns.

Recall

Students are required to recall and reconstruct elements of a text. The purpose of the recall is to highlight significant features of the text.

Reference training

Students need to learn to use reference works – dictionaries, grammars and study guides.

What possible starting points are there?

If learners are to search language for useful generalizations they need a starting point. If teachers are to help learners organize their language insights they need to provide reference points for that organization. The diagram on the next page summarizes a number of possible starting points.

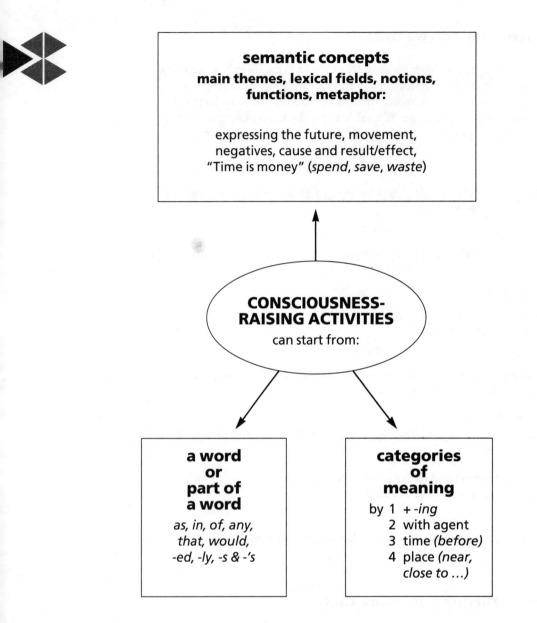

Some examples of C-R activities

C-R activities based on a written text

Auto-pilot

The flight ran several times a week taking holiday-makers to various resorts in the Mediterranean. On each flight, to reassure the passengers all was well, the captain would put the jet on to auto-pilot and he and all the crew would come aft into the cabin to greet the passengers.

Unfortunately on this particular flight the security door between the cabin and the flight deck jammed and left the captain and the crew stuck in the cabin. From that moment, in spite of efforts to open the door, the fate of the passengers and crew was sealed.

---

1 List all the phrases to do with aircraft and flying. What word occurs in nearly all these phrases? Why?

2 What does *would* mean in the second sentence?

3 What about *ran* in the first sentence? Would *used to run* give the same meaning? What about *jammed* and *left* in the second paragraph? Could *used to* be used here?

4 Cover your original text. Read the rewritten version of the text below. How has it been changed from the original?

Auto-pilot

The flight ran several times a week taking holiday-makers to resorts in the Mediterranean. On every flight, to reassure the passengers that everything was all right, the captain used to put the jet on to auto-pilot and he and all the crew used to come aft into the cabin to greet the passengers.

However on this flight the security door between the cabin and the flight deck jammed, leaving the captain and the crew stuck in the cabin. From that moment, despite efforts to open the door, the fate of the passengers and crew was sealed.

---

5 *Would* : Review
Here are some sentences with *would* which you have seen before. Find sentences in which
i) *would* is used as a conditional.
ii) *would* is the past tense of *will*.
iii) *would* means 'used to'.
How many sentences are left over?

a If you were designing a poster which two *would* you choose?
b Yes, I *would* think so.
c My brother *would* say, 'Oh your mother spoils you.'
d *Would* you like to ask us anything about it?
e Yes, yes, I *would* agree with that certainly.
f Not the sort of letter I *would* like to receive.
g *Would* people in your country talk freely about these things?
h Then we said that we *would* play hide and seek.

i   Often there *would* be a village band made up of self-taught players.
j   Some *would* write their own songs or set new words to tunes.
k   What advice *would* you give to a young person leaving school or University?
l   That's right, yes, and it *would* slow the ship down.
m   I never had the light on. My parents *wouldn't* allow it.
n   But now a new fear assailed him. *Would* he get caught in the propeller?
o   This brief report *would* best be understood by a listener who had read the earlier story.

Commentary

This shows only the language focus stage of the treatment of the text. Before reaching this stage the text will have been processed as a story. One obvious way to do this is to give students the story up to and including the word *Unfortunately* and ask them to predict the ending. This will generate a good deal of talk rehearsing the lexis in the text. Since the story is a fairly well known one some students may actually have read it in their own language.

Activity 1 focuses first on a lexical set as a way of helping students build up word associations and their knowledge of collocation. It also focuses on the use of the definite article. The word *the* occurs with all these items not because they have been mentioned before, but because a flight assumes *passengers, captain, crew, cabin,* etc. The starting point for this exercise is a semantic concept, a lexical field. The process is one of identification and consolidation.

Activity 2 focuses first on *would* meaning *used to*. This use is very common. In fact *would* with this meaning occurs almost three times as frequently as *used to*. The starting point is a word, *would,* leading, through a process of semantic classification, to a category of meaning.

Activity 3 is to do with discourse structure. It reinforces the analysis of *would* to show that the introduction to a narrative, the scene setting, often employs a particular use of the past tense. Whereas the past tenses in the first paragraph carry the meaning of past habit, those in the second paragraph, which carry the narrative, refer to specific actions in the past. The teacher needs to make this explicit. Students could then be referred to other narratives and asked to identify similar tense uses. This moves out of the text under study and links it to other texts the students have experienced. It might also be possible to make a useful comparison with the L1, a process of cross-language exploration.

Activity 4 is an example of a recall and reconstruction exercise which brings together a number of language points. Obviously students should not have immediate access to the original text while they are doing this exercise. There are a number of ways the exercise can be handled. Students can be given the rewritten text and then hear the original text as a dictation, making notes as they hear it. If they are to do this they should be given a double-spaced version of the rewritten text. This can be done as an individual exercise but works better with pairs or groups.

This question focuses on a number of useful points. It highlights a very common use of the word *various*. It relates the two determiners *each* and *every,* the two common fixed phrases *all was well* and *everything was all right* and later the phrases *in spite of* and *despite*. It underlines the work done earlier on *would* and *used to*, and illustrates a narrative use of the *-ing* form. Overall it gives students an opportunity to process the text again, focusing firmly on the language.

Activity 5 is a review exercise bringing together a number of examples of *would* and asking students to classify them. It takes a word as its starting point and works towards semantic categories. Examples are taken from texts which learners have experienced. With a word as common as *would* it is often possible to do this. My own 'answer' to this exercise is as follows:

*i) **would** used as conditional: a, f, g, k, l, n, o*
*ii) **would** as the past tense of **will**: h, m*
*iii) **would** meaning '**used to**': c, i, j*
*The sentences left over are b, d and e. These are fixed phrases. In b and e **would** is a marker of politeness. In d **would you like** is a very common way of making an offer.*

It is important to note that there is more than one possible answer. Sentence m, for example, could be read either as the past tense of *will* or as meaning *used to*. The two are, in fact, very close to one another. The phrase *would like* in f could be seen as a fixed phrase, although here I feel it certainly has a hypothetical or conditional ring to it. Sentence c could be either conditional or *used to*. In this particular case a check back to the text in which this occurs shows quite clearly that it means *used to*. The fact that these examples are somewhat open ended can be turned to advantage by the teacher. What we are trying to do is encourage learners to think about language and to formulate their own categories of description.

C-R activities based on a spoken text

The following is the transcript of a recording made to support a task-based lesson, the aim of which was to explore how different people feel about rain storms. Several pairs of native speakers were recorded doing the same task that the learners would be doing in class. This is how one conversation went.

RS: So, how do you feel about storms?

EL: Well, they are fine as long as – I don't really like being caught in the middle of them. I mean, as long as you're at home or even in a train. I like storms when you're in a train.

RS: Mhm.

EL: I was just, erm, going up north in a bus to Durham last week and er, it was absolutely pitch black outside and really pelting down. And that was quite fun. But if you're actually out in it, I find that – I don't like getting wet.

RS: Right. Yeah. I actually like storms. I love them except for the lightning, because I know it can be dangerous.

EL: Right.

RS: But erm, I think particularly if you've had really hot steaming weather and then the storm breaks, it's just something!

EL: And you like being out in the middle of it?

RS: Lovely, if it's – as I say – if there's not much lightning or anything, that'd be fine.

EL: Mm.

> RS: But it's a bit – I tend to be sort of sensible and stay indoors.
> EL: Right.
> RS: Erm. Thunder can be quite scary sometimes but I'm not too worried.
> EL: Do you get headaches in thunder? Some people get really bad headaches.
> RS: No, no …

The lesson might begin with a brief introduction to the topic of storms – perhaps with pictures, and/or a personal anecdote from the teacher. The Pre-task phase could then continue with some initial C-R activities, like this:

The learners each think of a storm they remember (from real life or television, film or book), then write down five words and phrases that they associate with stormy weather. The teacher collects these, talks about them, and writes them on the board, eg *heavy rain, strong wind, clouds, dust, lightning, scary, dangerous, raining, pouring with rain, dark, get wet*. The class, in pairs, finds ways to classify them, for example into words describing weather, feelings, verbs and so on.

Next, in the Task cycle, learners first in pairs, and then as a class, share experiences of storms and say how they generally feel about them. The purpose is to find out whether people have positive as well as negative reactions to storms. Before or after the task, depending on the class, students can hear the recording of the task on tape. To make this easier, they can listen in pairs, each person paying particular attention to what one speaker says.

Once learners have managed to pick out each speaker's main reactions to the storms and compared them to their own, they are ready to continue to some C-R activities based mainly on the written transcript. Examples follow. The first is an example of one starting from a semantic concept; the others start from a word or part of a word.

1 Phrases describing reactions to storms
Listen to the tape once more and write down any phrases you can catch about their feelings about storms, eg *They're fine as long as …*

Compare with a partner. Then read the transcript and see if you can find eight phrases altogether. Which are positive and which negative? What about the phrase *It's just something …* ?

2 Words ending in -ly
Find and underline seven phrases with words ending in *-ly*. Now listen to them on the tape to hear where the main stress falls in each phrase.

Choose any three of these phrases. Write them down without the word ending in *-ly*. Do not leave a gap. Read them to your group. Can they remember (without looking) which word fits where?

What does the word *actually* mean? Look it up in a dictionary and see how it is typically used.

*3 Find five phrases with **be** and **being***
What verbs do *be* and *being* often follow?

4 Common verbs
Find all the verb phrases following the word *I*. (There are thirteen.) Classify them as
follows:
- expressing like/dislike (5 or 6)
- beginning a story (1)
- expressing the idea of *usually* (1)
- two very common short phrases. Do you have parallel phrases in your language for
  these? (*I mean …, as I say …*)
Which ones are left over? What would you say in your language for these?

5 Typical words in conversational English
Find these words in the conversation: *And, But, So, Well*. What do they all have in
common?
What might you say in your language for each of them?
What about the function of the words *Right, Yeah*, and *Mhm* and *Mm*?

Commentary
Activity 1 shows how in addition to common verb phrases with *like, love*, etc we can use
words like *Lovely!* (instead of *I do*), phrases like *that was quite fun*, and phrases with
adjectives such as *fine, scary*, to express how we feel. Thus learners have a wider range
of expressions to draw on and generate from.

You may want to stop and explore the meaning of *as long as* at this point. Ask students
where else in this conversation it could have been used. (If they search for the *ifs* they
will find one in RS's turn: *Lovely …*)

Activity 2 focuses on *-ly* adverbs commonly used in conversation for emphasis, and
their possible positions in the clause (grammar of structure). The word *actually* has a
slightly different function, signalling something contrary to what might be expected.
Learners can form their own hypotheses and then check them out by looking in a
dictionary or usage book.

Activity 3 focuses on very common collocations *can be, would/'d be*, ie *be* after modals;
tend to be may be new for some learners and can be focused on in context; the form *being*
after *like* can be picked up and extended to other verbs, eg *don't like getting wet*.

Activity 4 uses the word *I* as a starting point to highlight a number of verb phrases that
are highly frequent in spontaneous talk. It naturally recycles some phrases already
focused on. Some learners may notice the use of the impersonal *you* in the same
sentence as an *I*. This might stimulate interesting comparisons with their own language.

Activity 5 draws attention to the meanings and uses of single words that are typically
used in spontaneous interaction to begin an utterance (*Well, So, And, But*) and those
which acknowledge what the other speaker has said (*Right, Yeah, Mm*). These are vital
words that are often overlooked. Without them, learners' conversations often sound
stilted and abrupt.

If learners wish to gain fluency in spoken English as well as written English, it is
essential for them to have exposure to features that are typical of spoken language and
that they have time to reflect on these features. Using the transcripts allows learners

time to notice features that may not be noticed for a long time if only heard in the flow of real-time conversation.

At the end of a series of C-R activities, it is a good idea to let learners make their own personal record of the points they have covered. They may also want to practise the pronunciation of some of the common phrases; they may want to hear the recording again, or read a related text. They may benefit – in a later lesson – from repeating the task with a different partner or writing their own version of a similar experience for others to read. It is unlikely that they will immediately assimilate and put to use all the features they have covered in the activities, but their consciousness will have been raised and they will be more likely to notice these linguistic features when they occur in future input.

Summary

We need to develop a systematic approach to C-R. In the long run this entails syllabus design procedures in line with C-R – almost certainly a data-driven approach based on the analysis of a relevant language corpus.

Meanwhile we have tried in this article to suggest a methodical approach to written and spoken text which will enable us to identify and exploit useful learning opportunities. In approaching a text we need to ask ourselves the following questions:

- What aspects of the language are exemplified here?
- Do we need supplementary data to illustrate these points and to link them to previous learning?
- What starting points will make these insights accessible to learners?

The benefits of these procedures go far beyond a single lesson. By encouraging learners to observe and analyse language for themselves we are reinforcing their natural tendency and ability to make sense of language and to systematize it. We are encouraging learners to learn for themselves.

Professional development and teacher training

f the ELT profession is to take up the challenges laid down in the first two sections of this book there are clear implications for teacher training. Teacher training should not be a transmissive process in which newcomers are initiated in a set of values and attitudes which will stand them in good stead for the foreseeable future. There is nowadays a growing emphasis on the developmental nature of training programmes. As part of this development teachers must be encouraged to take a critical look at existing practice.

Scrivener (Paper 8) offers us a way, to take Woodward's words (Paper 1), of 'looking at what we already do in a new light'. Taking the problems of the PPP sequence as a starting point, Scrivener argues against substituting yet another prescriptive approach. He wants to offer his trainees 'a description of the variety of approaches to lessons' so that trainees can create, describe and analyse lessons in a non-evaluative way. He puts forward the ARC model, the letters standing for *Authentic, Restricted* and *Clarification and Focus* respectively. In '*Authentic'* activities the learners can freely use all the language they have at their disposal. In '*Restricted'* activities the language available for the learner to use or understand is controlled or constrained by the teacher. *Clarification and Focus* occurs when learners look closely at some specific pieces of language, with or without immediate teacher help, with a focus on form. The components of the ARC model can be used to describe activities 'in which the main aim is towards better understanding and use of grammar and other language systems, rather than lessons where the main aim is improving specific language skills'. Scrivener applies the model to six different types of lesson, and illustrates how, by using ARC as an analytic tool on training courses, trainees can become more aware of what they and their learners are actually doing, so that the impetus to change and look for variety comes from the trainees themselves.

Kerr (Paper 9) begins by reviewing research which reveals 'the contrast between the initial trainees' view of grammar and the way CTEFLA trainers look at grammar'. This contrast in itself is not so surprising; what is worrying, though, is the finding that 'what trainers say and what trainers do are not necessarily the same thing'. For one thing, most trainers seemed to converge strongly towards their trainees' view of grammar, and to adhere to a 'transmission' model of both language learning and teacher training – one that has been questioned by many, including Skehan (Paper 3) and Willis (Paper 6) (and sometimes even the trainers themselves). For another, their emphasis on 'sentence level, verb-based grammar' flies directly in the face of current findings in linguistic research – the evidence for lexical phrases (Lewis, Paper 2) and broader perspectives on discourse and grammar as outlined in Willis and Willis (Paper 7). Kerr goes on to describe a variety of attempts to provide alternative starting points and argues finally that such a change 'will not be effected by a bolt-on solution', reminding us of Woodward's early warnings of the nature of paradigm shift, and inferring that the way forward may consist of 'swapping one paradigm for another'. Indeed, it would be interesting to relate Kerr's findings more exactly to Woodward's description of the stages in change in Paper 1, to find out how far along the road of change we are.

Edwards (Paper 10) addresses a central question. How do we train teachers to operate confidently with the existing paradigm and at the same time encourage them to question that paradigm and look for alternatives? Edwards goes on to develop an interesting analogy between language teaching methodology and teacher training methodology. She talks about 'the basic *vocabulary* of language teaching – a basic set of core techniques and skills … that can be employed in a number of classroom situations to achieve a number of objectives.' She refers later to 'the *grammar* of teaching'. Just as the language learner needs a few powerful grammar rules in order to get started, rules to do with things like basic clause structure, so the novice teacher needs to understand 'some of the fundamental principles of language learning and teaching' – for example the four basic conditions for learning referred to by Jane Willis (Paper 6), and the uses of language in the classroom elaborated by Dave Willis (Paper 5) and Scrivener (Paper 8).

As Edwards develops her analogy, the teacher training process, as she herself points out, begins to echo Lewis's process of *Observe – Hypothesize – Experiment* (Paper 2). Trainee teachers need exposure – they need to observe classes. They need to hypothesize, to evaluate classes in the light of their experience and their reading. And they need to experiment by working with classes of their own and finding what works and what doesn't. Trainees have their own 'first language' – they are all experienced learners and teachers in a variety of roles outside the language classroom. Just as learners have their grammars and dictionaries to call on so we, as teachers, have a valuable body of literature to draw on to extend and illuminate our practice. Once Edwards has established the analogy it begins to take on its own momentum. It prompts questions which go beyond Edwards' basic analogy and it suggests answers to those questions. Is there a Universal Grammar of teaching? Do developing teaching routines go through processes of 'syntacticization' and 'relexicalization'? Like the best training courses and teaching programmes, Edwards' paper provides a powerful framework for learning by discovery, a theme that will be taken up again in the following section by Özdeniz (Paper 11), who explores her own learners' reactions to a new approach.

ARC: a descriptive model for classroom work on language

8

Jim Scrivener

Introduction: the problem

Many teachers believe in PPP because they were trained to; the roots of their faith are in the initial training courses they took. A trusting trainee might suppose that they had been initiated into a methodology their tutors used themselves. The paradox is that many tutors who use PPP as a training paradigm don't actually use PPP much in their own English language teaching. But PPP is resilient on training courses, not because it is a true reflection of actual classroom practice, but because it is convenient and useful.

Many trainers will recognize the problem:

- What can I tell course participants on initial teacher training courses about the teaching and learning of grammar and other language systems? What can I tell them that is clear, comprehensible and true?
- Should trainees be offered clear, prescriptive 'route maps' for lessons? Route maps that they are then encouraged to follow when planning their own classes? Or is it better to introduce them to a range of teaching strategies, lesson types and activities and then encourage them to use their own insights and understandings to create their own lessons?

It's often difficult to get the balance right between prescription and encouraging intelligent experimentation, especially on short four-week courses. Prescription seems to trap new teachers within ritualized routines. Yet not telling them 'what to do' can feel like an abdication, leaving them to flounder.

PPP – a prescriptive paradigm

The PPP paradigm offers a single, simple, clear, workable lesson model, but it has serious drawbacks if it is presented as an ideal to be aimed at rather than as a description of different modes of classroom activity. It only describes *one* kind of lesson; it is inadequate as a general proposal concerning approaches to language in the classroom. It entirely fails to describe the many ways in which teachers can work when, for example, using coursebooks, or when adopting a task-based approach.

The PPP process from beginning to end is seen as a smooth and logical progression from the teacher's selection and teaching of discrete language items to the fully integrated use of these items in the learner's own language, and from close teacher control of language to the learner's independent use of the language to express his or her own communicative needs in the real world outside.

Indeed, a curious by-product of many current training courses is that trainees schooled in PPP come out believing themselves to be trained in 'communicative language teaching'. The dilution and subsumption of CLT within a PPP framework raises serious questions about the lack of principled thought behind much current classroom work.

PPP seems to assume that the speaking skill will arise naturally out of sufficient work on discrete grammar items. It assumes that learning is 'straight-line', that following a certain routine will guarantee the required results; in this respect it is essentially behaviourist, and therefore largely out of step both with discoveries about second language acquisition and with a lot of current classroom practice.

More worryingly for trainers who are eager to encourage course participants to think more about classroom events from the learner's perspective, with PPP the entire sequence of classroom events is described from the teacher's perspective; it is possible to plan a lesson entirely without reference to the learners.

For many trainees on initial training courses the PPP model is problematic because of its apparent prescriptiveness and lack of flexibility. This prescription is not necessarily explicit. However, trainees who have been offered a fairly rigid model often create the prescription internally, interpreting PPP (rightly or wrongly) as the way their tutors expect them to teach.

There may seem to be a limited number of teaching options, all of which can be pre-planned; in this respect many courses are actually training teachers not to consider the range of options that are based on responding to real events in the classroom. Variations in sequencing of the three stages disturb the underlying logic of progression from control to free use and seem to be discouraged.

The three components of the model (Presentation, Practice and Production) do not appear to cover the varieties of approach possible or common in an ELT classroom. Consider, for example, the term 'Presentation'. What happens mid-lesson when a student asks about a problem? Or when we return to a language item from a few weeks back? Or when one learner explains a grammar point to another? The essential common factor is not 'Presentation' – in this work we are helping students to become clearer, to focus in on areas, to analyse and sort out and categorize and resolve difficulties, to notice and *understand*. When using the three PPP components we are often unable to analyse what actually happens in the classroom.

From prescription to description

Many trainers no longer seem comfortable to offer such a 'formulaic and prescriptive and rigorous … straitjacket' model (Wajnryb 1989) for trainees. But what alternatives are there?

One option is for trainers to select and present to trainees an alternative route map, one that they believe more accurately reflects both their own teaching and current understanding about language learning. Task-based learning cycles, described else-where in this book, are one such option. It may be worth bearing in mind, though, that any such model offered as a single approach on a training course would still be implicit-ly prescriptive, suggesting specific ways of organizing a particular kind of lesson.

In the real world outside the training room, teachers use a great variety of teaching approaches, drawing inspiration and information from many sources. A training course which simply exchanges PPP for another route map is perhaps only straitjacketing a new generation of trainees into the current orthodoxy. If the history of ELT shows us one thing, it is that the pedagogic truths of one year tend to look more uncertain 15 or 20 years later.

What is the most effective way to teach a second language? We don't know, and because we don't know, I believe that, at initial training level, the priority is not to train trainees into any single 'way' ; rather, we need to find ways to value the intelligence and insights that course participants bring to their course and to encourage them to continue exercising this intelligence through the course and in their future teaching. An eclectic training course, providing an introduction to a range of core techniques, adopting a reflective, practice-driven approach, stands a better chance of producing autonomous, thinking teachers than a course focused around mastery of one kind of methodology.

One key to the success of such a course might be the availability of a simple, clear, flexible way of describing what teachers and learners do when working with language in the classroom.

The move from prescription to description is a small step, but with immensely powerful results. By removing the idea that there is such a thing as an ideal or 'right' way to teach, we free people. We free teachers and trainees to explore and learn and find the best ways for themselves and for their students. We free them to analyse and reflect on what is actually planned, or what actually happens, in terms of its own effectiveness, rather than by comparing lessons against a pre-set model of what makes a good lesson. We remove the shadow of evaluation against idealized, misunderstood or invisible goals and allow lessons to be evaluated more objectively against the teacher's or trainer's own criteria.

Four objectives

I know what I'd like:

- I'd like to be able to offer my trainees a simple description of the *variety* of approaches to lessons (and parts of lessons) that are possible.
- I'd like a description that *enables* this variety, rather than straitjackets into one workable, but restricting formula.

- I'd like a description that allows myself and the trainees to create lessons in the way that many experienced teachers do, by putting components, like building bricks, together in different orders.
- I'd like a description that also allows us to clearly analyse what is going on – to see the possibilities and the gaps, to see which arrangements of stages work and which don't, but which does not itself imply an evaluation.

One way of achieving these aims is to use the ARC model. This alternative analysis was originally devised for use in initial training, though it has now been used by many people on a variety of courses and programmes around the world. It is, I hope, quick to learn and simple to grasp; the surprise is that such a straightforward analysis can be very powerful in use.

Eight key features of ARC

A single lesson
The analysis is based on the range of things that happen in a single lesson, or part of a lesson, where the teacher or students are working with language.

Descriptive
It describes what happens, rather than prescribes one approach.

Three building blocks
What happens in class is analysed in terms in which trainees and many teachers think of lessons – as building blocks or separate components, that together add up to a complete lesson. There are three of these component blocks in this analysis.

Four skills
The analysis extends across the four skills.

Flexible
The analysis is flexible and enabling. Variations in the number of components used and in the order they occur are clearly possible. The analysis does not presume anything – for example, it does not presume pre-planning or pre-selection of language items to work on.

Non-evaluative
Although the analysis clearly describes sequences, and actively encourages reflective analysis as to what is effective or not, it does not itself imply any judgement. A descriptive analysis can be made of any lesson working on language, whether apparently successful or not.

Language
The analysis is based not on the degree of 'teacher control' (as in PPP), but in terms of the *language* available for the student to use, or to understand.

Variety of viewpoint
The analysis can be made from either the teacher's viewpoint, the student's viewpoint or an observer's viewpoint. The three analyses may be different in some respects.

ARC

ARC seen from the learner's perspective

In these diagrams the circles represent the language that a learner knows. The shaded areas show how each ARC category relates to this total knowledge.

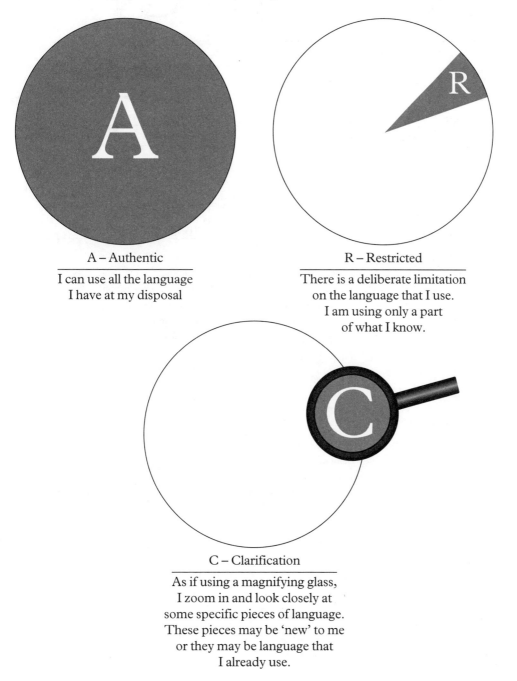

A – Authentic

I can use all the language
I have at my disposal

R – Restricted

There is a deliberate limitation
on the language that I use.
I am using only a part
of what I know.

C – Clarification

As if using a magnifying glass,
I zoom in and look closely at
some specific pieces of language.
These pieces may be 'new' to me
or they may be language that
I already use.

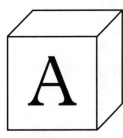 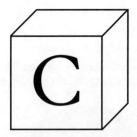

Authentic

for:
Meaning
Communication
Fluency
Real-life
Pleasure

Restricted

for:
Form
Practice
Accuracy
Testing
Display

Clarification

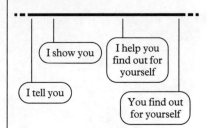

| | I show you | I help you find out for yourself |
| I tell you | | You find out for yourself |

Example activities

Speaking:	Communicative activities	Drills
	Discussions	Language Practice Activities
	Conversations	Elicited dialogues
		Jazz chants, poems, texts
Writing:	Stories	Copying
	Poems	Exercises
	Essays	Guided writing
Reading:	Novels	Examples
	Newspapers, articles	Coursebook texts
	Stories	Exercises
	Leaflets, notices, ads	
Listening:	Conversations	Discrete sounds, words
	Radio, TV	Sentences
	Narratives	Coursebook tasks
		Examples from coursebooks

Tools and techniques

Rules
Examples
Reference information
Diagrams, time lines
Substitution tables
Translation
Questions about meaning (concept Qs)
Questions about form
Questions about use
Problems and puzzles
Error analysis
Sentence analysis
Explanations, lectures
Demonstrations
Gestures, mime
Pictures, flashcards, visual aids
Cuisenaire rods, building bricks
Contexts and situations
Repetition
Elicitation
Voice, intonation, silence
Discussion
Personalization
Models, toys

It is possible to describe the ARC model very simply. (I find that a basic introduction to trainees usually takes 4 or 5 minutes.) Everything that happens in the classroom can be categorized under one of three headings, all of which refer to ways that *language* is being used in the classroom:

Restricted

The first component is *Restricted*. The language available for the learner to use or understand is in some way restricted, often in order to exemplify particular grammatical items. This Restriction may come from the teacher, the coursebook, an exercise, a text, etc. It may be self-imposed by the learner. It may arise because, for example, the teacher has decided to drill a specific grammar pattern or because a coursebook text has been written deliberately to include a number of examples of selected target language items.

This *Restricted* category, therefore, includes oral drills, many written exercises, copying from the board, elicited dialogues, reading coursebook texts and so on. Restricted activities are those that offer opportunities for language practice, for improving accuracy, for testing, for display. The emphasis will tend to be on form over meaning. In Widdowson's terminology, we may be more concerned with 'usage' (structurally correct and possible language, but with limited context, appropriacy or communicative purpose) than with 'use' (language that communicates meaning in specific situations).

A teacher may be mainly concerned that learners are engaged, challenged and that, by working intensively on using one language area, they *notice* problems and internalize new learnings that they were previously not aware of.

Note that the analysis includes language work across the four skills.

Authentic

The second ARC component is the converse of the first; *Authentic* activities are ones in which the language available to the students is *not* restricted – where students have opportunities to use all the language they know to really communicate or to understand what they are reading and hearing. They will be no attempt to control language so as to include specific grammatical or lexical items. In the classroom this is essentially the same as Skills work. *Authentic* is for communication, fluency, real-life, pleasure. Transmission of meaning is more important than correctness of form.

Clarification

The third and final building brick concerns the parts of a lesson where the learners need to really focus in on one (or more than one) language item – to see it, think about it, understand it better, become clearer on its form, its meaning and its use.

Whereas *Restricted* is concerned with learning about language by using it, *Clarification* concerns looking at language more analytically, from outside. Thus, 'teacher explanation', 'reference to a grammar book', 'elicitation of target sentences' and so on fit into this category.

Clarification is not simply another name for 'Presentation'. 'Presentation' is one option, meaning 'I tell you' or 'I show you'. If I position this at one end of a scale, then at the other end I can place 'You find out for yourself' (ie self-directed discovery). Somewhere towards the middle of the scale is 'I help you to find out for yourself' (ie guided discovery).

Depending on your beliefs about how people learn a second language you might wish to equate *Clarification* with an attempt to build 'linguistic competence', ie a theoretical knowledge of how the language works, whereas *Authentic* and *Restricted* might be seen as more concerned with improving 'performance', ie the ability to use language. Having said that, I'm sure that many would argue that any of the three categories might equally be responsible for building either competence or performance.

ARC

I now have three basic building bricks, simple to grasp in meaning – but surprisingly powerful in use. I can refer to each component by its initial letter (ie 'A' for Authentic; 'R' for Restricted; 'C' for Clarification). In order to distinguish the letters clearly from other abbreviations, when I annotate lesson plans or make other notes using ARC I have adopted the practice of drawing a box around each letter, eg

As a teacher, colleague, trainer, observer, inspector or head teacher, I can now look at any activity in any lesson and make a decision about which box it best fits, ie what is the main characteristic of that stage of the lesson? Is the language restricted? Is the language relatively unrestricted and natural? Is the language narrowed down to one specific area for the purposes of focusing attention and raising understanding?

The decision as to how to categorize an activity may not be clear cut; there is a certain degree of overlap and integration in every activity, and different people will interpret the relative importance of features in different ways. When watching the same lesson they may come to different conclusions as to what happened. In practice such different viewpoints and the subsequent different ARC categorizations have proved to be an interesting and useful aspect of this model. Discussions about making an ARC description have a very useful role in raising awareness for both trainee and trainer. So don't worry too much if you can't definitely decide on an ARC component; choose the one that seems to you to fit best.

By using the three ARC components I can describe a wide variety of ways of working with language in the classroom. It is of primary use in describing lessons and activities in which the aim is towards better understanding and use of grammar and other language systems, rather than lessons where the main aim is improving specific language skills. Here are some common lesson types:

Type 1 lesson

1 The teacher presents information about an item of language.

2 The students then work on oral practice of examples of these items.

3 The students do a written exercise to practice these items.

4 The students are given the opportunity to use these items, along with the other language they know, in communicative activities.

This procedure uses the three components in the order: CRRA (Clarification; Restricted; Restricted; Authentic). Sometimes this approach is characterized as 'Teach-Test'. It is essentially the same as the PPP model.

Options and possibilities
But already the description is different from PPP. It is flexible. It is already helping to show up options and possibilities. A few random examples:

• The Clarification and Focus could be student led.

• There could be an additional Restricted writing activity.

• The lesson could be reading-/writing-biased rather than oral-biased.

Type 2 lesson

1 The teacher selects an activity requiring use of specific language points. The students do the activity. While they are speaking the teacher listens in discreetly and notes down problems.

2 After they have finished the teacher uses the sentences he/she noted down to focus on and discuss difficulties and teach potentially useful language items that were avoided during the activity.

3 The teacher follows on with a similar activity to the first one. The students now have better resources to deal with some of the problems they may have faced.

This procedure uses the three components in the order: RCR (Restricted; Clarification; Restricted). This starts by encouraging the students to use the language they know and only then focuses in on specific problems or difficulties. Note that the teacher did not select the specific sentences to work on until he/she had listened to the students talking. Sometimes this approach is characterized as 'Test-Teach-Test'.

A small but significant variation would be to change one or both of the R activities for A; this is the Type 3 lesson.

Type 3 lesson

1 The teacher selects a communicative activity. The students do the activity. While they are speaking the teacher listens in discreetly and notes down problems.

2 After they have finished, the teacher uses the sentences he/she noted down to focus on and discuss difficulties and teach potentially useful language items that were avoided during the activity.

3 The teacher follows on with a similar communicative activity to the first one. The students now have better resources to deal with some of the communication problems they may have faced.

In the Type 3 lesson the order is: ACA (Authentic; Clarification; Authentic). I have now categorized the first and third activities as *Authentic* rather than *Restricted* because the teacher did not require or invite the students to use specific items of language.

Although the teacher might have chosen material likely to provide work on specific problem areas, he/she is less able to predict exactly what the main objective of the lesson will be than was the case with lesson types 1 and 2. He/She is prepared to work on *whichever* area turns out to be most important or useful.

Although the ARC description is itself non-evaluative, a trainer might well wish to use the description to raise points and compare approaches. (However, do note that any interpretation is added by the user rather than being implicit in the model.)

A trainer comparing CRRA and RCR might, for example, decide to point out that (a) CRRA is more likely to be used if an item is assumed to be completely new to the students, and that (b) with this approach the teacher is able to plan the lesson around specific example sentences selected before the lesson.

Type 4 lesson

The fourth type of lesson is based on textual or taped material, often in a coursebook. This material has been specially selected to include lots of examples of the target language items:

1 The students read the text (or listen to the tape).
2 The teacher focuses them in on specific language points.
3 The students do a follow-on exercise or communicative activity.

This lesson involves: RCR (or RCA) (Restricted; Clarification; Restricted/Authentic). The first Restricted activity here involves reading (rather than speaking).

Type 5 lesson

This lesson follows a task-based model:

1 Learners use whatever language they have at their disposal to do a task.
2 They plan a report, helped by the teacher where appropriate.
3 They report to other learners.
4 They listen to competent users working on the same task.
5 They study specific language problems arising from earlier activities, practising language patterns where appropriate.

The sequence here is: A – A/C – A – A – C/R. The first four activities involve no imposed restrictions on natural uses of language. In the report writing, for instance, the main aim of the learners is to communicate meaning as clearly as possible (A), perhaps with assistance from the teacher at various points (C).

As this example shows, any one lesson stage might involve more than a single ARC component. While students are performing a task (A) the teacher might intervene with corrections or explanations (C) or ask learners to repeat a pattern sentence (R). While using ARC to describe a lesson you will need to decide whether you consider that the stage is still predominantly within one category, or if its defining characteristic is that two or three categories are involved.

Type 6 lesson

1 Learners take part in natural conversation with other learners and the teacher.

This, of course, is: A.

Using ARC as a descriptive tool in observation

Although we have so far only considered a few lessons, note that the order of the three components is quite different in each. The strength of ARC is that the other possible combinations are infinite.

ARC has value in the seminar room as a way of introducing, describing and analysing a range of route maps such as those above. However we can also now, without judgement, describe many different kinds of actual observed lessons, both successful and problematic. Once we have a simple, clear overview of what has happened in a classroom (in an observed Teaching Practice lesson for example), we can then quickly move on to encouraging trainee reflection upon why options were chosen, what principles and beliefs underlie them, what the balance and relationship between stages was, what alternatives there might have been.

A trainer observed a weak trainee teach the following lesson:

1 The teacher chatted with the class while they waited for latecomers.
2 The teacher explained a grammar point.
3 The students wrote answers to an exercise in their books.
4 The teacher explained a grammar point.
5 The students wrote answers to an exercise in their books.
6 The teacher explained a grammar point.
7 The students wrote answers to an exercise in their books.
8 The teacher explained a grammar point.
9 The students wrote answers to an exercise in their books.

The ARC sequence as noted by the trainer was ACRCRCRCR.

A more complete description of a lesson is possible if we include :

- details of which skill areas are involved in the R and A categories
- information about how the Clarification was done
- a note on interaction patterns

This information could be noted when writing down the ARC sequence, for example: A (Informal chat) C (Teacher lecture) R (Written exercise) C (Teacher lecture) R (Written exercise) C (Teacher lecture) R (Written exercise) etc.

Alternatively, a form, such as the one below, could be used.

ARC	Skill area / further details	Interaction	Time
A	Chat about the weekend	T and Ss	1 min
C	Teacher explains grammar point	T>Ss	4 mins
R	Written exercise	Ss individ.	5 mins
C	Teacher explains grammar point	T>Ss	6 mins
R	Written exercise	Ss individ.	11 mins
C	Teacher explains grammar point	T>Ss	4 mins
R	Written exercise	Ss individ.	5 mins
C	Teacher explains grammar point	T>Ss	6 mins
R	Written exercise	Ss individ.	8 mins

Although the ARC description itself involves no evaluation, the trainer was able to use it as an important starting point for post-lesson discussions with the trainee about what she regarded as an essentially limited teaching routine. This is how the trainer used the ARC description to facilitate a reflective and non-judgemental feedback session after the lesson:

Recall
She first asked the trainee to recall the lesson and write his own ARC sequence for it.

Comparison
The trainer and trainee then compared their (slightly) different perceptions of what had happened and discussed why the trainee had believed that some stages involved students using language for communication (A) whereas the trainer had seen them as essentially practice of specific items (R).

Reflection
They then considered the sequence of activities in the lesson and particularly what beliefs about how people learn lay behind the trainee's choice of teaching strategy. As it turned out the trainee had not considered his rationale in any great depth.

Making conclusions
During the conversation the trainee was encouraged to make some tentative conclusions about the lesson. He decided that maybe (i) explanations and written pattern practice alone did not guarantee that learning had taken place; (ii) the lack of oral work on the language might have been an important omission; (iii) the repetitive sequence of activities and the limited interaction patterns had been somewhat predictable and unmotivating from the students' perspective; (iv) more varied approaches to using coursebook written exercises might be worth looking into.

Planning
The trainer asked the trainee to consider how he might approach a grammar-focused lesson next time he taught. The trainee made some concrete suggestions.
It is worth emphasizing that the trainee's conclusions were relevant to this specific situation. In a different school or in a different country or with different learners or a different teacher or different aims or different attitudes a similar ARC sequence of CRCRCRCR might have been entirely valid and appropriate. The description alone is no evaluation.

Implications for a training course

A descriptive model is an important starting point. It provides a tool to help us analyse lessons (i) as a theoretical model in seminars, (ii) at a planning stage, (iii) in execution and (iv) retrospectively.

Use of such an analysis may have wider implications for a training course.

Course programmes can start increasingly to reflect the way that teachers really teach. We no longer need to describe (or avoid describing) a simplified 'training' model for grammar teaching. Many of the seminars currently timetabled in many centres (ie drilling, communicative activities, etc) can remain as they are, but can now be linked into the flexible possibilities of ARC.

We do not initially need to change our course programme at all – just add in ARC as another ingredient, as a descriptive tool for the training we are offering. However, once ARC is being used, there may then be opportunities for evolving a slightly changed course around it. Consider, for example, lesson planning, observation of experienced teachers and personal skills:

Lesson planning
Assisted lesson planning can make use of ARC as an analytical tool to clarify, to both trainee and trainer, what is being planned.

This might enable us to avoid unhelpful rules and generalizations, such as – 'You need to select your target sentences before you teach'. In acknowledging that an ACA sequence is a viable grammar lesson (see 'Type 3 lesson' above), trainers will be able to accept that language items to be focused on are *not* necessarily always selected before the lesson.

Observation of experienced teachers
Trainees observing experienced teachers can analyse the lessons in terms of noticing and analysing what actually happens, rather than attempting to fit the lesson into a possibly false or inappropriate PPP framework. A blank ARC grid (such as the one used in the ACRCRCRCR lesson above) is a very powerful observation instrument.

Personal skills
As a result of more flexible planning options, trainee's lessons can become more responsive to learners' needs and less a demonstration of ability to operate certain possibly inappropriate or unrealistic models.

We can also start to concentrate on some important non-methodological aspects of our lessons: qualities such as engagement, rapport, intentional listening, and being 'in touch' with the learners; qualities that often become relegated to side-issues when we are over concerned with getting fixed methodological routines correct.

Implications within a school

As my main concern in this chapter is with initial training courses, I shall only make this one suggestion: if ARC is found to be relatively straightforward to grasp, maybe it can also be offered to *learners* of English. By giving my class a copy of the ARC diagram as an overview map of possibilities for English lessons I can raise awareness about the range of classroom activities available. In discussion we can then start to address the differences or similarities between the ways that various students wish to work. For example, a learner who believes that analysing grammar is the only way to make progress might notice that other possibilities do exist. With guidance from the teacher (and maybe having heard other students voice their views), she might begin to consider the possibility of trying out alternative strategies and being less dismissive of classroom activities that do not match her initial expectations. And whatever conclusions she eventually reaches, the raising of an awareness that other learners have different attitudes or expectations is probably valuable in its own right.

Conclusions

ARC may provide teachers, trainers and trainees with answers to some common problems. I don't believe that it in any way illuminates the whole truth about a lesson, but its essential simplicity and clarity has proved a valuable key to new insights and understandings in many training rooms. And maybe it is closer to the truth than any single paradigm can be.

Maybe ARC can allow us to run courses that are more honest to our beliefs about what English language teaching really involves. Maybe we can increasingly run training courses that involve trainees in intelligent, reasoned approaches to their work. Maybe we can give permission to new teachers to think for themselves from day one.

ARC is not a new methodology. A lesson described by ARC is not implicitly 'good' or 'bad'. ARC is nothing more than a description. But maybe describing what we already do is a good starting point for training a new generation of teachers.

Jim Scrivener is a teacher and teacher trainer at International House, Hastings. He is author of *Learning Teaching* (Heinemann 1994). He is interested in the skills of training and feedback and in the role of personal development as a concomitant of professional growth.

Acknowledgements
I am very grateful for research by and advice from my colleague Pete Redpath. Thanks also to Tim Bowen and Adrian Underhill for some excellent advice.

Grammar for trainee teachers

9

Philip Kerr

ll teacher training courses must achieve two conflicting goals at the same time. They must provide trainees with the confidence they need to make decisions in the classroom. But training courses must also equip trainees to learn from experience. There is a tension between certainty and security on the one hand, and open-mindedness and the ability to develop on the other. Trainees need a basic methodology which they can apply from the moment they begin teaching. But they must also be able to question that methodology and to experiment with alternatives. Without this there can be no professional development. The same applies to language description. Trainees need an understanding of basic pedagogic grammar, something they can apply to their teaching from the start. But they also need to question generalizations about language. Without this ability they cannot respond appropriately to queries and problems raised by their students, and, even more important, they are not in a position to learn from the continued exposure to language which is part of any teacher's day-to-day experience.

In my own view, and it is a view supported by research and observation, there is a serious danger that many teacher training courses aim at security at the expense of future development. In terms of language description, training courses, particularly at the basic level, transmit an accepted view of language and of priorities in language description, but do not equip trainees to question this view. Most trainers nowadays stress the importance of learner independence and of preparing learners to draw conclusions for themselves from the language to which they are exposed. But paradoxically they fail to provide such opportunities for their trainees. In this paper I will examine the approach to language description on basic training courses and will ask how this approach might be extended to encourage teacher development. In doing this I will look closely at practice on training courses leading to a particular qualification, the RSA/UCLES initial training course, the CTEFLA.

Trainees on the RSA/UCLES CTEFLA (see Andrews 1994, for further information) typically find that upwards of 20% of seminar time is devoted to what is known as 'language analysis'. It is clear, therefore, that an understanding of language systems is regarded as an important part of initial teacher training. But what such an understanding might entail and which language systems it might be appropriate to analyse are questions that it would be healthy to ask, particularly in the context of a determinedly practical initial training course.

When, in 1992, 100 such trainees were asked (Kerr 1993a) to write what they understood by the expression 'language analysis', many of them described it as the breakdown of language into a number of constituent categories, most prominent of which was labelled 'grammar'. Some trainees saw grammar as something different from form, structure, function, syntax, meaning, concept, etc, but most often 'language analysis' and 'grammar' were seen as synonymous: 'a less terrifying word than "grammar" ', as one put it. Only ten trainees made any reference to the teaching and learning process, or to the students themselves.

Not only did most trainees equate language analysis and grammar, they also had very definite ideas about grammar. It was seen as a set of rules to be learnt, an 'out-there' body of knowledge (Grundy 1989) concerning the organization of language at the sentence level. ('How to describe clearly the precise grammar in each phrase/sentence,' was one suggestion.)

These findings were hardly surprising, reflecting what might be described as a prototypical or 'folk' (Taylor 1989) understanding of grammar. Chalker (1994) describes the beliefs of practising teachers in similar terms: grammar is seen as a set of awe-inspiring rules, derived from the structuralist tradition, that are waiting to be discovered. There is, however, some evidence that teacher trainers take a rather different view of grammar. In a survey carried out by Andrews (1994), CTEFLA trainers, when asked to characterize grammatical knowledge/awareness, made more frequent reference to teaching and learning processes and revealed a significantly less product-oriented view than the one I have described above. They referred, for example, to the selection and grading of language for teaching purposes and to the anticipation of learners' difficulties.

It seems, therefore, that most trainers recognize the complexity of language description and language learning. One would expect this recognition to be reflected in the content and methodology of training courses. But what trainers say and what trainers do are not necessarily the same thing. The way trainers actually treat grammar seems to be based on a view much closer to that expressed by trainees than that expressed by the trainers themselves. A survey of 'language tasks' from the application forms of 15 CTEFLA centres indicates a preoccupation with the candidate's declarative knowledge of language descriptors and grammatical rules. Candidates for the course are interviewed, and tasks similar to those of the application form are often set. The most frequently used task in these forms asks applicants to label particular verb forms and state their meaning in the context of an example sentence. The trainers/interviewers are then usually asked to provide written comments on the candidate's language awareness. Most commonly, these comments evaluated the candidate's language awareness in general terms, eg 'She had it', 'a bit superficial', or in terms of how long it took the interviewee to get 'it', eg 'Took him a long while', 'quick to see it'. The 'it' in question was usually the ability to describe the meaning of a particular verb phrase in a particular sentence. Successful candidates were often those who knew the rules: 'he knows his stuff', 'she's done her homework'.

During the course itself, the language component of the syllabus often boils down to the 'analysis of the verb phrase in the context of a presentation and practice lesson' (Kerr 1993a and cf Shaw 1979). A typical seminar might consist of an analysis of the problems of meaning, form and pronunciation of, say, the 'three' types of conditional sentence, followed by an investigation of how this language area could be presented to a class, perhaps with reference to one or more contemporary coursebooks. One outcome of these sessions is often a set of prescriptive rules – often of questionable validity.

The organization of teaching practice in these courses usually reinforces the approach of the input sessions. Trainees are directed to teach a range of lesson types (grammar, vocabulary or skills), each of which follows relatively set procedures. Language is dealt with in presentation and practice lessons and these often inspire fear in the trainee. Skills lessons, however, where the focus is on the development of spoken fluency or the sub-skills of listening, reading and writing, are seen as quite separate from the tricky business of learning and teaching grammar: they are seen as the easy option.

The view of grammar that emerges is one that may be characterized as follows:

- Grammar is at the centre of language learning.
- Grammar consists of rules that can be taught and learnt.
- Grammar is concerned with the construction of discrete sentences.
- Grammar is mostly about verbs.
- Grammar is acquired through practice (controlled and freer). The acquisition of grammar is not a problem-solving activity.
- Grammar exists independently of other aspects of language such as vocabulary and phonology. It can therefore be taught independently of language use. This is why the learning of grammar in the grammar lesson and the application of grammar in the skills lesson are seen as quite separate activities.

The view of language learning implicit in this approach is informed by the 'transmission' model and is mirrored by the view of learning implicit in the training approach. 'Talk-and-chalk' has become taboo (indeed, 'teacher talking' is presented as a 'bad thing' and student interaction a 'good thing') but it is clear that the teacher (or trainer) sets the agenda, and the learner's role is to internalize and then output the information that is presented. Trainees are required to reproduce a limited set of generalizations about language rather than encouraged to think about language for themselves.

The CTEFLA is essentially a practical induction to teaching and must prepare trainees as realistically as possible for the work that they are likely to face. This is often referred to in terms of the students they will teach and the books they will use. The product-oriented view of grammar promoted by initial training courses, coinciding as it does with the 'folk' understanding of grammar, is likely to meet many learners' expectations of language teaching/learning. In addition, as Batstone (1994a: 226) points out, 'such a structured and systematic approach can provide the learner with a strong sense of purpose and direction, and this in itself can generate a much needed feeling of security and purpose which can have a motivating effect'. By the same token, it may provide the trainees with a sense of measurable achievement and a handle on what can be a bewildering and confidence-draining experience (Rinvolucri 1991 and Pearce 1991). There is a clear correspondence, moreover, with best-selling texts such as Murphy (1985) and the demands of many public examinations. Alternative approaches, it is argued, can be left until later in a teacher's career.

But approaches which produce short-term results are not necessarily the most effective in the long term. The grammar of teacher training courses depends, as it must, 'on critical assumptions about the nature of language and its relationship to language learning' (Tomlin 1994:141). However great the immediate practical expediency of a particular approach may be, its adoption will remain problematic if it can be shown to be based on demonstrably false assumptions, and is likely therefore to be to the long-term detriment of both language learner and teacher trainee. Attacks on the language focus of these courses (eg Grundy 1989; Lewis 1993; Kerr 1993a) have concentrated on the demonstrable limitations of the approach to language description (incorrect, inadequate or irrelevant rules) and the lack of any grounding in second language acquisition theory. The assumptions outlined above concerning the nature of grammar and language acquisition are not as readily accepted as they once were. Indeed, the recent research consensus (eg Bygate et al 1994; Odlin 1994; Batstone 1994) would seem to weigh heavily against such an approach. Whilst the grammar of popular grammar exercise books may be what learners like, it is not necessarily what they or their teachers need (except from a very short-term market perspective). If the grammars of the functional grammarians or the discourse analysts, or the proponents of grammar as process (eg Rutherford 1987), provide a more complete and convincing picture, should this not be on the menu for trainee teachers? Is it either fair or respectable to promote a view of language and language learning which has so little theoretical underpinning? Even the contemporary coursebooks (eg Bell and Gower 1991), from which trainees are often required to teach, are often incompatible with the presentation-and-practice approach of traditional training programmes.

These criticisms of the language focus of many CTEFLA courses may be well founded. But it is arguable that such criticisms fall into what Skehan (1994:181) calls the 'linguistic fallacy': the belief that there is a straightforward relationship 'between how grammatical systems are described and how they should be used practically'. The fact that teachers' grammars should not directly mirror a grammar for learners does not necessarily entail that it should be replaced by a more academic grammar. 'We could usefully begin,' writes Leech (1994:17), 'by seeing teachers' grammar as some kind of mediation between [academic grammar and grammar for learners].' It is not, therefore, a question of promoting either the product of learners' grammars or the process of academic grammarians and acquisition theorists, but of establishing a relationship between them.

Leech (1994) and others (eg Wright and Bolitho 1993) have attempted to provide an alternative by spelling out what a teacher needs to be able to do in behavioural terms. These do not refer to particular classroom techniques, but are equally observable and measurable nevertheless. Leech (1994:18) provides the following list:

A 'model' teacher of languages should:

- be capable of putting across a sense of how grammar interacts with the lexicon as a communicative system (both 'communicativeness' and 'system' will need independent attention);
- be able to analyse the grammatical problems that learners encounter;
- have the ability and confidence to evaluate the use of grammar, especially by learners, against criteria of accuracy, appropriateness and expressiveness;

- be aware of the contrastive relations between native language and foreign language;
- understand and implement the processes of simplification by which overt knowledge of grammar can best be presented to learners at different stages of learning.

Wright and Bolitho (1993), in a more directly practical vein, suggest a list of activities that will train the language awareness of teachers. The point of departure is what teachers need to do, not the rules they need to learn. Clearly, if trainee teachers are to do things with language, some kind of selection of particular language areas is inevitable. They will need to learn for themselves, within the contexts of particular teaching situations, what kind of language focus is appropriate for their students. In a practical teacher training scheme, such as CTEFLA, the starting point for the linguistic development of teachers will therefore need to be the language output of the students in teaching practice, on video and in observation, rather than the diet offered by the published grammars for learners.

Attempts such as these to describe the grammatical awareness needed by language teachers do not provide a blueprint for immediate implementation in initial teacher training courses. The particular nature of the CTEFLA scheme (like any other) will impose restraints and limitations. It will be some time before piloting and trialling leads to an effective and accepted modus operandi, and it is not likely to be one that will remain static. However, the dethronement of sentence-level verb-based grammar and its accompanying model of presentation-and-practice teaching seems likely in initial EFL teacher training. The shift would already seem to be away from telling and drilling to supervised 'doing'. It encompasses, rather than rejects, previous models and bridges the theory/practice divide, which has so often been a problem in teacher training courses. It also finds an echo in the new CTEFLA syllabus (1994). This syllabus, the product of extensive consultation, reflects a situation that is already extant. Change is at the top of the agenda.

A change such as this will not be effected by a bolt-on solution. Trainees struggle hard enough as it is in their efforts to fit in and pass, to make sense of the mass of information that is sent their way, without having to cope with further, contradictory paradigms. Any attempt to take on board the recent developments in grammatical theory will have implications for the training process itself. A more process-oriented view of language learning will sit ill with a transmission model of teacher training. Almost inevitably, the transition will be a rocky one (see Woodward, Paper 1): firmly established and reassuring practices in many centres (where, for example, training seminars are kept in central files and delivered by different trainers to different groups of trainees teaching different groups of students) will have to be changed. Staff will have to be retrained, materials rewritten, money invested. The change will, in its way, be as significant to the profession as the introduction of practical training courses over 30 years ago.

Finally let me offer just one example of an activity which might be used on training courses to encourage learners to look critically at language and make generalizations for themselves. The extracts were taken from a sequence of correspondence leading up to an international seminar.

Look at these extracts from two letters. Underline those words and phrases which refer to the future and discuss ways in which you might classify them:

Extract A

> I would like to confirm that the British Council will contribute £500 towards your visit to Singapore to this year's RELC Seminar. Our Specialist Tours Department should contact you within a week or so with details of payment. Please let me know as soon as you have fixed your travel plans so I can make sure you are properly looked after on arrival.

Extract B

> I am planning to make arrangements to arrive on Sunday April 21st and to leave either pm April 30th or am May 1st. I have been in touch with the British Council Washington about the payment for my ticket and I am hoping to finalize those details this week.
>
> I do not know yet whether I shall be staying with Vijay Bhatia. I'll let you know as soon as I have heard from him.

There is plenty of room for discussion here. There are a number of expected references to the future such as the modals *will; should; can; shall*. There are less predictable ones like the present perfect *(as soon as you have fixed; as soon as I have heard)*; present simple *(you are properly looked after)*. There are four expressions which focus on the future *(I would like to; I am planning to; make arrangements to; I am hoping to)*. The prepositional phrase *on arrival* clearly refers to the future. The word *yet* in *I do not know yet* clearly has implications for future action.

An exercise of this kind teaches a good deal about how future reference is encoded in English, particularly in correspondence. It suggests a much richer description than is usually offered in student grammars. Most important of all it shows that trainees can learn a great deal for themselves by looking critically at language – a message they might also usefully pass on to their students.

Philip Kerr is a teacher, teacher trainer and Director of Studies at International House, London. His current interests include curriculum development and teacher training processes.

Learning to learn how to teach: developing expertise through experience

10

Corony Edwards

Introduction

once went to a workshop for teacher trainers on the relationship between input sessions, teaching practice and TP feedback. We were asked to form groups and come up with definitions for 'Input' and 'Feedback'. One (very experienced) participant stood up to give her group's contribution: 'Input is telling trainees how to do it. Feedback is telling them how they should have done it.' Of course, everyone laughed, but the implication is a serious one. Is this, in essence, what happens on teacher training courses? If so, does it have to happen this way?

In this paper I consider typical approaches taken on initial courses in TEFL in terms of the course content, or syllabus, and the training methodology used to deliver this. I will argue that just as PPP has become the dominant model for 'communicative' lessons, a received model of training has also evolved, and that like PPP this model has some serious drawbacks that need to be addressed if course providers are to fulfil their responsibilities to the profession. In Paper 9 of this volume, *Grammar for Trainee Teachers*, Philip Kerr reconsiders the way that language awareness raising and grammar teaching should be dealt with in initial training; this paper will focus mainly on how development of trainees' classroom techniques and methodology could be more effectively achieved, particularly in the light of the opportunities offered by newly revised syllabuses for language teachers. (The changes in the RSA/UCLES exam syllabuses for teachers, for example the CTEFLA – Certificate for the Teaching of English as a Foreign Language to Adults – are good examples.) Ideas from second language acquisition theory will be extrapolated to apply to 'teaching skills acquisition'. My aim is to describe an alternative framework for the content and methodology of teacher training courses using the emerging approach to second language teaching as a metaphor. Just as language teaching is moving towards a learner-centred, problem-solving methodology, so training is, and should be, moving towards a trainee-centred methodology which relies more on self-examination and less on transmission.

Language acquisition and teacher training

I believe that the process of learning to be an effective teacher in many ways parallels the process of learning to be an effective second language user. For example, it is now widely accepted that you learn a language through using the language. Effective language lessons include communicative activities to provide language learners with opportunities to learn through language use. Likewise, you learn to teach through teaching, and effective teacher training courses include teaching practice activities to provide trainees with the opportunity to learn through teaching. Language acquisition theory and research tell us that learners need meaningful exposure to language; trainee teachers need meaningful exposure to the teaching/learning process through directed classroom observation (and experience as second language learners themselves). Language learners also need the chance to produce language in a meaningful way, and to stretch their output in order to make progress; trainees need to try out new techniques, to take risks, in the TP classroom. Both groups, of course, need motivation to engage in their learning activities. There are far more initial teacher training courses nowadays which insist on a generous proportion of the timetable being devoted to real TP. These provide initial trainees with just the opportunities they need, and most trainees are indeed well motivated.

The more contentious issue is what role and form *instruction* should play in the process: should trainers devise a syllabus that, like an atomistic approach to language teaching, consists of a list of discrete items to be presented, maybe practised through peer teaching, and then produced in the TP classroom? Or should an approach analogous to a language awareness-raising, learner-training approach to language teaching be followed? Should TP performance be assessed by an 'expert' (the trainer) and the trainee given the verdict in feedback notes or meetings after TP, or should trainees also (alternatively?) be developing the skills to evaluate and develop from the TP experience for themselves, and if so, how can trainers foster the development of such skills? I believe that on a short course it is particularly important to focus on equipping trainees with the ability to develop their own expertise with experience.

Why we need to change

What I have to say applies, I believe, to any teacher training course, whether it is aimed at in-service development or aimed at external certification, whether it is an introductory course or an advanced course for experienced teachers. Let us, however, take one specific situation as a case study. Over the last ten years the outline syllabus set by RSA/UCLES for the CTEFLA has remained the same, and has only recently come up for revision. However, the way that this syllabus has been realized through the course programmes of approved CTEFLA centres has, I believe, become increasingly complex and overcrowded as centres attempt to squeeze in new sessions on whatever happens to be the latest discovery of applied linguistics or language teaching methodology, often encouraged by the comments of their external assessors. The inclusion of sessions on discourse analysis, learner training, using video, CALL and so on have all crept in over the years until the resulting course is in danger of becoming a cluttered kaleidoscope of one-off sessions. Comparing centres' programmes from the early 1980s with those of the early 1990s bears some witness to this, but even these quite detailed documents do not give the full picture, since the title of a session such as 'presentation techniques' (which occurs in nearly all programmes regardless of date) could cover either a very limited or very wide range of issues. Those closely involved with the planning, delivery and assessment of this or similar courses, however, will recognize the trend towards diversification and complication of initial teacher training curricula.

The situation trainers now find themselves in is not dissimilar to that of the language teacher and materials writer. Our knowledge and understanding of language is much richer now than a decade or two ago, as is our understanding of language acquisition. There is a tendency nowadays (evidenced in many coursebooks) to attempt to include in our syllabus, and teach, not just sentence grammar, but many of the other aspects of language systems that have recently been brought to our attention by linguists – language functions, cohesive ties, signals of clause relations and phonological features. This linguistic knowledge is a difficult load for both teachers and students to cope with, and the amount of teacher input that becomes student intake becomes proportionately less and less.

Perhaps it is inevitable that courses training teachers in a presentation approach to language teaching will reflect this approach in their own syllabus and training methodology. Indeed, it would seem desirable to do so, since a good training course should surely employ what is considered to be good language teaching practice. But if we are to consider alternatives to PPP, then by the same token we need to consider alternatives to teacher training. They are two sides of the same coin.

One alternative approach already mentioned in this collection rejects the explicit teaching of systems, and instead starts with meaningful input of language (through use of familiar topics, contextualization, etc), and allows learners to investigate the language they have just processed to discover for themselves the patterns that exist. This does not mean trying to guess the form or the rule that the teacher or coursebook already has hidden up their sleeve, but encouraging learners to look more closely at the language to see what they are ready to see. This awareness-raising approach does not depend on a pre-determined (and possibly inadequate or even inaccurate) pedagogic grammar, but on the learners' perceptions. Arguments for a similar approach to teacher development have also been put forward, eg Wallace's reflective teacher (Wallace 1991).

Syllabus

In terms of the initial teacher training syllabus, where does this leave us? Well, initial trainees are rather like beginner students. They have to start somewhere. Like beginner students, they need a basic *vocabulary* of language teaching – a basic set of core techniques and skills with a high surrender value that can be employed in a number of classroom situations to achieve a number of objectives depending on the context and the way they are used. For example, basic classroom management skills such as setting up groupwork and pairwork, using teaching aids, attracting and holding students' attention are obvious candidates (just *how* these might be included will be discussed later). Also in this 'essentials' list I would include being able to: use published materials, conduct a choral drill or question and answer session, give clear instructions, control one's language so that students can understand instructions and explanations and so on. And of course, the ability to plan and time a lesson could not be omitted. This does *not* mean learning to plan a lesson based on a specific model such as PPP. The CTEFLA syllabus has never stipulated this – it has simply required trainees to demonstrate that they can 'plan appropriately for parts of and for complete lessons within a sequence of lessons'. It does, however, *imply* a PPP format in its fourth criterion: 'The candidate has demonstrated an ability to … provide appropriate presentation, practice and production activities.' In the new syllabus, even this implication is removed, and is replaced with 'the selection and evaluation of appropriate exercise types, activity types, and tasks, for specific lessons'. It is encouraging that while the 'PPP' element has disappeared, the word 'appropriate' has remained. I suspect that it will be much easier for trainees to plan appropriate learning opportunities for their students without this (intentionally or otherwise) implied restriction. This is a clear signal to centres that the freedom exists to encourage trainees to plan not according to any complete lesson formula, but according to other, more fundamental, criteria. This could result in a whole variety of lesson types – including those that appear incomplete in themselves, as they may be part of, for example, an on-going project involving meaningful and motivated exposure to, and output of, language at various stages, with instruction inserted as and when it is needed. The key is that if the trainee considers the activity to be appropriate, they should be able to justify this in terms of their learners' needs, interests and level, and in terms of what the trainee knows about language and how language acquisition is facilitated.

The CTEFLA initiated will be thinking that most of the above list is pretty much the same as already exists; it *is*. These are basics that language teachers following any number of different approaches and methods might employ. The difference is firstly that I would not worry about the omission of some, or even several, more specialized techniques, such as 'using songs', or 'chain drills' (there is no mention whatsoever of anything so specific in the new CTEFLA syllabus). Secondly, I would be more concerned with how we ask trainees to *apply* the techniques we include (the CTEFLA syllabus *does* require trainees be able to select and evaluate *appropriate* exercise types, activity types and tasks).

My doubts are directed here towards courses aimed at the CTEFLA, but, as I have said, the same doubts could be raised about courses at other levels and about courses which are not specifically designed to meet the demands of an outside body like RSA/UCLES. In-service courses are often designed to enable trainees to implement a specific teaching programme, not to enable them to question that programme and to contribute to its development. Training courses at an advanced level are often designed simply to impose a 'new' orthodoxy rather than to encourage teachers to develop and assert their own values within that orthodoxy.

Training teachers to survive on their own

Let me return to a focus on initial training courses. I am not suggesting that a minimal list like the one I have outlined above will be adequate for the rest of a trainee's teaching career; but then no teacher of beginner language students would claim that the lexis covered in the first 100-hour course will turn them into fluent speakers. What the teacher might well do, however, is train the students to use reference books, especially dictionaries, to help them learn more for themselves in the long term, and to survive in the meantime. The field of ELT is spoiled for choice when it comes to 'books for teachers'. What I *would* like to see included in initial training courses is a much greater emphasis on trainees using such books to find out about specific techniques for themselves. They should leave a course knowing about the range of resource books available, and how to use them in an informed and critical way. TP planning workshops would be an ideal forum for this, since trainees would be employing their referencing work for a genuine teaching activity. By the end of a course all participating trainees would have learned about and used, or observed others using, a range of specific techniques, but the precise range for each trainee will be different and will depend on individual teaching needs, preferences and styles.

Increasing the real learning and removing the guilt

At this point I anticipate cries of 'But there wouldn't be enough time!' or 'They need a clear model for lesson planning!' By paring down the amount of formal input, there *would* be more time for trainees to do *real teaching activities,* which is what lesson preparation is. It is comparable to a learner training session on using reference works where the activities the students are engaged in are helping them to complete a real task. This is very different to 'drilling' trainees in a prescriptive and rigid type of lesson format that they are very likely to find impossible to apply. Such prescriptive approaches may appear to offer survival teaching strategies, but ultimately prove to be a false investment. They leave novice teachers feeling inadequate and even guilty for not doing it the 'right way'. Instead of evaluating how effective a lesson is in terms of what the students are getting out of it, whether there is a good learning atmosphere, whether the learners are involved, whether they are being given opportunities for real communication that encourage them to stretch their communicative capacity, the teacher will be worrying about the fact that they didn't stick to the lesson plan, or did something in the 'wrong' order. They become, in some cases, quite obsessed with their own performance, instead of evaluating their lessons in terms of how their *students* fared.

Developing pedagogic competence

Initially, novice teachers are likely to use the techniques they learn about in input sessions and reference books in a fairly naive way, just as a beginner will use lexical phrases in an rough and unanalysed way to achieve a communicative purpose. But with experience and reflection they will begin to understand *what* such techniques can achieve and *when* it is appropriate to use them. They will begin to see how one technique might be used in different contexts for different purposes, and conversely how similar teaching/learning objectives can be achieved through a range of techniques, like language learners becoming aware of the different form/function relationships of language. This is likely to happen in spite of when and how they have been told to use them by their trainers. In supervised TP on a 'PPP course' a trainee will no doubt try to stick to the prescribed stages of the lesson: they will be teaching for display purposes. Compare this with a learner who has been taught a rather complex and difficult-to-apply rule of grammar; they obligingly apply the rule as best they can during practice activities in class. But as soon as the need for genuine communication arises, the learner forgets the newly learned rule and gets on with using the language they have in any way that works to get their message across – just like the newly qualified teacher who, with 25 or more hours a week of teaching, has no time for meticulous lesson planning and so is forced into making spur of the moment decisions and falls back on intuitive improvisations. Indeed how many experienced teachers, trainers and examiners who were trained in PPP still closely follow this format? I suspect that the vast majority have adapted, if not completely changed, their approach to structuring lessons, and very few squeeze in a neat sequence of the three stages in their 50-minute slots. Yet they would still claim to be able to evaluate those lessons in terms of whether they were useful for their students or not. So why ask trainees to do it, and leave them feeling they have under-achieved? Surely instead we should be helping them develop their 'pedagogic competence' in a more realistic way.

The grammar of teaching

This does not mean that we should ignore structured approaches to teaching altogether. For the beginner language learner a *small* number of the most powerful grammar rules are likely to be an invaluable addition to a basic vocabulary: how to make negatives, for example. The equivalent for the trainee teacher would be the understanding of some of the fundamental principles of language learning and teaching. Here I have in mind the four basic conditions for language acquisition: meaningful input, meaningful output, motivation plus, ideally, instruction, and understanding of whether classroom language is *really* communicative or not (ie is student output really meaningful?) through the use of a descriptive model such as Scrivener's ARC (Paper 8). Trainee teachers, like students, have a need for security. Students often find security in the form of learned rules. Trainee teachers likewise need some basic criteria by which to evaluate their teaching activities, and by which they can be evaluated for assessment purposes. I believe the four basic conditions listed above can adequately provide these criteria. The resulting course, with its combination of core techniques plus basic principles, is equivalent to beginners learning a core vocabulary of the most frequent or useful lexical items together with a minimal number of the most powerful language rules.

Training methodology

The methods used to deliver the type of course I have suggested have been hinted at in places already. I have mentioned 'trainee-training' in using reference books for teachers, for example. In addition I would encourage trainees to take a 'data-driven' approach to their development, deriving their teaching methodology more from classroom experience than from 'experts' delivering input sessions, however interactive these may be. The analogy here is that of a data-driven or awareness-raising approach to language teaching instead of a presentation-based methodology. *No* trainee comes to a course without knowledge and experience of classrooms and learning, and most will have extensive experience of language learning. This knowledge could be exploited far more overtly than is often the case, and provides the obvious starting point from which trainees can structure classroom-based experience, to ensure that this becomes 'meaningful input'. Input session time could be used for trainees to reflect on learning and teaching experience, both pre- and in-course, with the agenda for reflection set by the tutor or negotiated with trainees in order to ensure an appropriate range of issues were covered during the course. Trainees would be encouraged to raise questions and form hypotheses about a given aspect of teaching and learning, and then focus on these issues in the following observation sessions. How, for example, do learners behave when engaged in groupwork? Do they actually use the target language? Do they correct one another? Do they show any concern for formal accuracy? The answers to these questions can only be found by careful observation of learners at work. And what about observing fellow teachers at work? At what stages of the lesson do experienced teachers correct and shape learner language? How do they compromise between on the one hand encouraging learners to use language for themselves and on the other hand providing language input? Answers to these questions may be found by observing experienced teachers and peers, analysing in a critical way their approaches, and taking the ideas which emerge as the starting point for developing pedagogic competence. In many cases techniques observed will need to be adapted to suit the specific context of each trainee's TP class, so trainees will find themselves in an informed position for experimenting in TP. A much more central role for structured observation is implied, with discussion of this being built into TP workshops or feedback sessions as well as input sessions.

The relationship of TP and feedback would also change with this approach, in order to develop teachers who are better able to evaluate their lessons and to learn from experience. On many courses this *appears* to happen already, but closer scrutiny reveals that the main activity in TP is to evaluate the experience (or be evaluated) against criteria of questionable value implicitly or explicitly laid down by the 'experts'. During their report on 'So how do you think it went?' trainees try to guess what the TP tutor has written in their comments with the idea that in subsequent sessions they will try to 'correct' the 'errors': the focus is on teaching for conformity (see Willis, Paper 5). The TP feedback session turns into a kind of confessional, albeit in the most supportive of atmospheres, and trainees are left feeling that there are so many things to get wrong. I think that this is less a problem of the approach taken to feedback than of the type of criteria used to evaluate the TP experience being discussed. In centres where I have observed feedback taking as its starting point the *students'* learning experience two interesting things seem to happen: the trainees appear much less anxious about whether their lesson and teaching performance was 'good' or 'bad', and at the same time they are developing a very student-centred approach to their teaching. Most training centres have moved towards this type of approach in a number of ways – for example, few still have sets of pre-determined TP points to form the trainees' TP syllabus regardless of how appropriate they may be to the students in the TP class. We need to keep moving in this direction.

This *experience*-centred approach is based on the same premises as Lewis sets out in his Observe – Hypothesize – Experiment cycle. A related way of looking at it would be to see the process as a sort of task-based learning cycle: preparing for TP, possibly with a peer-teaching walk-through of the lesson, can be seen as the task and report preparation stages (in private; redrafting for improved product); doing the TP lesson is the report stage (in public; prepared); feedback is the reflection and analysis stage. Trainee diaries provide another opportunity for reflection, but in private. Some trainers may feel uncomfortable about not giving any traditional (ie direct) input. One input technique that exploits the 'experience followed by reflection' staging is 'loop input' (Woodward 1991), where a technique is demonstrated through the technique itself – for example, a jigsaw reading activity for the trainees to do on the subject of jigsaw reading. Woodward emphasizes the importance of trainees being able to *experience* the process they are being taught about, to be on the receiving end in order to better evaluate it. Loop input followed by discussion and reflection is a very efficient way of doing this. Another rich source of experiential data is a foreign language course which trainees attend in parallel to their TEFL course. Again, many centres already have at least one lesson in a foreign language built into their programme. It is worth considering whether more such lessons would pay more dividends than some traditional input sessions. In fact, the approach I have described above could be viewed as a broader version of loop input, where the assumptions, principles and values of good language teaching permeate the teacher training course.

Assessment

Communicative language testing relies on ascertaining how successfully a candidate completes a task, focusing on accuracy only in the sense used by Willis (Paper 5), ie how successfully a message has been conveyed. Assessment of trainees based on how effectively they fostered learning would be the training equivalent, and Stevick's (1976) summary of what he hopes for in a classroom would be an excellent starting point in drawing up criteria for this. Conversely, assessment based on the trainees jumping through a number of hoops often with the aim of achieving a neatly planned PPP lesson to please outside assessors is the teacher training equivalent of monitoring for conformity to please the teacher. A 'communicative' approach to assessing trainees would not, in my view, be incompatible with up-to-date assessment criteria. A skim through the RSA/UCLES CTEFLA syllabus and objectives for successful candidates shows that here the assessment criteria could, without difficulty, accommodate the training approach outlined above.

Overcoming resistance

Language learners embarking on a language course that takes a learner-centred, *truly* communicative approach, with lots of built-in learner training, may well resist such an approach if they come to the classroom with strong, traditional expectations about how a language is learned. After all, for most learners, learning a language in the classroom has meant learning the rules of sentence grammar. Trainees and trainers are just as likely to resist a trainee-centred approach to training – or, in Wallace's terms, development. Woodward and Jennings and Doyle discuss the difficulties of introducing change elsewhere in this volume, but it is worth reminding ourselves here that teachers who, twenty years ago, switched from a purely grammar translation methodology to one that involved students actively communicating *did* succeed in 'selling' their new approach and changing their learners' mindsets in terms of what should be on the repertoire of language classroom activities. For many language learners, after a short period of acclimatization, the new approach was a huge and welcome relief from the boredom and pressure, if not threat, of the old one. New trainees too are likely to have some quite fixed ideas about teaching, and therefore what they think they should be doing on their training course. These beliefs need to be discussed and challenged as part of the training process. No-one should have a methodology imposed upon them without being given the chance to hear why it is being used.

Conclusion

In summary, I have argued the need for an *experience-driven* approach to teacher training: direct experience of learning and teaching, and experience of observing others teaching and learning, playing a much more central role in the process of developing reflective teachers. This experience may take a number of forms, needs to be structured, and must be followed by reflection and the opportunity for further experience if it is to be useful. It aims to turn novice teachers into explorers of the teaching and learning process. It parallels the approach to language teaching that the trainees are increasingly likely to meet, where language learners are encouraged to become language explorers, and be able to take responsibility for their own continued development after a course has ended. Both are based on the premise that unless the learning/training *process* is based on an understanding of how people learn, then the product will be less than adequate. Both recognize that over-full, content-based syllabuses which teachers have to try to transmit to their students are doomed to, at best, very limited success, and they therefore require drastic pruning. Some trainers are already taking steps in this direction. I hope that many more will follow.

Corony Edwards lectures at Birmingham University and has been involved in teacher training in the UK since 1986, and is an assessor for the RSA/UCLES CTEFLA scheme. She has also taught on short courses and workshops in Spain, Hong Kong, Hungary and Argentina.

4 Investigating new approaches

I n the first paper in this section, Özdeniz picks up the theme of teachers exploring and reflecting on the teaching and learning process. For practising teachers with regular classroom routines, change can often appear threatening. Özdeniz sets out in detail a framework which can help in-service teachers to explore and investigate what they are doing in class, enabling them to face the challenge of innovation. Working with secondary school teachers in Turkey, she applied Allwright's (1993) model of exploratory teaching to investigate her class's reactions to task-based learning. Her procedure puts an emphasis on enquiry and on teacher-student co-operation. She does not initially decide to implement task-based teaching. She decides to try out task-based teaching and to test carefully her students' reactions to the experience.

Depending on the outcome of this evaluation stage she is prepared to modify her initial approach to task-based learning, or to abandon it altogether. An important outcome is that 'the exploratory process empowers learners by enabling them to participate in making decisions about what happens in their classrooms'. It contributes to learner training by making learners more aware of the learning process and their own preferred styles. It also provides an engaging topic for language use in the classroom.

The procedures for a programme of innovation within a single class show striking similarities with the curriculum innovation procedures described in the final section by Jennings and Doyle (Paper 16). In both cases an open enquiry provides solutions to subjects of enquiry, and at the same time directs attention to other areas of enquiry. In both cases development prompts further development. This reinforces the message highlighted again and again in this volume. If it is undertaken in a spirit of enquiry the search for innovation brings its own reward. After evaluation, we may modify or reject the proposed innovation. What is certain is that we will learn from the process.

The next two papers take up the theme of task-based learning, and each sets out to investigate different aspects of it. It is implicit in the methodology described by Jane Willis in Paper 6 that planning and repetition of task make a difference to task performance, that they allow for more concern with language form and lead, therefore, to greater accuracy. This seems an entirely reasonable assumption, but do things actually work out that way in the classroom?

Bygate looks at the effect of repetition on task performance. A student saw a short cartoon on video and was then asked to tell the story. After an interval of three days, and without prior warning, she was asked to tell the story again. Bygate predicted that the second telling would 'show greater accuracy, a broader [linguistic] repertoire and greater fluency'. Bygate devised a number of objective criteria to measure changes in performance. The second telling was more accomplished in a number of ways than the first telling. From this Bygate draws interesting conclusions about eliciting spontaneous language in the classroom and about procedures for testing.

Although, as Bygate himself is careful to point out, this is small-scale research, the results are encouraging for those who propose a task-based approach. It seems that learners do deploy more effective language and more effective strategies when faced with the repetition of a task. It is reasonable to suppose that they will transfer elements of this improved performance to the way they tackle other tasks. If this is the case then task performance does lead to language development.

Foster looks at the effect of planning time on task performance. She used three different tasks, and for each task compared the performance of three groups of students. The first group had no planning time; the second group had planning time but no guidance as to how this time might be used; the third group had planning time and guidance.

Foster then compared the performance of the three groups on the three tasks in terms of fluency, syntactic variety and complexity, accuracy and lexical variety. Like Bygate she was obliged to devise objective measures to assess student performance. Her analysis, like Bygate's, has implications for both teaching and testing. She links her results to the model of language development outlined by Skehan (Paper 3). Basically her conclusion is that planning time does encourage students to pay attention to both form and content, and that it leads to students attempting a wider range of vocabulary and syntactic forms, suggesting that students could be engaged in interlanguage restructuring. There were, however, some unexpected findings concerning accuracy.

The Bygate and Foster studies are valuable for a number of reasons. They are valuable, of course, for what they tell us about learning and about student behaviour. They are valuable because they both propose measures of student performance which are more subtle and revealing than a simple count of student errors. This suggests that teachers too might look beyond error for a more positive assessment of student performance.

There is another possibility which we find exciting. The experimental nature of their work meant that Bygate and Foster could not take students into their confidence without compromising their results. It might, however, be possible to reproduce aspects of their work not only for experimental purposes but also as part of our on-going classroom procedures. We could use categories similar to those devised by Bygate and Foster in order to measure improvement in learner language, taking care to ensure that students know exactly what is going on. This could have the valuable effect of directing learners towards specific areas of improvement in their performance and of encouraging them to appreciate the value of planning in terms of enhanced performance, not simply of error reduction.

11 Introducing innovations into your teaching

Denise Özdeniz

Innovation and exploratory teaching

xploratory teaching as described by Allwright (1991) is a procedure by which teachers can investigate the teaching and learning taking place in their classrooms through a process which involves reflecting on an aspect of their practice, gathering information about it and interpreting this information so as to come to a better understanding of what occurs. Exploratory teaching was initially developed to help teachers explore existing classroom phenomena which puzzled them in some way, hence Allwright's use of the term 'puzzle' for the phenomenon to be investigated. A typical 'puzzle' might be why a certain activity works well whilst another similar activity often fails.

Allwright originally developed and refined the criteria for exploratory teaching with Brazilian teachers in Brazil as a way of trying to integrate research and pedagogy, and 'using already familiar pedagogic activities to investigate teacher and learner "puzzles" ' (Allwright 1993). From the experience I have had working with teachers in Turkey, I have found that the procedures involved in exploratory teaching can also be used by teachers when trying out things which are new for them or in other words when introducing innovation into their existing classroom practice.

In this chapter I will describe how the procedures used for exploratory teaching as set out by Allwright (1993) can be modified slightly and employed to research 'innovatory puzzles'. I will provide guidelines aimed at helping teachers unfamiliar with this type of practice to embark upon such investigations. In order to illustrate the procedures in action, I have included a flow chart summary of the stages followed when I first introduced a class of Turkish students to task-based learning. This innovation was based on the first two phases of a task-based framework similar to that described by Willis in Paper 6.

Preparing for exploratory teaching

The main goal of exploratory teaching is to help practitioners become more aware of the teaching and learning situation in which they operate, for 'being a good teacher means being alive to what goes on in the classroom, alive to the problems of sorting out what matters, moment by moment, from what does not' (Allwright and Bailey 1991:xvi). Whilst the extent of our awareness increases as we explore our classrooms, the initial act of being able to identify what to investigate and how to begin explorations also requires a certain amount of insight into where we are at present and where we wish to get to. Becoming aware involves a process of naming: stating what you know about an aspect of your teaching in as much detail as possible; questioning: trying to account for what is done or believed; and reconceiving: seeing things differently from new perspectives and/or proposing alternative ways of doing things and thinking about them (Freeman 1992). Mentally exploring teaching in this way can appear difficult to teachers unfamiliar with an approach which emphasizes learning from experience. This is especially true if they are trying to reflect on their teaching for the first time and simultaneously to carry out the stages involved in working their way through their first exploratory puzzle. For this reason, if you are a relative newcomer to this type of self-exploratory work, I recommend that you begin to reflect on your classroom practice by working through some of the activities below.

Here are some aspects of your work that you may wish to focus on while doing these activities:

- your ideas about what makes a good teacher and what leads to good language learning
- what you actually do in the classroom, eg when introducing new vocabulary or when carrying out a reading lesson
- the beliefs and theories behind the materials you use
- the ideas about successful teaching held by your colleagues, school and education system

Activity 1

Brainstorm: what and why?

Choose one of the four areas above, for example, an aspect of your present teaching practice, such as introducing a listening or reading comprehension lesson, and brainstorm all ideas connected with it. Next note down the reason why you do each thing. On the next page you can see an example of the kind of thing you might end up with.

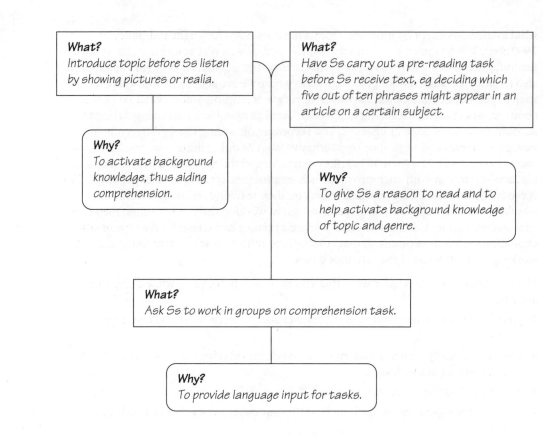

Finally, try to make connections between the various sections of your mindmap: for example, I could link the reason why I set a pre-reading task with my rationale for introducing the topic before starting a listening activity.

Activity 2

a) Becoming aware of your own classroom practice
Tape one or two of your lessons. Listen to them, then analyse critical parts of them using a grid as in the example given here:

Description of lesson	Your rationale for doing this	Things to consider
In groups Ss decide on 5 words from the text they would like to know the meaning of.	– To discourage Ss from insisting on knowing every word in a text – To encourage S to S vocabulary teaching	Do Ss define words for other Ss in L1 or L2?

b) Becoming aware of the theories behind the materials you use
Repeat the above procedure using the Teacher's Book unit outline of a lesson you have taught in place of the lesson you tape-recorded.

Activity 3

Ask colleagues to comment on what good and bad teaching entails, or collect statements about teaching and learning from books. Categorize these into statements you agree and disagree with. Justify your groupings. This whole activity is best done with several fellow teachers rather than on your own.

For further such activities refer to Wajnryb 1992 and Parrott 1993.

Comments

I have found that working through activities of this type helps teachers to become critically aware of their teaching, as the example below illustrates. The transcript that follows is from a recorded interview with a teacher who believed that she taught 'communicatively', but upon analysing her own lesson she discovered that she was placing a higher priority on a knowledge of grammatical terminology.

> Teacher A: I think I teach in a communicative way. Yes, talking is very important for me. I make my students talk a lot …

(A few seconds later)

> Teacher A: I don't say the grammar too much. When we do the exercises I give my students a context and I pay attention to the meaning not to the grammar.

(A few seconds later as Teacher A analyses the following extract)

> Teacher A: Oh, I say the grammar a lot and I'm very bossy!

Extract from Teacher A's lesson

> T: What is the man doing?
> SS: Ögretmenim, Ögretmenim, *or* Teacher, Teacher.
> T: Yes, Ali.
> S1: He look the picture.
> T: Present continuous, Present continuous. Say it again.
> S1: He looking the picture.
> T: Where's the verb? Mehmet, you say it.

Both the greater insights into their classroom practice and the increased ability to articulate classroom procedures which such activities stimulate, help teachers to set the scene for exploratory teaching.

A step by step guide to exploratory teaching

When trying to comprehend the exploratory teaching process, it may be useful to visualize it as a journey. Imagine you have a roughly drawn map of unknown territory through which you must travel in order to reach a destination you have never been to before. Your point of departure, which you can see and describe in detail, represents your present teaching practice; the previously unvisited destination is the time in the future at which the innovation has been tested out in practice and you have come to an informed decision about it; the vaguely mapped out terrain through which you must form a route, possibly meeting dead ends or realizing that you are heading off course, is the actual exploratory process itself. On some journeys, especially if you are using exploratory teaching to investigate a problem you have, you may feel that you never quite reach your intended destination, but you will almost certainly have made a few discoveries along the way. This should not dishearten you, for successful teaching and learning is not borne out of the accumulation of new skills and techniques but out of the increased awareness that a careful exploration of the classroom situation affords.

What follows here is a stage-by-stage account of the exploratory process. There are four basic stages, each containing three or four steps. I have chosen to illustrate each stage with a flow chart representation of a task-based learning innovation which became my 'puzzle' to investigate. Throughout this flowchart Teacher action and reaction are shown on the left and Student action and reaction on the right.

Stage A: Identifying the innovatory puzzle

Step 1   Identify what it is you wish to explore.
Step 2   Identify what you hope to discover in exploring this puzzle.

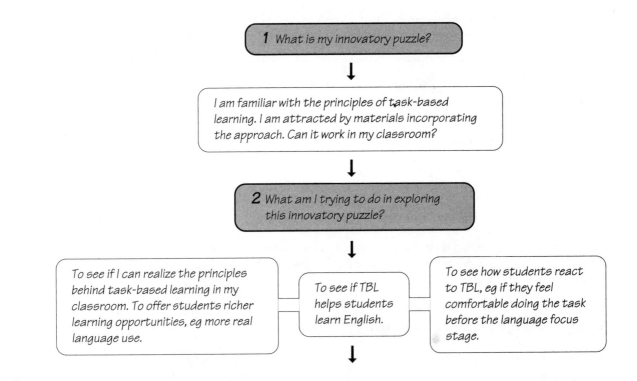

Here is a list of exploratory questions which may assist you when considering Steps 1 and 2. I have included the answers to several of the questions based on my own TBL exploratory puzzle.

Checklist of exploratory questions on starting an innovatory puzzle

1 What do I know about the innovation at present?

2 Where can I find more information about the innovation?

3 Is the innovation new to the students or new to the teacher, or both?
   Answer: In my case the innovation was new to the students and to the teacher.

4 In which ways might the innovation differ from my present teaching practice?
   Answer: Under the PPP paradigm, I normally present new language first, and then get students to practise it to gain accuracy. Only then do I ask them to use it to communicate real messages. In the TBL cycle, students will start by trying to communicate, using what language they have, and then focus in detail on aspects of that language afterwards.

5 What possible effects could implementing the innovation have on my students, the learning situation, etc?
   Answer: Students may feel uneasy about being required to complete the task drawing on whatever linguistic resources they have, rather than being told what language forms to use. They may need reassuring that the message is of most importance and that the main thing is to try to achieve the task, not to worry about mistakes.

6 Is there any aspect of the innovation or my present practice that I can foresee having to alter in any way so that the integration of the two is successful?
   Answer: Maybe emphasizing that the language focus stage will come after the task, and maybe dealing with this stage in a less teacher-controlled way.

Stage B: Identifying ways of gathering information about the innovation as it is tried out in the classroom

Step 3   Identify the type of information needed to enable you to come to informed conclusions about whatever you wish to discover in answer to the Step 2 question 'What am I trying to do in exploring this innovation?'
   – Identify how you will gather this information.

Step 4   Draw up lesson plans incorporating the innovation and information-gathering methods.
   – Carry out the explorations.

The flowchart overleaf follows on without a break from the previous flowchart section. It shows how these steps can happen in practice. The step numbers refer to the steps in this stage. Notice, in Step 3, the methods I, as teacher, use to gather data for myself (left hand box) and to get my students to provide data (right hand box). In Step 4, I summarize my lesson plans.

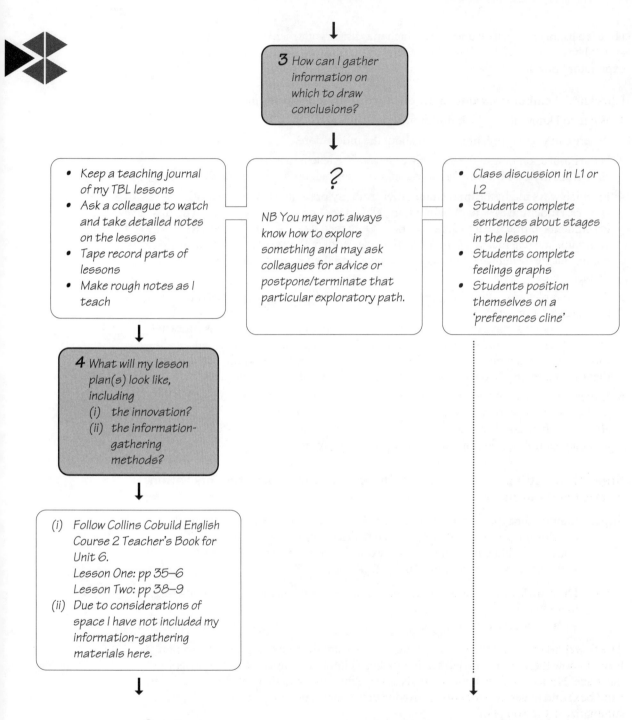

3 How can I gather information on which to draw conclusions?

?

- Keep a teaching journal of my TBL lessons
- Ask a colleague to watch and take detailed notes on the lessons
- Tape record parts of lessons
- Make rough notes as I teach

NB You may not always know how to explore something and may ask colleagues for advice or postpone/terminate that particular exploratory path.

- Class discussion in L1 or L2
- Students complete sentences about stages in the lesson
- Students complete feelings graphs
- Students position themselves on a 'preferences cline'

4 What will my lesson plan(s) look like, including
(i) the innovation?
(ii) the information-gathering methods?

(i) Follow Collins Cobuild English Course 2 Teacher's Book for Unit 6.
Lesson One: pp 35–6
Lesson Two: pp 38–9
(ii) Due to considerations of space I have not included my information-gathering materials here.

Comment

It has long been recognized that in order to maximize our awareness of what occurs in our classrooms and how our learners respond, teachers need regularly to collect data documenting what has taken place and obtain feedback from class participants concerning this (Allwright and Bailey 1991; Nunan 1992). However, busy teachers may find it extremely difficult to add the role of researcher to their job descriptions if this necessitates a knowledge of traditional research skills such as using real-time coding devices or observation grids. Designed to assist teacher researchers, exploratory teaching attempts to reduce the burden that traditional research adds to the workload by 'fully integrating research into teachers' normal pedagogic practices' (Allwright 1993:125). Thus instead of having to familiarize themselves with, and draw up, conventional data collection materials in addition to their normal lesson planning and work sheet preparation, teachers are encouraged to 'exploit already familiar and trusted classroom activities' (Allwright 1993:125) when gathering information about the puzzle they are exploring. Such activities may include:

- discussions
- interviews
- roleplays
- student diaries
- student letters
- sentence completion
- grouping or ordering according to preferences
- surveys

We noticed, for example, in the flowchart above how students were asked to complete sentences showing how they felt after each stage of the task cycle.

Due to the integration of pedagogy and exploration, however, Steps 3 and 4 above often merge simultaneously with information-gathering methods growing out of classroom activities that suit the lesson objectives and its plan.

For example, if students have been working with adverbs of frequency, they could carry out a survey to provide the teacher with information about the class's study habits and/or exposure to English outside class with questions such as:

How do you usually learn new vocabulary?
How often do you watch films in English?
Do you ever speak to people in English outside school?

At this point I should add that experience has taught me that it is easier to use familiar classroom activities when collecting data on student attitudes and reactions than when focusing on yourself as teacher and on your own teaching. The latter still necessitates the deployment of more traditional research tools such as audio or video recordings of lessons and teacher's field notes (rough notes jotted down during the course of teaching). Furthermore, teacher-focused research may even require the use of an outside observer to conduct an ethnographic transcript which consists of the observer writing out a descriptive verbatim account of what happens in the lesson or filling in observation schedules. For a more comprehensive treatment of such data collecting techniques see Allwright and Bailey 1991 and Nunan 1992.

Stage C: Interpreting the data

Step 5   Examine the information gathered to discover more about what exactly took place during the teaching/learning event and to find out how students reacted to it.

The flowchart now continues below, illustrating how this stage can work. What I noticed in particular were the ways the students used the transcripts and then redrafted their reports. It was interesting what the students said they felt about using the transcripts. To fully appreciate the students' data referred to, you will need to look at Appendices A, B and C, where I have collated the results in order to analyse them.

> **5** *What have I discovered from the information gathered?*

My reflections on how the TBL lessons went

- I was impressed at how much interaction and negotiation occurred during the task and planning stages.
- Initially students only circled new words on transcripts, but proceeded to underline useful phrases on their own initiative, whilst using the transcripts to write or re-draft reports.

eg 1   draft 1   Travelling by bus is slow and exhausted.
         draft 2   (after referring to transcript)
                      Travelling by bus is slow and you feel exhausted.
eg 2   draft 1   I looked at her bag to learn her address.
         draft 2   I had a look in her bag to find her address.

- Some students didn't listen to other groups reporting back.
- I feel unsure of how much input to give in the planning stage.

Students' reactions to the TBL lessons

- Students enjoyed the amount of interaction lessons afforded.
- 6 out of 7 students favoured having new vocabulary and grammar presented before doing tasks (see preference cline, App. A).
- No-one disliked the TBL cycle in general, but some felt less enthusiastic about certain stages than others (see graphs in App. B and C).
- When completing sentences students said that:
  - looking at transcripts to help write reports 'helped with new words', 'became helpful', 'was not very easy'.
  - speaking in small groups made one student feel 'like a boss, self-confident, being power strong'.
  - reporting to the class made them feel 'nervous', 'well'.

Comment

Analysing and interpreting the information gathered is one of the most difficult aspects of exploratory teaching (Allwright 1993:133). It is almost impossible to be totally objective about your own classroom. However, teacher researchers should try to evaluate all data equally and not be biased by isolated fragments which support previously held ideas. Nor should they jump to hasty conclusions. Rather they should try to view the information from as many different perspectives as possible and reflect on the feasibility of any interpretations that emerge.

One way of generating multiple perspectives is to analyse the data together with other colleagues or the students themselves. A useful by-product of such discussion is that whilst talking about classroom data, teachers and students alike are forced to be specific about what they mean by terms such as 'grammar' or 'error correction' and thus a common classroom language develops which facilitates further exploratory teaching.

Here are a number of procedures that might help with the interpreting process.

Procedure 1

Transfer anything in the data which attracts your attention onto individual slips of paper. Group this information in any way you wish, for example, according to similarity of opinion, of subject matter, of your reactions to it, or arrange opposing ideas together. Try to visualize the many different interpretations and/or implications that such groupings suggest and decide how you can explore them further. Do not be disheartened by contradictory data such as in the examples below. Contradictions help you to see alternatives and to really explore the many different sides of an issue, eg 'I hate the grammar to learn it' versus 'I need to memorize vocabulary and grammar'. Possible implications of this are:

- classes consist of different types of learners,
- perhaps these people have had different language learning experiences in the past,
- these students may be learning English for different reasons.

Procedure 2

Use a statement or statistic from the data as the basis of a discussion with colleagues or students. Two examples follow.

a) When commenting on a task-based lesson one student wrote:
   'I expect the teacher to support/to encourage for expanding our ideas, explanations while we were talking to the teacher or friends.'

   A useful class discussion could ensue on exactly when and in which ways students felt teachers should intervene and on the positive and negative effects this might have on their communicative development.

b) Six out of seven students favoured having new vocabulary and grammar presented before doing the tasks in the initial TBL lessons.

   The teacher and the students could discuss whether this was because they were used to the old way, and were showing reluctance to change, or because they felt a bit lazy and were trying to avoid the difficulty of having to think what to say for themselves.

Procedure 3

Highlight anything in the data which interests you and ask yourself questions around it. For example, the comment in example a) in the last activity may generate the following:

Q On what occasions might students want a teacher to help them complete an utterance?

A When they think
   - that the teacher probably understands what it is they want to say;
   - that there is a better expression that they have already been taught, but that they cannot retrieve;
   - that there is a grammatical rule they should apply here but they don't really remember it clearly or understand how to apply it.

Q What does 'to support/to encourage' mean here?

A It could mean :
   - to take over and complete the student's utterance,
   - to show that you understand the student by nodding and agreeing in the right places.

Stage D: Further explorations

Step 6 On the basis of your findings from Step 5 decide which areas of the innovatory puzzle require further investigation.

Step 7 Repeat Steps 3 to 6 where appropriate as many times as is necessary for you to gain a clear picture of the innovation operating within your specific teaching context.

Step 8 Reflect on all of the information you have gathered and the conclusions you have drawn from it. What is your overall assessment of the innovation in relation to your teaching style and your students' learning preferences?

These steps are illustrated in the flowchart opposite. You will notice that, having interpreted the data, I decided to explore three specific areas; the first one in order to encourage students to listen to each other, the second to examine more closely the Planning stage and the effects of teacher intervention. The third is a much larger area and could well form the basis of a whole new puzzle. I am also planning to observe students' reactions to the addition of a language focus slot after the task cycle. Here I also noted down my overall conclusion. It is important to stand back from the data in this way, and take a wider view of the results.

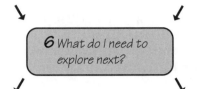

6 *What do I need to explore next?*

- *See what effects building a natural reason for listening (eg a competitive element) has on student attention during the report stage.*
- *Monitor the effects of varying degrees of teacher intervention at the planning stage.*
- *Experiment with ways of error correction. (This requires a new puzzle.)*

- *In my first two TBL lessons I omitted the language focus slot. Will students reposition themselves on the preference cline (see p 124) as they become familiar with the TBL cycle and see there is overt grammar practice in the final stage? It certainly seems vital to reassure students that language study still has an important part in the TBL cycle. If assured of this, will they suspend judgement?*

7 *Repeat Steps 3, 4, 5 and 6 as appropriate as many times as is necessary.*

Due to considerations of space I have not included this section of my exploratory teaching here. →

8 *What overall conclusions have I come to?*

- *Students appreciate the amount of spontaneous speaking time permitted by the task stage.*
- *Students recognize that the planning stage is accuracy-focused and exploit transcripts, the teacher, dictionaries and other students to greater effect than when first introduced to TBL.*

Stage E: Future directions

Step 9   According to your overall assessment of how the innovation operates within your classroom, decide whether or not you will incorporate it into your teaching repertoire and, if so, whether either the innovation or your teaching needs to be modified in any way so that they concord with one another.

Step 10 You may wish to write up your teaching puzzle and circulate it among colleagues or have it published in a teaching journal so that other members of the profession can profit from your explorations. This is in fact what I have done here by writing this paper and sharing my exploratory teaching with you.

The last part of my flow chart follows, illustrating Step 9 of the process, and detailing the decisions I took at that point in time.

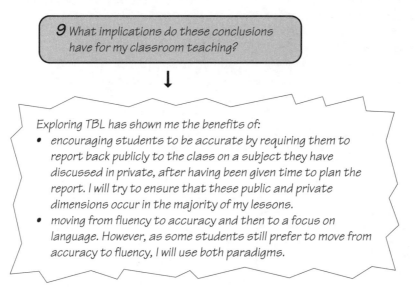

9 *What implications do these conclusions have for my classroom teaching?*

Exploring TBL has shown me the benefits of:
- *encouraging students to be accurate by requiring them to report back publicly to the class on a subject they have discussed in private, after having been given time to plan the report. I will try to ensure that these public and private dimensions occur in the majority of my lessons.*
- *moving from fluency to accuracy and then to a focus on language. However, as some students still prefer to move from accuracy to fluency, I will use both paradigms.*

Some suggestions for future explorations

Having read this book, you may have identified some areas which you or your teachers might like to explore. You might, for example, like to carry out a small scale 'replication' of the work reported by Bygate (Paper 8) or that of Foster (Paper 9). You may like to attempt to examine how far Lewis's *Observe – Hypothesize– Experiment* paradigm accounts for what students are doing in your classes. In this short section, I have listed some other examples of puzzles that interest me and that you could adapt for your own use.

- I would like to focus more on collocations and phrases which will help students communicate, rather than on words in isolation. How can I do this?
- My students are not used to carrying out tasks in groups, and they tend either to abandon the task or do it in L1. Can I enable students to complete group tasks in L1 by increasing their stock of useful classroom phrases, such as *'It's your turn next'*, *'OK, shall we start?' 'Does anyone know the answer for number 2?'*?
- Would banning the use of L1 altogether in groupwork inhibit or encourage longer-term use of L2 in groups? On what occasions might it be seen as enabling?

- I realize I spend far too much time explaining and checking that students understand classroom instructions. How can I encourage students to follow the instructions written in their coursebooks? Would this then help them become more independent learners?

- I have observed how a 'public' report stage after a task encourages students to rehearse and improve their spoken English. I would like to explore other ways of increasing this public dimension in my lessons, ways that are meaningful and motivating for my students, and to monitor how my students react to them.

- Whilst working with non-native-speaker trainee teachers on short courses, I have noticed that many of them want to speak more accurately and ask to be corrected but I feel I cannot do this in front of their colleagues. Could I get them individually to record themselves on video giving a short report of an activity or a task and then observe what they do in the planning stage and playback stage?

Sometimes puzzles can involve the learners directly and explicitly. Turkish school children, for example, have made their own collective class decisions on the following issues:

- how best to tackle the problems of using too much L1 during group and pairwork activities
- how much and what kind of homework they wish to be given
- how they want written work to be corrected (given the constraints on teacher's time) and the various ways in which they would like to receive feedback.

The benefits to be gained from exploratory teaching

Many teachers have found exploratory teaching to be of great use in helping them 'know what they do, how and why' (Orem 1981, cited in Freeman 1990:103) and in increasing their sense of professional worth. Practitioners capable of investigating their own classrooms and of monitoring the effects that different approaches, methodologies and techniques have on their teaching are no longer at the mercy of policy changes or paradigm shifts, for they are capable of assessing innovations and of coming to informed decisions, supported by evidence, about the innovation in relation to their work. Thus teachers are empowered to control how they incorporate new ideas into their teaching as opposed to having new ideas forced upon them.

Similarly the exploratory process empowers learners by enabling them to participate in making decisions about what takes place in their classrooms. By being asked to comment on their responses to various activities they become more aware of their own preferred learning styles and of what learning involves.

And finally, the collaborative act itself, in which everyone's opinions are equally valid, creates a bond between teachers and learners which enhances motivation and co-operation and makes teaching and learning a more rewarding process.

Acknowledgements
I would like to thank Ann Haznedar for all the hours of work and discussion with her which have contributed so much to my understanding of self-directed teacher development, Carole MacDiarmid for her assistance while I was writing this paper and all those who read draft copies for me.

Appendix A

Finding out student reactions to TBL using a preference cline

Students positioned themselves along the cline according to how they related to the two statements placed on the wall. They then commented on why they stood where they did.

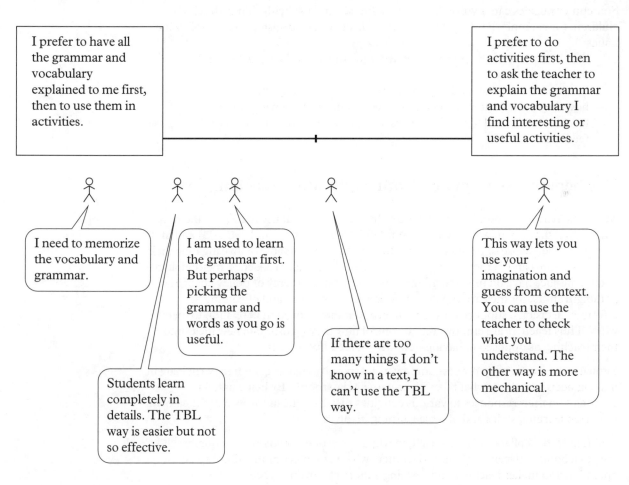

I prefer to have all the grammar and vocabulary explained to me first, then to use them in activities.

I prefer to do activities first, then to ask the teacher to explain the grammar and vocabulary I find interesting or useful activities.

I need to memorize the vocabulary and grammar.

I am used to learn the grammar first. But perhaps picking the grammar and words as you go is useful.

Students learn completely in details. The TBL way is easier but not so effective.

If there are too many things I don't know in a text, I can't use the TBL way.

This way lets you use your imagination and guess from context. You can use the teacher to check what you understand. The other way is more mechanical.

Appendix B

Finding out student reactions to TBL using a feelings graph: positive reactions

Three students reacted positively to the task, planning and report stages. The three kinds of line each represents one student.

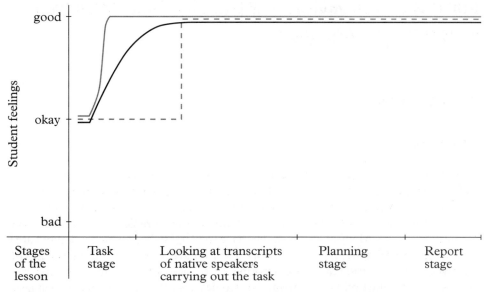

Appendix C

Finding out student reactions to TBL using a feelings graph: mixed reactions

The four lines show the mixed reactions of four students to the task, planning and report stages.

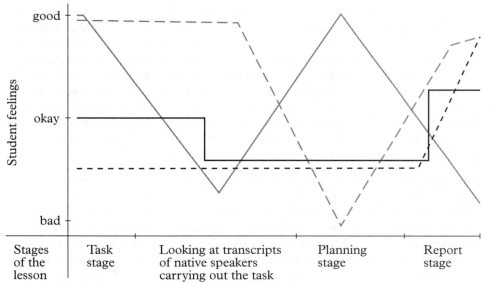

Denise Özdeniz is a teacher trainer for the British Council in Istanbul. She works closely with Secondary School teachers, designing and implementing a wide variety of courses. She also tutors on a British Cultural Studies programme.

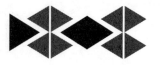

12 Doing the task better: how planning time influences students' performance

Pauline Foster

Introduction

In much description of a task-based approach to language learning the classroom teacher appears to have the relatively passive role of selecting and administering the task (ie making sure the students understand what to do), while it is the task itself which generates the conditions favourable to Second Language Acquisition (SLA). Many research studies have tried to establish which task types are most effective, and most justified by theory. Claims have been made for the benefits of tasks where students need to transfer information to each other (information gap exercises). From the results of experimental studies it is confidently expected that tasks like these will produce healthy amounts of 'negotiation of meaning' (students checking and clarifying problem utterances), and that this in turn will produce healthy amounts of the Comprehensible Input (Krashen 1981a, 1982) that is claimed to be vital to SLA (see, for example, Long 1983a, Doughty and Pica 1986, Varonis and Gass 1985).

But as any teacher soon suspects, and as many critics of task-based learning enjoy pointing out, students in classrooms may not necessarily perform in tasks as the task-designers would wish them to, or as research would predict that they should. They may not realize (or care) that their task partners do not properly understand what they are saying. They may cheerfully ignore gaps in their own understanding, and allow much Input to remain Incomprehensible. They may focus upon transmitting their meaning through simple or formulaic language enhanced by gesture, facial expression and/or intonation. Language does not have to be well-formed to be meaningful, and human beings are adept at communication strategies that can substitute for syntax. The fact that so many second language learners fossilize before advancing very far in the syntax of the target language is convincing evidence of this, and suggests that there are problems in task-based learning which need to be addressed.

An approach that lets students take care of the task, while assuming that SLA will take care of itself, is therefore rather dangerous. Clearly it is important for any theory of task-based language learning to be underpinned by sound research into how students actually perform when transacting classroom tasks, and whether their performance can be influenced by the methodology of the teacher in ways that are likely to advance SLA. Skehan (Paper 3) maintains that task-based learning needs to be implemented in a way that discourages the learner from focusing on form at the expense of meaning, or meaning at the expense of form, but encourages instead a focus that shifts between the two. Skehan suggests that if teachers give students time before a task to prepare what they are going to say and how they are going to say it, this will act against any tendency towards careless fluency and provide space for students to consider language forms. This article will report a study designed to discover how the fluency, accuracy and complexity of students' language is affected by planning time.

Investigating the effects of language planning

Some exploratory research in this area has had encouraging results. Ellis (1987) has shown that the regular past tense is used more accurately when students have had planning time, and Crookes (1989) has shown that planning time can lead to students attempting more complex language and using a more varied vocabulary. Ellis's study has been criticized for comparing speaking with writing tasks, and the improvement shown in the students' performance may have been as much a result of the shift from speaking to writing as it was a result of planning time. Crookes' study used tasks (involving maps and Lego bricks) that cannot be generalized easily to classrooms, and therefore the implications of his results for teachers are not clear. The study described here was designed to investigate the same area, ie the effects of planning time, but on students' oral production only and using tasks that any EFL teacher would be able to use in the classroom. Moreover, the study was conducted on EFL students during their normal scheduled classes. This is somewhat unusual in SLA research, but means that the data is as authentic as possible, and the findings can be more justifiably applied to ELT practice.

Three tasks were chosen for the study: personal information exchange, narrative and decision making. These task types were chosen because it was reasoned that each would require a different level of attention from the students, with the progressively less familiar and less predictable content of the narrative and decision-making tasks giving students much more to think about than the (presumably) familiar content of the personal information exchange. The way in which task complexity influences performance could then be measured.

The personal information exchange required students to describe to a partner how to get from the college to his or her home. This was considered to be the task with the simplest content, allowing the greatest amount of planning time to be devoted to language forms.

The narrative task was based on a series of pictures that were loosely but not obviously connected, from which the students had to construct a story-line. This task gave greater scope for more complex language, but the unfamiliar content meant that less attention could be devoted to form.

The decision-making task involved the students acting as judges at the trials of a list of offenders and having to agree with a partner on a suitable prison term. This task required students to evaluate a lot of new information and defend their decisions. It was considered most likely to demand complex language from them, while at the same time the difficult content would allow the least scope for attention to be paid to language form.

Eight students from each of four intermediate level classes at Richmond Adult and Community College took part in the study, making a total of 32 students. They were aged between 18 and 30 and came from a very wide variety of language backgrounds. All but three were female, and overwhelmingly they were in England as au pairs or wives of foreign businessmen. All intended to pass the Cambridge First Certificate examination. They were, in short, typical of the very large number of young people who come to Britain every year and attend part-time courses in English for General Purposes. Given their backgrounds and temporary residence in the UK, they are also broadly comparable to many people learning English post-school in their own countries.

The students were asked to do one task a week for three weeks during a normal scheduled class, each time working with the same partner. To combat any effect that practice might have had, each of the four class groups did the tasks in a different order. Two of the class groups acted as controls and did the tasks after only a brief introduction to ensure that the students understood what was required. (These will be referred to as the non-planners.) The other two class groups received the same brief introduction and were then given ten minutes individual planning time. To ensure that they used this time for task planning, the students were asked to make brief notes, but were told that they would not be allowed to use these during the task. To investigate whether the type of planning would have a significant effect, half of the planning students were given some suggestions on how they might use their ten minutes (eg considering the vocabulary they might need, the grammatical structures, the organization of the content). We will refer to these as the guided planners. The other half were given no guidance and told simply to plan; these will be called the unguided planners.

Details of two of the tasks and the actual instructions that each group of students received to help them plan are set out in Figures 1 and 2 on pages 129 and 130.

Each pair of students was recorded doing the tasks by means of a small dictation machine placed on the desk in front of them. Because the whole class did the task at the same time (as is normal in classrooms) and because the recording equipment was unobtrusive, it was felt that the students would not be affected by self-consciousness and would produce language as close as possible to their normal standard. Informal observation during task completion seemed to confirm this. The tasks took on average around ten minutes to complete.

The first five minutes of each piece of recorded interaction was then transcribed using a fairly broad system, eg pauses were not timed using specialist equipment. The transcripts were then coded for measures of fluency, complexity and accuracy.

Figure 1

PERSONAL INFORMATION EXCHANGE TASK
Sending somebody back to turn off the oven!

It is the afternoon, you are at school, and you have an important examination in fifteen minutes. You suddenly think that you haven't turned off the oven after cooking your lunch. There is no time for you to go home.

Explain to a friend who wants to help:
• how to get home to your house
• how to get into the house and get to the kitchen
• how to turn the oven off

Non-planners	*(Students do the task after a brief introduction, with no planning time)*
Planners (unguided)	You have ten minutes to prepare for this task.
	You can make notes during the ten minutes, but you won't be allowed to use these notes while doing the task.
	Be sure you can explain the decisions that you make to your partner.
Planners (guided)	You have ten minutes to prepare for this task.
	You can make notes during the ten minutes, but you won't be allowed to use these notes while doing the task.
	These are things you can do to help you prepare: • Think what problems your listener could have, and how you might help her. • Think about how your listener can understand the order of the things she has to do. • Think of ways to make sure your friend won't get lost. • Think what grammar you need to do the task. • Think what vocabulary you need to do the task. • Think how to avoid difficulties and solve problems with grammar and vocabulary.

Figure 2

DECISION-MAKING TASK

You are a judge. You have four decisions to make. For each decision, you must decide how long to send the accused to prison for. The maximum is a real life sentence. The minimum is three months. You can also set them free.

1 The accused found her husband in bed with another woman. She took the bread knife and killed him.

2 The accused is a prisoner of war. Your country has just defeated his. He was a pilot. He dropped an atom bomb on your tenth largest city, killing 200,000 people and injuring many more.

3 The accused is a doctor. He gave an overdose (a very high quantity of a pain-killing drug) to an 85-year-old woman because she was dying painfully of cancer. The woman had asked for the overdose. The woman's family accuse the doctor of murder.

4a Three teenage boys were having a fight with a fourth boy near a swimming pool. They threw him in the water and then stood on him till he drowned.

4b Five adults were sitting not far from the pool and watched the fight. They did nothing to help the fourth boy.

Non-planners	*(Students do the task immediately on reading the instructions)*
Planners (unguided)	You have ten minutes to prepare for this task.
	You can make notes during the ten minutes, but you won't be allowed to use these notes while doing the task.
	Be sure you can explain the decisions that you make to your partner.
Planners (guided)	You have ten minutes to prepare for this task.
	You can make notes during the ten minutes, but you won't be allowed to use these notes while doing the task.
	Be sure you can explain the decisions that you make to your partner.
	These are things you can do to help you prepare: • Think what you already know about each of the questions for judgement. • Think about different parts of each problem. • Think of different judgements that are possible; of reasons for these different judgements; and of why these reasons could be wrong. • Think about why your partner may not agree with you. • Think what grammar you need to do the task. • Think what vocabulary you need to do the task. • Think how to avoid difficulties and solve problems with grammar and vocabulary. • Think how you will deal with *'talking'* to someone, how you will say what you want to say and stop the other person from talking all the time.

Results and discussion

Fluency

It was immediately clear that students who had been given time to plan spoke with far fewer pauses and were far less likely to lapse into silence. The effect was weakest (though still significant) in the personal information task where the students were dealing with familiar material requiring little or no reflection, and where the scope for complex syntax was somewhat limited. The non-planners paused on average 19.2 times during the five minutes, and were silent on average for a total of 32 seconds. By contrast the planners paused on average only 10.8 times and were silent for an average total of 17 seconds. In the decision-making task the effect was much stronger, with the non-planners pausing much more often than the planners (an average of 37 times to an average of 17.3 times) and for very much longer (an average total of 91 seconds to an average total of 28 seconds). The effect was greatest in the narrative task where the non-planners made an average of 30 pauses to the planners' 12, and produced on average a very startling total of 120 seconds silence to the planners' total of 24 seconds.

It had been predicted that the task presenting the greatest cognitive complexity would cause the non-planners to pause longest and most often while they pondered what to say, and it had been assumed that the decision-making task would be the most difficult. In fact it was the narrative that caused the most problems to the non-planners because so many of them were unable to find a way of connecting the pictures. They remained silent for long stretches (sometimes for over 30 seconds) while their imaginations tried to find something they could talk about. By contrast the students who had had time to plan all found ways of creating a storyline from the pictures, and could spend the task time putting their ideas into words.

Another measure of fluency used in the analysis of the transcripts was repetition of words or phrases. Repeating a word or phrase (without altering it at all) is a way of gaining time while you think about what to say next. For all three tasks the non-planners repeated themselves significantly more often (a composite average of 45.3 times to the planners' composite average of 30.1 times). It was the decision-making task that showed the most significant difference between the two groups, with the non-planners repeating themselves almost twice as often as the planners.

Syntactic variety

Syntactic variety was investigated to see whether planners were more willing to take risks by using more challenging forms. An analysis was made of the tense, mood and voice of the verbs used by the students. Taking composite scores for all three tasks, it was clear that the students with planning time were significantly more likely to select tenses other than the simple past when referring to past time, while the non-planners tended to rely excessively on the simple past. Planners were also more likely than non-planners to use the perfect aspect and the passive voice. It was the decision-making task that showed the most significant differences, with the conditional and the modal *have to* also used more often by planners than by non-planners. That the decision-making task should involve the greatest variety of verb forms is not surprising considering the nature of the content and the complexities of opinion that the students might need to express. It was therefore notable that while the planners used a wide variety of verb forms, the non-planners (undoubtedly with equally interesting and complex ideas to express) were more likely to rely on a restricted syntactic range.

The effects of planning are less obvious in the narrative task, although the planners were significantly more likely to select the present perfect tense. For the personal information exchange there was even less in the way of significant difference between the two groups of students. This result was entirely expected as the nature of the task – telling someone how to get from the college to your home – is likely to require mostly active, indicative and present tense verbs. It was interesting to note, however, that in both the narrative and personal information exchange tasks, the students without planning time were much more likely to use references to the immediate context. That is, instead of *go out of the main entrance and turn left*, they might say *go out there, and turn here* (with appropriate gestures). Or, instead of *the picture where the man is filming the wedding* they might point and say, *this one, with the wedding*. This communication strategy is common to most languages, but perhaps not one to be encouraged in the classroom. It could be significant that planning time seems to reduce the need to resort to it.

Syntactic complexity

It was also thought necessary to examine the complexity of the language which was used, on the assumption that more complex language is likely to be associated with an underlying interlanguage system that is changing and developing rather than comfortably fossilizing. Each student's language production was measured for the total number of independent grammatical propositions (known as communication units, or c-units) and also for the total number of clauses. Complexity of language was calculated as the ratio of clauses to c-units. (The simplest language thus consists of c-units each with a single clause, more complex language will have c-units with two or more clauses, for example, a main clause with its related subordinate clauses.) Results for all three tasks show that students with planning time produced language with greater syntactic complexity than those without planning time, and that this difference increased in significance with the cognitive difficulty of the task. Moreover, this was the first measure for which a significant difference could be found between the guided and the unguided planners.

For the personal information exchange task the non-planners produced on average only 1.11 clauses per c-unit, the unguided planners produced an average of 1.16, and those with detailed planning guidance produced an average of 1.26.

For the decision-making task the scores rose from an average of 1.23 for the non-planners, through 1.35 for the unguided planners, to 1.52 for the guided planners. An even greater change was observed in the narrative task where the non-planners managed on average only 1.22 clauses per c-unit, while the unguided and guided planners scored 1.42 and 1.68 respectively. These results are shown in Table 1 opposite.

Table 1: Planning and language complexity

	Narrative	Personal	Decision
no planning	1.22	1.11	1.23
unguided planning	1.42	1.16	1.35
guided planning	1.68	1.26	1.52

Scores in the table represent average no. of clauses per c-unit.

Here task type and planning condition are combining to produce a very remarkable effect: the least taxing task done without planning time leads to language whose syntax is almost as simple as can be; a more demanding task done with guided planning leads to language where more than half of the c-units contain a subordinated clause.

Accuracy

Given the greater syntactic variety and complexity in the language of the students who had had planning time, it might have been expected that they would make more mistakes than the non-planners (who were taking fewer risks). To measure this, the level of accuracy for each student was calculated as the number of error-free clauses compared to the total number of clauses.

When the average scores for each task type were examined it was found that there was in fact a general trend for the planners to be more accurate than the non-planners. Interestingly, when the two groups of planners were compared, it was those who had received no detailed planning guidance who were consistently more accurate than those who had. In other words, the unguided planners were more accurate than the guided planners. This was an entirely unexpected result and its implications for task-based teaching will be discussed in the conclusion below.

For the narrative task the increase in accuracy was too small to be statistically significant. A greater and more significant increase was observed in the decision-making task where the proportion of correct clauses in the language of the non-planners compared to that of the unguided planners rose from .63 to .73. For the personal information exchange the increase in scores for the same groups was .64 to .76. In other words, the unguided planning condition had led to an increase in accuracy on all of the tasks, and on two of them had increased accuracy from just under two-thirds to approximately three-quarters of the total clauses. As there was no measurable difference in the average English proficiency of the planners and non-planners, this difference in accuracy scores indicates that the planning condition had caused the planners to pay more attention to form. These results are shown in Table 2 overleaf.

Table 2: Planning and accuracy

	Narrative	Personal	Decision
no planning	.61	.64	.63
unguided planning	.66	.76	.73
guided planning	.58	.69	.71

Figures represent the proportion of clauses which are error-free.

Lexical variety

The analysis of the vocabulary used by the students is incomplete at the time of writing but preliminary results suggest that here too the students with planning time are performing better than those without. A count was made of the total number of different nouns, verbs, adjectives and adverbs (ie lexical types) used by each student. For the personal information exchange task the planners used on average more types than the non-planners, but the difference was too small to be statistically significant (57 to 51). For the narrative the average totals were significant (49 to 37). A great and very significant difference was also observed in the decision-making task where the planners on average used 63 lexical types compared to the non-planners' 44. As there is no reason to suggest that the planners had larger vocabularies of English words than the non-planners, it would appear that the planning time enabled them to access words less readily available to them in unplanned speech. This is not important in the personal information exchange tasks where the subject matter is limited, predictable and extremely familiar, but it is very important when dealing with the unfamiliar pictures of the narrative task, and the unfamiliar and rather unpredictable material of the decision-making task. The cognitive demands made by such tasks on students without planning time give little space for word-searching.

Summing up

A task done without planning time is more likely to lead to students choosing relatively undemanding language. It also increases the chances that they will rely on readily available vocabulary rather than trawling the less easily accessed parts of their English lexicon. Students without time to plan are very much more likely to pause frequently and at length. All these effects are stronger on tasks that are cognitively more demanding, presumably because students do not have the attentional resources sufficient to deal with the difficulties of both language content and language form at the same time.

Some conclusions

Requiring students to do tasks without planning, using material that is new to them, or complex, or both, is a format chosen by many oral examinations. Candidates are given pictures they have never seen before and asked to talk about them, they are set topics they may never have considered before and asked to discuss and evaluate them. The examiners are trained to give credit to candidates able in these circumstances to produce a flow of accurate, appropriate and suitably complex language. The results of this study suggest that such an exam format may well be creating a situation where candidates are most likely to produce language at the more undemanding end of their range, and are also more likely to need to pause while mustering their thoughts. Perhaps task-based testing should recognize that the extra cognitive burden imposed by unfamiliar subject matter may interfere with a fair assessment of the range and fluency of a candidate's language.

In terms of classroom practice, it is clear that without time to plan students may not be able to exploit tasks in ways that most benefit SLA. If a task is transacted successfully in language that is limited, simple and inaccurate (as many in this study were) then there is a risk that less desirable interlanguage forms may be inappropriately reinforced. If, as a result of planning, a student attempts language that is more varied and more complex, this surely acts against any tendency to fossilize comfortably at a premature and inadequate level. All language learners know more of the target language syntax and vocabulary than they can fluently use. If planning time makes it more likely that they will be able to call into use otherwise unavailable words and structures, then it is likely that such words and structures will be helped to shift from planned, thoughtful language use to extemporaneous speech (Ellis 1987).

A note of caution, however, is sounded by the finding that detailed planning appears to increase the complexity of the language attempted by the students, but to decrease the level of accuracy. It could be that the suggestions given to students on how to plan lead them into being rather too ambitious, attempting structures over which they have poor control even with planning time. Unguided planning may make it more likely that students will select language that is already close to making the shift from careful to extemporaneous use.

The results of this study suggest that tasks need to be used in the classroom in ways that avoid both unrehearsed fluency (so prized by much Communicative Language Teaching) and the very conscious use of certain target structures (so often expected in PPP style lessons). The goal of encouraging students to shift focus between fluency and accuracy in language production, outlined by Skehan (Paper 3), is apparently achieved in this study because planning time allows them to devote attention to both form and content, rather than forcing them to choose one at the expense of the other. Moreover, the fact that planning time leads to students attempting a wider range of vocabulary and syntactic forms suggests that they could be engaged in the third goal – interlanguage restructuring.

The encouragingly parallel results reported by Bygate (Paper 13) show how another form of planning – task repetition – also increases the variety, complexity and fluency of students' language. The scope for further research into task performance is wide, and it is to be hoped that future findings will indicate the ways in which teachers can most effectively exploit tasks in the classroom.

(A fuller statistical analysis and discussion of the results of this study can be found in Foster and Skehan (forthcoming) *The Influence of Planning on Performance in Task-Based Learning*.)

Pauline Foster has taught EFL in the United States, Japan and the UK. She is now research assistant to Peter Skehan at Thames Valley University, where she is working towards a PhD.

13 Effects of task repetition: appraising the developing language of learners

Martin Bygate

Introduction

Is there any point in asking a student to repeat a story-telling task a few days after doing it once? We often find ourselves giving students tasks to do, and then moving on to another, doubting the value of repetition. But what differences might there be in the learners' language, and what language learning processes might be involved, in task repetition? These are the questions I want to explore in this paper.

There are two main reasons for being interested in this. Firstly we need to know what learners do on their own, unprompted and unguided by the teacher, before deciding on appropriate forms of teacher intervention. Secondly, task-based approaches to learning require us to take seriously the need to examine how learners learn when doing tasks. How does language develop as a result of task-based language use, and why? This is an important area for our attention if language teaching is to take a responsible attitude to the methodology it proposes. This paper discusses some of the kinds of learning that may be occurring during communicative tasks, and especially the learning processes that tasks might activate.

Learning on oral tasks

Looking for signs of learning in recordings of students doing tasks leads us to consider what underlying learning processes might be occurring. The same question of course arises when as teachers we ask ourselves what kinds of learning we are expecting from students working on tasks. Let us consider for a moment a response to this question.

Task-based language use and language learning

Various writers are increasingly discussing language proficiency as made up of two kinds of knowledge: the first type is knowledge about the language, which can be stated in some way, and which is often called declarative knowledge (eg Littlewood 1992; Widdowson 1983). Let us call this language knowledge. The second type of knowledge is the knowledge of how to use the language, which generally cannot be stated, but is more likely to be demonstrated. This type of knowledge is often termed procedural knowledge, but let us call it language skill.

Now there is an argument that task-based practice can promote language knowledge. A number of writers have emphasized this view (see Gass and Varonis 1985, Long and Porter 1985, Doughty and Pica 1986, Pica 1987). For example, Pica, Kanagy and Faludon (1993) argue that interactive tasks may be particularly useful in enabling learners to pick up new vocabulary or grammar. They suggest this can occur when students check with each other on appropriate forms of language while carrying out a given task. This might be called the 'negotiation of meaning' perspective. Alternatively one could argue (eg White 1987) that one important aspect of learning involves identifying what one doesn't know, and that task practice could provide this information to learners. In this article I do not wish to pursue these questions. Instead I want to focus on the question of how language skills can be affected by practice on tasks and, in particular, by repetition of the same task on a later occasion.

Task-based language use and language skill

To consider the effect of task-based language use on language skill, it might be useful to draw upon an account of language processing proposed by Levelt (1978). Whether producing a first or second language, Levelt suggests that the process involves planning. The planning processes are complex and very fast, so that at first sight it might seem difficult to think of speech as involving planning (although it may not be such a problem to apply this view to writing).

Levelt distinguishes between three main levels of planning: conceptualization, the part of the process which focuses on the content of the message; formulation, which is concerned with finding words or phrases to communicate the message, with ensuring the selection of appropriate grammatical markers (including inflections and articles), and with planning the sound pattern of the utterance; and articulation, the execution of the precise articulation. These three types of planning are somewhat different, and precisely how they are connected to each other is not fully clear. It is however probable that planning at each level occurs simultaneously and over varying stretches of language (mostly more than a word at a time). For instance, planning a message may involve rough conceptualization of one's purpose and more precise conceptualization of specific utterances in turn. Planning the formulation of each utterance is then likely to involve selecting words or phrases one group at a time. Pawley and Syder (1976) suggest that this may take place roughly one clause at a time.

Evidence for the existence of these processes includes processing errors: for instance the fact that we are able to select and produce the wrong word, and then adjust it in line with our message (Færch and Kasper 1983); or that we can select and produce the right word but with the wrong grammatical form (Garman 1990). The occurrence of first language pronunciation errors also suggests that pronunciations are planned more than one word at a time. We are all familiar with 'spoonerisms' involving the exchange of consonants between words, such as Spooner's often quoted rebuke to a student: 'You have tasted the worm. You have hissed my mystery lectures. You must leave by the first town drain.' Mistakes of this kind suggest that we formulate meanings by selecting groups of words and preparing them for pronunciation together as groups, not one word at a time (Garman 1990).

Having suggested some of the key aspects of language processing, we need to consider how task repetition can help language processing skills develop.

How can task-based language use help?

The general prediction regarding the contribution of task-based language use to language skills is that performance is likely to be altered by repeating a task. We can expect to see this in a number of ways. For example, we might expect performance to be more fluent in terms of pausing and speed of words per minute. This is because all things being equal we would expect that doing the task a second time would involve less planning work. Also it is likely to have a different form: because the task has already been formulated previously, we can expect fewer false starts and self-corrections. And because the words have already been selected on one occasion, we might anticipate that the speaker would probably tend to produce fewer errors the second time around. Having succeeded in assembling language items once, the second attempt may be achieved with fewer errors.

There are other possible differences that could result from task repetition, however. These are mainly related to the possibility that the speaker, working without a script, could change the formulation on a subsequent occasion. One reason why this could happen is that familiarity with the content of the task might enable speakers to pay more attention to its formulation. For instance they might increase their range of vocabulary and reduce repetition of words; they could improve their choice of vocabulary; or they might use more syntactically complex language. How might this affect the recordings for this study?

The task in this study is a story re-telling task. The student is shown a short video extract and asked to re-tell the story. The speaker has witnessed a related sequence of events; will have understood the sequence of events (since there is no language in the input); has to work from memory; is free to divide the sequence up, or focus it, as they wish; and works without prompting in terms of the language to be used. When asked to do this, the speaker is likely then to have to deal with a number of problems. These would include processes such as remembering; focusing on key episodes in the story; selecting appropriate information to communicate for each episode; formulating the selected information; producing the relevant utterances; and monitoring the whole process to ensure the pragmatic qualities of adequacy and accuracy in the discourse. To summarize, the problems for the speaker are to recall something from the story which represents an episode; find a way of formulating it; and then articulate it. Second time around would, then, quite conceivably result in changes in performance. Such changes could be important for both teacher and student to be aware of. They could influence the learner's general language improvement.

Hence there are a number of possible outcomes from comparing two versions. Firstly there may be no difference between the recordings. This might occur because the speaker's performance is begun anew on each occasion, the performances reflecting general proficiency rather than task familiarity. Alternatively, one previous exposure to a task may not be enough to affect a subsequent performance. Thirdly, there may be random differences between the recordings, some language being well selected and formulated on the first occasion, and other language formulations being more successful on the second occasion. Fourthly, according to Levelt's model it is possible that having done a certain amount of work on a communication problem on one occasion, on a second performance the speaker can shift attention from the familiar aspects of the task to others. This would give rise to a different – and perhaps to a generally more satisfactory – performance on the second occasion.

In the following sections we report and discuss recordings collected from a single speaker, and some of the possible interpretations of the findings.

The study

Data collection

Our data consists of the language produced by one learner narrating a video extract on two separate occasions immediately after viewing it. The two occasions were three days apart. As far as possible the conditions were identical on each occasion: the instruction was the same ('Could you tell me what happened in the video?'); the video extract was identical, as were the interlocutor, the room and the conditions. In addition, on neither occasion did the student know what she was going to be asked to do; she had had no practice or opportunity to prepare herself for the task before either occasion, since the request to repeat the task was totally unexpected; the interlocutor was equally familiar with the extract on each occasion; and on neither occasion did she receive any feedback (other than 'OK, that's fine, thank you'). The key difference between the recordings was that on the second occasion the learner was familiar with the story from the previous encounter.

The video sequence was a 2'50 extract from a *Tom and Jerry* cartoon. This was selected for three main reasons: 1) the cartoons generally contain no dialogue, the advantage being that this simplifies the task since incorporating dialogue into a narrative is likely to give rise to grammatical and functional complications; 2) the cartoons are well known to many different cultures, and would therefore probably not pose acute problems of interpretation, of unfamiliarity, or contain a strong cultural bias; 3) the cartoons tend to involve few characters, limiting the complexity of the narrative. (Brown and Yule 1983 and Anderson and Lynch 1988 found this to be advisable.)

The data collected on the two occasions follows here, in the form of transcriptions of the recordings.

Time 1

I saw a little film about a cat and a mouse and the cat would like to eat the mouse but the mouse disliked this and she escape and she run up the wall and there was a board who was covered over and over with plates and and bowls and the mouse put it down and the cat was afraid that the plates are break damaged and she tr she erm catch all the things and in the end there was er a big a big I don't know a big hill with the dishes and the cat stand there and try to hold the dishes to save it but the mouse smiled and she comes up over the plates and she erm played with the tail of the cat she took a bath in the cat's milk and then she took the tail of the cat as a towel and she erm took the hairs from the cat away and she gave her erm she touch her with her feet and then the landlady come and the mouse erm touch the cat with the feet and the cat couldn't hold the dishes and all the plates and the bowls break and go go down and all the things was damaged and the landlady took the cat and go to punish to give punishment to the cat and the mouse were very happy and she took erm she took a board over her door who stand er a nice house ( ) so that's all [2'47"]

Time 2

I saw a very nice cartoon about Tom and Jerry and er the cat tried to catch the mouse the mouse er run up to a ca... to a cupboard cupboard and there were a lot of dishes especially plates and the mouse put up the plates and tayed (?) down and the cat wun to take off the plates because he had fear that the dish will get break and the cat collected all the dishes and in the end there is a lot and um very high just like a hill and the mouse come down came down and she jump jumped on the cat's nose and then she jump in the milk from the cat and she took a bath and after that she used the tail from the cat as a towel and she took the hairs away and she kicked the cat and all the dishes falling down and all the plates are broken the house lady came and she saw this and she picked up the cat (clears throat) to give her a terrible punishment I think so and the mouse was smile smiled and she go to erm to a hole and she put a sign where stand stood this is a nice home my sweet home [2'25"]

Features to be analysed

The specific features of oral language focused on are listed in Table 1.

Table 1: Indicators of task performance

	Repertoire	*Accuracy*	*Fluency*
vocabulary	range (type-token ratio) evaluative comment	selection collocation	repetition
discourse	range of connectors		
grammar	verb forms syntactic complexity	errors	

Repertoire refers to the range of language features used by the student, including: the variety of lexical items ('type-token ratio'); evaluative comment by the speaker; the variety of discourse connectors ('cohesion ratio'); verb form selection and syntactic complexity. *Accuracy* refers to: the adequacy of the choice of lexical item, collocation and overall errors. *Fluency* refers to the amount and type of repetition (pausing and speed of production could also serve as indicators, but are not referred to in this study). Of the many possible types of repetition, two in particular are distinguished: the first – verbatim repetition – occurs when hesitating, creating time to find an appropriate word; the second – substitutive repetition – seems to be employed when correcting a word or grammatical feature.

Expectations

The question we start from is whether a student's second performance would be significantly different from the first performance. The prediction is that all things being equal, the second performance would show greater accuracy, a broader repertoire, and greater fluency (or processing capacity), reflecting a shift in attention in the processing task.

Results of the analysis

Our results are reported in Table 2, and are discussed by category below. Note that they refer to one subject and therefore cannot be taken to be representative of what other learners would do.

Table 2: Results

	Time 1	*Time 2*
Total words	244	205
Error	9.4%	8.2%
Verb form selection		
Tense usage		
simple present	3	3
simple past	16	18
regular	3	7
irregular	8	10
BE	5	1
stem	10	4
V-ing	0	1
modal	2	1
passives	2	2
Grammatical complexity	4	7
Lexical repertoire		
type:token ratio	19	24
cohesion ratio	7:28	12:26
evaluative comment	0	5
Lexical selection/collocation		
– inappropriateness	16	8
– relative appropriateness	6	18
Disfluencies		
verbatim repetitions	9	4
substitutive repetitions	5	6

Errors

The expectation regarding errors is that proportionally fewer errors would occur at Time 2, and this expectation is confirmed. However, the margin of improvement is quite small, so it is necessary to remain cautious as to whether this direction would be confirmed over a larger group of learners.

Verb forms

Verb forms are often a particularly significant part of a speaker's performance. In narration, simple past is an important device for signalling narrative sequence. Ellis (1987) and Crookes (1989) each found that, given more planning time, learners produced regular forms more accurately than when under pressure (irregular forms were not similarly affected). The conditions of this study affect planning time, in that previous experience of a task would alter total planning time: the second performance can capitalize on the planning undertaken for the first performance.

Our results show three related changes. Firstly there is an increase in the number of simple past forms. This seems to relate to a drop in the number of stem forms, the speaker using inflected verb forms more often on the second occasion. The second change is that although irregular and regular past forms of lexical verbs both become more numerous, the increase in the use of regular past forms (over 100%) is far greater than that for irregulars (25%). This is consistent with the findings of Ellis and of Crookes referred to above. The third change is the sharp drop in the use of *be* past (by 80%), and a corresponding increase in the number of lexical verbs used (by over 50%), which also reflects the improvement in lexical selection. However, the drop from 5 to 1 of past *be* forms on the second performance also precisely parallels the increase from 3 to 7 in the occurrence of regular past forms. It is possible to conclude therefore that some lexical items may not have been used on the first occasion because it is easier both grammatically and lexically to use the rote-learned past form of *be* than to use a regular past form derived from a rule. In other words, the changes in performance may be due to a combination of two factors – grammatical regularity + problems of lexical selection. The lexical verb may require more retrieval work; and what's more, regular verbs may require more work to inflect correctly.

Grammatical complexity

The prediction that the speaker would use grammatically more complex structures on the second occasion was also borne out, the increase being of the order of 75% in the number of subordinate clauses.

Lexical repertoire

The next set of features concerns the choice of lexical items. Remember that here the expectation was that by the second occasion the speaker would already have carried out substantial content planning and would therefore have more time to think about lexical choices. One possible indication of this would be a greater variety of vocabulary at Time 2. This can be measured by calculating a type-token ratio, expressing the number of different vocabulary items (ie types) as a proportion of the total number of words used (ie tokens), a higher score indicating features such as less repetition, more adjectival or adverbial modification. The results show just such an improvement of

Time 2 over Time 1. The speaker seems to have a wider range of vocabulary items on the second occasion.

In order to explore this a little further, a second measure reflects the range of cohesive devices. This includes expressions such as *then, so, because, since, besides, at first, finally.* When these cohesive expressions are analysed and calculated as a proportion of the number of clauses, we find that the speaker has used a greater variety (though not a greater number) of these at Time 2.

The third measure concerns the use of evaluative comment. By 'evaluative comment' is meant the use of an adverb or adjective to indicate the speaker's attitude to an aspect of the story. Here again we might expect that speakers heavily concerned with communicating the content of the story would have little time or attention to spare for commenting on what they are describing. There are no obvious examples of evaluative comment in the first version of the narrative, but five on the second occasion.

Lexical selection/collocation
The next measure, lexical selection or collocation, is intended to reflect the extent to which the speaker has succeeded in selecting an appropriate word, expression or collocation to communicate the content. This is clearly a somewhat subjective measure. However most teachers and learners will agree that a substantial element of 'language learning' – both first and second – by definition entails the learning of other people's patterns of expression. 'Lexical selection' reflects the extent to which learners' vocabulary converges towards that of native speakers. Readers can check this assessment for themselves in the appendix.

First, all instances of relatively inappropriate or imprecise expressions were identified. The criterion for assessment was how the speaker's choice of expression compared with the choice made on the other occasion. Sometimes this is a matter of precision, as when, for example, the speaker refers to the video excerpt as 'a little film' on one occasion and 'a cartoon' on the other; or the speaker says 'comes up' when the opposite direction is the correct one ('came down'). At other times both expressions may be erroneous in some way, but one of the two is more *idiomatic* in the sense of being closer to a native speaker's choice, for instance: 'put it down' at Time 1, and 'taked down' at Time 2. The mouse is seen lifting plates off a shelf, and for this the use of the verb 'put' is less normal than the verb 'take'. Sometimes one expression is quite abnormal compared with the other (eg 'covered over and over' versus 'there were a lot of'); sometimes the speaker uses an unusual expression but improves it on one of the two occasions by the addition of a lexical item (eg 'gives a punishment to the cat' is improved by the addition of the adjective when phrased 'gives a terrible punishment to the cat').

16 expressions were identified as inappropriate at Time 1, while only 8 were classified as inappropriate at Time 2. On the other hand, 6 expressions were more appropriate at Time 1 (one of them not appearing at Time 2), whereas 18 were more appropriate at Time 2 (one not appearing at Time 1). In other words, the speaker seems to have reduced oddness at Time 2, and the speaker's choice of vocabulary seems more native-like on the second occasion.

Disfluencies

An analysis of the total number of word or phrase repetitions, calculated as a proportion of the total number of words, showed no change on the second occasion. However, more detailed analysis comparing the number of verbatim repetitions with the number of self-correcting substitutive repetitions yielded an interesting finding: self-correcting repetitions were significantly more frequent in the second version.

There is a possible explanation for this: on the first occasion the speaker may pay more attention to content planning, to deciding what meanings to express and to finding an appropriate word to express the selected meanings. Hence, verbatim repetitions, especially of grammatical words, would be likely to occur, giving the speaker time to access appropriate lexis. In contrast, on the second occasion the speaker would have already thought through the content of the narrative, and would therefore have more time and attention to monitor the choice of word or grammatical feature, giving rise to more self-corrections (substitutive repetitions) at Time 2. This explanation is strengthened by the earlier finding that lexical and grammatical selection improved on the second occasion.

Some conclusions

Although this is a study of just a single learner, there are a number of interesting patterns that emerge, particularly when we recall that the learner had no warning that either recording would take place, and was carrying out an unusual task which she would not normally have had any practice in. Firstly, overall there seem to be strong grounds for asserting that performance of a task on a second occasion may well be better than the first. In terms of *accuracy, repertoire* and *fluency* this learner seemed to perform better at Time 2. In other words, a pattern seemed to emerge which would support the idea that when first carrying out the task, the learner would be initially more concerned with planning the content of the message, and under pressure of time with finding the resources sufficient to communicate it. On the second occasion, on the other hand, having done the substantial conceptual work, the learner would be more concerned with paying attention to the formulation aspect of the task, that is with the selection of words and phrases, with their correct grammatical production, and where necessary with correcting mistakes as they occur. The contrast could be summed up as the distinction between accessing expressions at Time 1, as opposed to monitoring expressions at Time 2. (Morrison and Low 1983 discuss this use of the term 'monitoring'.) Finally, we could suggest that this shift, from a preoccupation with finding the expressions to a greater capacity for monitoring formulation, may be precisely what teachers might wish to encourage since it may enable learners to pay more attention to the task of matching language to concepts, and possibly to improving their knowledge and organization of the language.

Other explanations for the changes are of course possible. One is that the learner subconsciously or consciously rehearsed between performances. This is possible, but would still be consistent with the above explanation. Another is that the learner happened to have considerable latent proficiency from earlier learning experiences which she was rapidly reviving while in the UK. This is quite conceivable, and would deserve further exploration. However the fact that there is no pedagogically widely recognized pattern of performance for such tasks is a measure of how little we know about this aspect of task-based learning.

To summarize, we can tentatively suggest that the following principles emerge from the study and merit further attention:

1 Learners may learn through repeated experience of the same, or of similar or parallel tasks, and teachers may be able to use task familiarity to help learners' language to develop.

2 Task-based testing may be unreliable unless students are appropriately prepared, and unless testing procedures use similar tasks to those used in class.

3 Repetition of tasks may enable learners to move their attention towards improving their formulation, just as varying planning time can also affect performance (see Skehan, Paper 3).

4 Task-repetition may also lead to changes in learners' use of the language system, to increased fluency, and perhaps to increased awareness.

The effects discussed here are not likely to be limited to story-telling tasks (cf Willis, J., Paper 6), and it is also worth emphasizing that studies of learners' task-based language indirectly provide information about the nature of different tasks (cf Pica, Kanagy and Faludon 1993). A fuller study will explore some of these questions further. Meanwhile there are certain likely implications for the classroom.

One implication is that it is very likely that providing students with the opportunity to repeat a task – or a very similar task – is well worthwhile. Varying the amount of time between repetitions might affect later performance. In addition, it might well be worth trying a similar task with a different partner: different people will do tasks in different ways and a variety of partners could provide valuable learning opportunities. Finally, repeated experiences of given tasks could lead learners to become more aware of the communication problems that the tasks pose, and of the ways in which language can be used to solve them. Encouraging learners to discuss how they think the tasks are best tackled, or whether they have changed their own approach, may help to raise this kind of awareness.

In conclusion, studying learners' task-based language seems to show patterns of performance and development that are richer than what might be anticipated on simple inspection of the description of the task. Furthermore, this may provide a basis for looking afresh at the ways in which teachers might usefully intervene in task-based learning.

Acknowledgement
I am grateful to the Centre for Applied Language Studies, University of Reading for providing a research grant which made this study possible, and to David Perry, whose immaculate work on the data, and continual commitment, have been indispensable.

Appendix

Differences in lexical selection

Phrases judged to be the more appropriate are shown in italics.

Martin Bygate co-ordinates undergraduate, postgraduate and research courses in TESOL at Leeds University. His main interests are second language acquisition, task-based learning and classroom language. He recently co-edited *Grammar and The Language Teacher* with Alan Tonkyn and Eddie Williams.

	Time 1	*Time 2* (three days later)
	a little film	*a cartoon*
	a cat and a mouse	*Tom and Jerry*
	a board	*a cupboard*
	covered over and over	*a lot of*
	put it down	*taked down*
	was afraid	had fear that
	are break	*get break*
	she catch	collected
	a big hill	*just like a hill*
	comes up	*came down*
	played with	
	the cat's milk	the milk of the cat
	took [...] as a	*used [...] as a*
	she touch her with her feet	*she kicked the cat*
	couldn't hold	
	go down	*falling down*
	was damaged	*are broken*
	the landlady	the houselady
	go to give punishment to	*picked up [...] to give her a terrible punishment*
	was very happy	*smiled*
		go to a hole
	took a board	*put a sign*
	a nice house	*a nice home my sweet home*
More appropriate (idiomaticity or precision)	6	18
Comment	a little film	*a very nice* cartoon
	covered over and over with plates and bowls	a lot of dishes *especially plates*
	a big hill	*just like a hill*
	to give punishment to the cat	to give her a *terrible* punishment
		I think so
Clause complexity		
Complex verb groups	would like to eat	*tried to catch*
		want to take off
	was afraid that …	had fear that …
	are break damaged	*will get break*
		try to hold
Subordination	–	because …
	–	to give her a terrible punishment
	a board [...] who	a sign where

Assessing and managing change

Our focus so far has been the relationship between teachers, learners, methods and materials. We have been looking at the individual teacher as a decision maker. But teachers themselves work in a wider context. Their work is ultimately evaluated and sanctioned by outside bodies, by parents and employers and, perhaps most influentially, by examining bodies. We have included testing in this section on management because testing has a management function. It identifies learning goals and objectives. It seems, therefore, to impose constraints on teaching programmes and on teacher training programmes. Assessment programmes can be reactionary. They may simply reinforce an existing paradigm and stifle moves for change. But if assessment programmes are responsive to the profession as a whole they can be an agent for change. They can encourage and reward professional development.

How does an examining body take up these responsibilities? Lynette Murphy-O'Dwyer is Head of the TEFL Unit at the University of Cambridge Local Examinations Syndicate (UCLES). Dave Willis asked her about the ways in which the Syndicate maintains contact with the profession as a whole and attempts to reflect best practice and not simply reinforce the mainstream. Murphy-O'Dwyer accepts the dangers inherent in the assessment of practical teaching. Candidates may simply play safe and avoid experimentation and development. Tutors may be tempted to offer trainees safe 'recipes for successful lessons' instead of encouraging them to reflect on their practice. But Murphy-O'Dwyer believes that it is possible to involve the profession as a whole in shaping the way assessment is designed and carried out. This demands a lot of careful groundwork on the part of the examining body, and it demands the co-operation of practitioners and researchers, but if it can be achieved the benefits are considerable.

Wharton in her neatly titled paper 'Testing innovations' looks at the ways we test learners. She accepts that there are constraints inherent in the evaluation process but points out that these constraints are mitigated in two ways. First, we have a range of outside examinations to choose from. Wharton cites examinations which reinforce aspects of task-based learning in which, for example, candidates are required to interact freely with the examiner or with one another.

Secondly, even if an outside exam does identify goals and objectives there is more than one way of reaching those goals. One way to make the exam work for us is by taking learners into our confidence. This is particularly the case when students are assessed not by an error count but in terms of the quality of their performance. 'When an exam task of this kind is practised in class, learners as well as teachers can become involved in the negotiation that is a prerequisite to a judgement about the quality of the performance.' Interestingly, Wharton suggests that 'it could be very motivating for students to record themselves on the same or similar tasks at reasonable intervals in time and then to analyse their progress'. This parallels the research procedure adopted by Bygate (Paper 13) and suggests a productive interplay between research, teaching and testing techniques. Wharton is concerned throughout her paper to react positively to the demands of the examination. Her response is not 'Why do we have to do this?', but 'How can we exploit this to enhance student motivation and involvement?'

Jennings and Doyle document a programme of curriculum change in a particular institution, *The Language Centre of Ireland*. They stress the need for a proactive approach. The alternative, they say, is 'an unprincipled eclecticism, varying from teacher to teacher'. As managers they set out to identify 'a principled, coherent model for the management of change'. Their approach was based on the premise that change must involve the staff as a whole, 'that genuine commitment can only be generated through an understanding of and real participation in the process of change'. They set out to involve all staff actively in planning and working for change. They set up a sequence of identifiable goals to deploy and develop the skills required in an innovative teaching programme. They agreed the criteria for project appraisal and monitoring of the project.

They accepted that change takes time. The first stage was background reading and data-gathering to identify and evaluate possible courses of development. Once a new curriculum model had been agreed, all teaching and administrative staff were involved in detailing and documenting the curriculum goals, level descriptions and the other minutiae which support a teaching programme. The trial and training phase involved open discussion of classes and materials. The discussion was informed by reading and research. The implementation of the new curriculum was beset by insecurities – 'some teachers reported feeling "in limbo" and admitted to feeling "fear, apprehension and confusion" arising out of a concern that they may not be "doing it right" '. The answer to this was 'collaborative problem solving'. Problems were viewed positively 'as a basis for further development'.

For us the most positive thing about this development project is not simply that it has succeeded in tackling a complex management problem. The most exciting thing is that the machinery is still in place. Jennings and Doyle end their paper by acknowledging the problems that still exist and pointing out that these problems provide the basis for further action agendas, particularly for the teacher development programme. Change in turn produces further challenges.

Assessing the practice of teaching: a view from RSA/UCLES

14

Lynette Murphy-O'Dwyer and Dave Willis

Introduction

Like other professionals language teachers are subject to outside assessment and accreditation. Most Ministries of Education have training schemes designed to maintain and improve standards, and most of these schemes lead to a professional qualification and involve some sort of assessment. There are also a number of bodies which operate internationally and which are recognized internationally. One of these is the *Royal Society of Arts/University of Cambridge Local Examinations Syndicate* (RSA/UCLES). RSA/UCLES operates a number of schemes, of which the best known are the Certificate, for inexperienced teachers, and the Diploma, for teachers who already have some years of classroom experience. Obviously any profession should welcome the possibility of professional accreditation as one way of maintaining standards. But it is important that accreditation leads to real professional development and does not simply reinforce a given paradigm. It is not easy to balance the need for the maintenance of standards on the one hand, with the need for experiment and development on the other. Dave Willis asked Lynette Murphy-O'Dwyer, Head of the TEFL Unit at UCLES, about the policy of RSA/UCLES on this.

DW   *I know that this is a time of considerable change for RSA/UCLES with regard to the Diploma and Certificate qualifications in teaching English. Could you tell me what changes are in the wind and what prompts these changes?*

LM   Well, we haven't had a major review of the schemes as a whole for many years and there has never been an integrated review of the framework from pre-service up to in-service. We felt that it was important to review things thoroughly and possibly to make changes. The foundations for these programmes were laid in the late 1960s. Obviously attitudes towards language teaching are very different nowadays, some twenty years on, so we need to see how far we are still in line with the needs of the profession.

DW   *What are the major directions of change?*

LM   We need to allow for the fact that teachers come from a wide range of backgrounds and have a wide range of possible directions for career development. One person may start off teaching in Central London, say, with the intention of building a career overseas and moving all over the world. Another person may take a course in

149

Brazil, for example, wanting to prepare for a lifetime career teaching in that country. So we need to take account of the international and local contexts. We need to take account of teaching adults and of teaching young learners, of working perhaps with small classes in the private sector and with large classes in the public sector.

DW   *That's a change in the range of the exam. What about the values and principles that underlie the changes?*

LM   Well, we work through committees who represent a cross section of the profession. Some are academics, some are practising teachers, some are teacher trainers, and so on. We need to be responsible to the profession and we need to be publicly accountable. We need to consult widely and to listen to what people tell us. That doesn't mean that we are looking for change, even less that we seek to impose change – that we decide that a particular methodology or approach will be focused on. It is not the role of an examinations board, or indeed of any official body, to say what teaching is going to be like for the next twenty years. Our role is to respond to the profession, not impose values on it.

DW   *You mention consultation and you have a review of design processes whereby you consult people working in the field and then you try to take account of these, but isn't that inherently conservative, inherently reactionary?*

LM   It could be – and if you only ask those who are currently involved who have a major vested interest in retaining the current framework, then it would be. But we try to involve a wide range of people. We consult people internationally. Obviously we talk to people who use our schemes and people who work with us as assessors. But we also consult people who have no connection with the schemes, but who are respected professionals whose views are obviously important to listen to. Clearly some of the people we talk to will have a vested interest in maintaining things as they are, and will be suspicious of change. But we also talk to people who are doing innovative work in the field, and we try to take account of what they all have to say too.

DW   *There have been upheavals in the last twenty years in language learning theory and in language description. In very recent years, for example, there have been accelerating changes in language description as a result of the use of large computer-held corpora. How far do you take account of research findings in learning theory and language description?*

LM   Well, as I have said, we do try to talk to people who are doing innovative work. And it is important that we do this. We must listen to people who are involved in the field of research – I mean applied research, not pure academic research. I think there has always been a tradition in the profession of taking account of outside views, from education, applied linguistics, etc, including views that challenge basic assumptions. It is important that course tutors consider challenges of this kind. This doesn't mean that they will necessarily change what they do, but it does mean that they constantly review what they are doing.

DW   *In principle this would be very healthy because you would have an organization like RSA/UCLES, or another body, providing this kind of certification, acting as a conduit for change but with the profession having a sort of veto over this. You would have research carefully filtered by the practitioners on the ground. But does it actually happen? It sounds fine but does it work that way?*

LM   Yes, I think it does. We *are* publicly accountable. I don't think that anybody working within applied language research in this country would allow us to get away with ignoring research findings. We make a conscious effort to cast our net very wide. We have a bulletin list of almost 3,000 people, in this country and overseas. This bulletin enables people to see what we are doing and this supplements the process of consultation. Anybody and everybody is able to comment on what's happening within the review. So the bulletin and the consultation documents are not just sent to people who are going to say 'Yes, this is a good idea' — the whole idea is that we should have a balanced perspective. The people on our committees and working parties wouldn't let us get away with just re-inventing exactly the same courses. And we would not devote resources to such a thorough process of consultation and review if that did not have a real influence on our work. So what we aim at is real public accountability – having everybody involved. When I say 'everybody' I mean all the interest groups in the profession. We would like to make people feel that they can write in. And a lot of people do this. It's not always a comfortable process because it sometimes involves being told you've got things wrong. But when we are told that we've got things wrong it means we have to review what we are doing and then if change is needed we have to manage that change.

DW   *So you're suggesting that an organization like yours ought to, and in your case does, act as a catalyst for this spread of best practice.*

LM   I think it has to. I think that if we are going to be publicly accountable for our work and represent the profession internationally in that work, then we have to act as facilitators of best practice. Obviously we can't guarantee that everyone always applies best practice. But we do have to insist on high standards of professionalism. If an individual centre is delivering courses which are not acceptable according to our internationally agreed criteria then that centre will be required to withdraw from the scheme. Again this doesn't mean that we have to agree in every detail with what every centre does. But it does mean that centres have to work within an accepted professional framework and have to be prepared to justify departures from that framework.

DW   *Yes, but what happens? I mean, I can see that in principle, but what very often happens, especially when it comes down to the practical assessment, is that people play safe, and so they want the kind of lesson that they can go through safely. And that implies a lot of teacher control, because it is much safer if you control things. It's much safer if you plan a predictable lesson and set down very specific learning aims. So there are a lot of very understandable pressures pushing people in the direction of control and of predicting what is going to be learned and so on. And these are things which are very much called into question by a lot of learning theory.*

LM   There are a number of issues here. First of all we have to be able to offer an assessment. In other words we have to be able to say that what is being shown to us can be recorded against some description. So, clearly there is a danger here. If your description is prescriptive you have problems. Obviously we have no right to be prescriptive, to tell people what they ought to be doing in their own classrooms. But there's a more insidious danger in that it may be *perceived* that there is one way to do an RSA/UCLES lesson. I know that people are often quoted as talking about 'the RSA lesson' and that in some quarters there is a belief that you have to do an RSA lesson to pass the exam. It may also be the case that this 'RSA lesson' is perceived as basically PPP. Now we have done nothing to encourage this belief. In fact we try hard to counter it. But it may be that the perception is none the less there. That's one of the major reasons for the review we are engaged in.

Finally there is the danger you point to. The danger that teachers feel they are on trial and react defensively, simply try to avoid doing anything for which they might be penalized. But we are not in the business of penalizing poor performance. What we want to do is encourage a positive performance in a way that will have a positive backwash effect on everyone's day-to-day teaching. If we are to achieve that, we must get away from the idea that at the diploma level, in the space of two externally assessed practical lessons, you can actually reflect your whole experience and capacity as a teacher in the classroom. If we're simply looking at an isolated assessment of practice then people are always going to believe that you have to play the game if you want to pass. We don't actually advocate that, and the standardization of the assessors and the involvement of the course tutors and the candidates in that standardization doesn't encourage it. But I can understand that some people may none the less think that way. They are going to look for some sort of form and they are going to say you have to show this, you have to show that, you have to show the other, and if you don't show that, you won't pass. So, I can see that the backwash effect from this sort of snapshot assessment could be seen as being impositional and therefore you have the notion of an RSA Cambridge lesson.

But if you don't have to rely on a snapshot assessment then you can bring to bear in the assessment all sorts of things in addition to observation in the classroom. You can make it possible for teachers to show you how they are tackling all sorts of professional issues in their working life. An ideal assessment would give a general picture of a teacher's day-to-day working practice. But that's not easy to achieve. How we do that, finally, will clearly depend on what is accessible in the sense of what we can record either through observation or indeed through other means. It will depend on how you link, say, the teaching plan to the lesson; how the teacher's reflection and review of the lesson can then be taken into account. We must get away from the idea that though someone is a good teacher, if they go in for the RSA Cambridge lesson and they have a bad day, they're going to fail. Everybody has the occasional bad day. If it's a one-off they should not be penalized for it. The difficult thing is that we are dealing with people's perceptions. I understand the fear of failure and how people may react defensively to that fear. It's something we have to get away from.

DW   *So you feel that experience of a diploma course should encourage risk-taking?*

LM   Well, I think we must consider that people at diploma level are practising teachers of some experience in a variety of contexts. They want to become autonomous teachers, able to assess and regulate their own performance. The course shouldn't try to provide them with simple answers to everyday teaching problems. It should open their eyes to different views of practice and allow them the chance to review their own practice for themselves and to enable them to find out what works and doesn't work in particular contexts.

So it seems to me that the role of the course is to encourage experienced teachers to examine their practice. Sometimes this will reinforce what they actually do day by day.

They can leave the course at the end with an enhanced confidence in some aspects of their professional expertise. But they should also learn what is involved in being a TEFL professional. They should look at the various methodologies that they have never even considered before and review their own practice in that light. Teacher training always has to balance security on the one hand and change on the other. So the course should act almost like a practical experiment in lots of ways. People should go in as secure teachers with a lot of practical experience and then be able to find it exciting to look at new ways of viewing their own practice and the practice of colleagues.

Now I suppose that's not a very comfortable thing for a course to do. So you have to make sure that the course tutors give them enough security in their own practice and their own particular context of practice. Given this confidence they can view change from a position of strength. They won't be afraid of change, but they will assess possible approaches critically. They will reject the things that they consider, after careful review, would not be appropriate in their own working context. They can apply critically elements of practice which they think will be beneficial in their situation.

So we don't simply want to reinforce existing practice, but we do want to give teachers a secure base for experimentation, so they can take risks without a crippling fear of failure. They must be prepared to take risks. But they must recognize what they are doing. The autonomous teacher is one who develops gradually, with an awareness of what they're doing.

DW   *The RSA/UCLES Certificate is aimed at inexperienced teachers, isn't it? How does it differ from the Diploma?*

LM   Yes, I think that one has to look at the certificate being aimed at pre-service teachers. They don't have the basic tools of the trade. That means that the aims and objectives of that certificate are to introduce people to the profession. They are not in a position to review their established practice and learn from it. So the process is slightly different because it has to support their learning and their introduction to the profession. But at the same time it is a real dilemma for course tutors as to whether they should confuse the issue and present to all candidates fifty different ways of teaching, or whether they should restrict it. There is a view that the CTEFLA has restricted the experience of candidates to the PPP model. Now, again it reflects the fact that on most courses the PPP model has been used as the model that introduces candidates to their professional skills. But this doesn't mean they have no experience of any other models. It's important to show that PPP isn't the only answer to teaching. But there is still a dilemma. When you're preparing a teacher in such a short time, you have to enable them to go into the classroom feeling relatively secure. But you must also encourage them to question if it's the only way. I would suggest, or I would hope, that through our system of checks and balances and monitoring the courses and course approval and reapproval, the training provided on certificate courses isn't stagnant. The training must be supportive, but by the end of the course participants must realize that they don't know everything about teaching. They should recognize that what has happened is that they have been introduced to one or two models and that they have a lot to learn.

DW   *If that actually happens, fine. But there is a danger that what they get is one or two recipes, that they are told 'This is how you do it', 'Go in and do this', without being equipped to question what they are doing.*

LM   Well I think we are agreed that part of the job of the Syndicate is to support best practice. This involves a heavy infrastructure. We have to make sure that we monitor centres. We train and brief our assessors. We give opportunities for course tutors to have annual/bi-annual conferences where the focus is to give people a professional shot in the arm. One of the main topics of the current review is the notion of professional development. We need to provide an initial incentive towards making teachers into questioning professionals. We don't want teachers or teacher trainers or anybody involved in the field to start with the CTEFLA and do nothing else at all – do no other professional training, have no other professional discussions or insights, never ever pick up a book. What we need to do is to encourage them to think about what they're doing. We shouldn't just give them recipes, but that's a start. You need to go beyond that, of course. If we truly represent the profession, the profession is not going to allow us to encourage people to do teaching by numbers and leave it at that. Again, that's one of the reasons for the review. We recognize these problems and we want to find answers.

DW   *Can I just ask a final question about the practical difficulties of doing this? You have some centres where there's a lot of very lively innovative teaching going on, and then they have to get an outsider to come and do assessment for their courses and they think 'Oh, dear me, if we're going to get someone from the outside, then we've got to go very much with the mainstream. We've got to do something which can't be challenged and called into question,' and so on. So it pushes them back to something perhaps like PPP. How do you avoid that? It could act as a sort of disincentive.*

LM   Well, it would act as a disincentive to centres if in fact the assessors where chosen from people who were not themselves involved in the course and indeed not themselves monitored, standardized in that sense, standardized positively to open their eyes rather than to just receive recipes. It would happen if you didn't monitor performance of assessors and centres. It would happen if you didn't allow people in the profession to ask questions. Actually, it would be much easier for us to be able to say, 'Right, this is the way we're going to do it. Here it is, accept it or not.' It's not comfortable to have a series of schemes that are based on consultation and based on feedback from the practitioners who are actually delivering the courses, and indeed from the candidates themselves. So it's not an easy model, but I think that if you have an infrastructure which is publicly accountable, which allows people to question what's happening, and if you ensure that accountability is part of your process, then people will be realistic about what the Certificate or the Diploma aims to do. If they themselves are involved in it, they will also know the dangers of going towards a recipe-driven methodology. Of course we could do things in a recipe-driven way. Life would be much more comfortable if we did it that way. But we wouldn't be able to hold up our heads professionally, so what would be the point?

Lynette Murphy-O'Dwyer has been involved with the RSA/Cambridge TEFL schemes since the 1970s. She is now head of the TEFL Unit at UCLES and has responsibility for the Cambridge Integrated Language Teaching Schemes.

Testing innovations

15

Sue Wharton

Introduction

As teachers we have considerable control over the way language is taught in our classrooms and institutions, and many of us use this independence to extend methodologies in ways which we feel will benefit our learners. We may have less control, though, over the way that students' learning will eventually be tested: in many contexts, learners are working towards assessment via an external examination. As this moment moves closer, the teacher who has worked for methodological change may face doubt and frustration: it may seem that developments in exams have not 'kept up' with the methodology of the classroom. Reservations about the exam format may be compounded by resentment of the fact that it is being imposed from outside, that the teacher's priorities and deeply held values might not be shared by the examiner. Factors such as these make many teachers uneasy about exams and tests.

And yet, validation of achievement by an outside body is important for students. For some, the goal of passing an exam is in fact the main motivation for attending classes. In these circumstances, the challenge for the teacher is to respond both to the broad goal of helping students to learn more, and to learn more effectively, and to the specific goal of helping them to pass the exam.

It is sometimes said that the two goals defined above are inherently contradictory. The expectation of certain examination formats can produce a backwash effect in the classroom, whereby teachers and learners spend too much time on narrow exam practice at the expense of other activities possibly more beneficial to actual learning. There are, then, two assumptions here: firstly that exam practice does not help learning, and secondly that classroom activities which do help learning are not in themselves sufficient for passing exams. In this chapter, we will look at both assumptions in detail and will show that they do not always hold true.

A mismatch between testing and learning?

Exams are based on theory. It is impossible to write a test without consciously or unconsciously bringing in our views about the nature of language and also the nature of learning. In this section and the next one we will take an overview of some of the positions on language and on learning represented in this book, and we will compare these to the positions represented by some exams. In each section we will look first at language and then at learning.

Language

It is useful to think about language from two angles: the exposure that learners receive, and the output that they produce. In terms of exposure first of all, contributors to this book emphasize the importance of a wide variety of written and spoken genres; of authentic language; of lexis as well as syntax; of a bias towards frequently occurring items with a consequently high surrender value; and of interaction with language problems rather than imitation of language solutions. In terms of output, emphasis is placed on the use of whatever language the learner has available; communication of own meanings rather than formal accuracy; integration of skills (both macro and micro skills); and the opportunity to use both private and public genres.

In external exams, though, learners may find a different approach to language. For example, preliminary research conducted on a corpus of reading passages from a well-known examination (A-Angeles 1993) suggested that the reading comprehension passages were drawn from a very limited range of genres, and that authentic materials related overwhelmingly to British culture.

A-Angeles also worked with a corpus of items tested by the multiple-choice cloze question of the same examination, many of which are grammar items. The corpus was made up of papers from 1984–1993. A-Angeles compared the most frequently tested items with the most frequent words of the COBUILD corpus; these, of course, are mainly grammar words too. It was found that a number of frequent items in the COBUILD corpus did not appear in the cloze item corpus. Other items which did get tested by the cloze questions were not particularly frequent in COBUILD. A-Angeles' research suggested, therefore, that the cloze question of the exam privileged some language items which may not be particularly frequent in everyday life.

In situations like these, there is the possibility of negative backwash. If the language content of the exam is allowed to dictate the syllabus content, teachers and learners may find themselves concentrating on relatively rare items and constructions at the expense of more frequent items which, as has been shown by COBUILD research (see eg Willis 1990), have a high surrender value.

Moving now from language *per se* to language acquisition, a recurring theme in this book is that teachers can never know exactly when a learner will be ready to acquire a new language item. One can never assume that an item will have been acquired simply because it was present in the exposure, even if it was the subject of particular attention. Many public exams, though, provide lists of the grammatical items and functions that they will test. This can be seen as helpful information (and it is certainly requested by both teachers and learners!) but it can also lead to an inappropriately atomistic and synthetic view of language. It may encourage teachers to 'teach to the test' using a presentation methodology, and this is the subject of the next section.

Methodology

In the area of methodology, the approaches described in this book have tendencies in common. Emphasis is placed on the importance of collaborative learning; on a positive view of error; on the importance of learner input; and on the role of the teacher as resource. If we look at exams, we may again find apparent mismatches.

The pressure of an upcoming exam may lead to a concentration on past papers or exam practice books, and this in turn may push the group to spend a lot of class time working as individuals. Most exam tasks, after all, require that students respond without collaborating, and this is reflected both in rubrics and in task design. Collaboration in exam practice may therefore not be seen as legitimate by students; a sense of competition may come to dominate the class instead.

For example, many tests designed to test listening and reading do so largely by multiple choice questions. The questions are designed so that there is just one correct answer, and no room for debate about which that is. When tests of this nature are practised in class, the teacher is cast in the role of knower of the correct answers, with learners relegated to more passive roles. Open-endedness is deliberately avoided. Such open-endedness may lead to rewarding discussion in a learning situation, but it is seen as unfair in an exam.

In this section, then, we have seen that there may be certain mismatches between learning goals and exam practice. In the next section we will look at some trends in test development which are very much in sympathy with the approaches described in this book. Again, we will look first at language and then at methodology.

Testing as an aid to learning

Language

The view of language ability underlying recent tests has broadened considerably from the traditional focus on grammar and lexis to include the value of actual utterances in context. Candidates may be asked, for example, to listen to a conversation and answer questions which focus not only on the understanding of content, but also of speaker attitude and intention (see for example excerpt 1).

Excerpt 1
(Taken from PET guidelines)

Question 12	The listening material for this question usually consists of a conversation between two or (at most) three people. The people may discuss holiday plans, buying a house, or another subject of mutual interest. Sometimes the people will become involved in remembering an experience which both have shared. Whatever the subject of their discussion, they will often agree or disagree about certain related matters. Consequently, the 5–6 written questions which are based on the conversation will be designed to test students' understanding of the language used to express agreement or disagreement, apologies or complaints, etc. as well as their understanding of the gist of a conversation. The questions themselves will generally take the form of simple True/False statements or Yes/No questions.

The following is an example of the beginning of such a conversation which students will hear.

Woman: I'm just going round to the garage to fill the car up with petrol.
Man: Why? You're not thinking of driving tomorrow?
Woman: Well, yes. I thought it'd be quicker, door to door.
Man: But the train only takes two hours.
Woman: But then I have to allow half an hour to get to the station, and the same at the other end, so that'll be three hours.
Man: But you don't know the way. You might get lost.
Woman: Don't be silly. I've done it before. It's almost the same as if I were going to Jamila's house.
Man: No, it isn't, not after the first half hour.
Woman: Well, anyway, it won't be difficult ….

Students read:

If you agree with the statement put a tick in the box under "TRUE". If you do not agree put a tick in the box under "FALSE".

	TRUE	FALSE
1. The woman is planning to travel by car tomorrow.	☑	☐
2. The woman agrees it would be quicker to go by train.	☐	☑
3. The woman has made the same journey before.	☐	☑

A concern with authenticity of exposure is reflected by the language of input of some tests of reading and listening, even at lower levels. Some tests include, for example, sections based on public notices displayed in context (see excerpt 2). Authenticity of task is also a consideration. The Preliminary English Test Speaking Test guidelines (UCLES) explicitly state that tasks have been chosen which could be useful to candidates in real-life situations.

Excerpt 2
(Taken from KET Handbook; Reading and Writing Paper)

Part 1

In Part 1 candidates are tested on their ability to understand the main message of a sign, notice or other very short text. These texts are of the type usually found on roads, in railway stations, airports, shops, restaurants, offices, schools, etc. Wherever possible these texts are authentic and so may contain lexis which is unfamiliar to the candidates, but this should not prevent them from understanding the main message.

Questions 1–5 are multiple choice (3 options). Candidates are asked either about the likely location of the text, or about the likely target reader.

Example 1

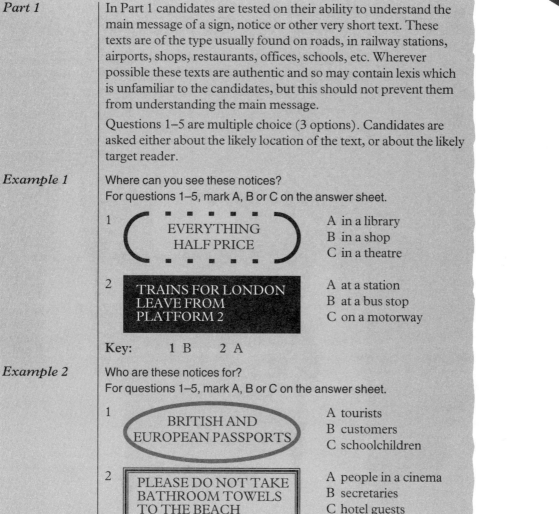

Where can you see these notices?
For questions 1–5, mark A, B or C on the answer sheet.

1 EVERYTHING HALF PRICE
A in a library
B in a shop
C in a theatre

2 TRAINS FOR LONDON LEAVE FROM PLATFORM 2
A at a station
B at a bus stop
C on a motorway

Key: 1 B   2 A

Example 2

Who are these notices for?
For questions 1–5, mark A, B or C on the answer sheet.

1 BRITISH AND EUROPEAN PASSPORTS
A tourists
B customers
C schoolchildren

2 PLEASE DO NOT TAKE BATHROOM TOWELS TO THE BEACH
A people in a cinema
B secretaries
C hotel guests

Key: 1 A   2 C

In many tests the language of input and of response is not tightly circumscribed. For example, in the individual version of the PET Speaking Test section II candidates participated with the examiner in simulated tasks, such as buying an item in a department store. Examiners had an approximate script to follow, but were free to alter or adapt their responses to fit with what the candidate said. The candidates, then, were able to use any language at their disposal to complete the task, and were assessed on the success of the transaction rather than on formal accuracy. Although the situation and therefore the *type* of language is circumscribed in this situation, the exact linguistic realization of the task is not (see excerpt 3).

Excerpt 3
(Taken from PET guidelines, Speaking Test★)

| **Section II** | In this section students are required to give directions, talk about time, discuss their needs, and make and reply to requests, offers and suggestions. All these tasks are performed in simulated situations. The examiner describes a situation and then hands a card to the student, giving the context of a situation (usually a picture). The examiner then briefly describes the roles and outlines the tasks to be performed. |

In the following example, the examiner tells students that they are in a big department store and want to buy a travelling-iron. The examiner then gives students a picture of a certain type of iron (as shown below).

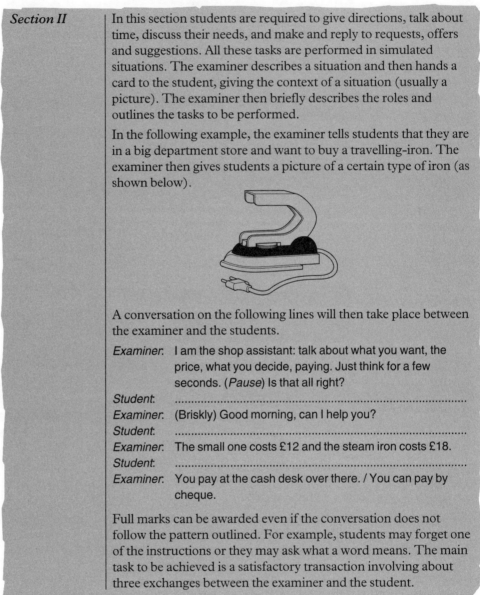

A conversation on the following lines will then take place between the examiner and the students.

Examiner: I am the shop assistant: talk about what you want, the price, what you decide, paying. Just think for a few seconds. (*Pause*) Is that all right?

Student: ....

Examiner: (Briskly) Good morning, can I help you?

Student: ....

Examiner: The small one costs £12 and the steam iron costs £18.

Student: ....

Examiner: You pay at the cash desk over there. / You can pay by cheque.

Full marks can be awarded even if the conversation does not follow the pattern outlined. For example, students may forget one of the instructions or they may ask what a word means. The main task to be achieved is a satisfactory transaction involving about three exchanges between the examiner and the student.

(★*Note*: this individual test format was discontinued by UCLES in 1996. The standard paired format now adopted by UCLES provides candidates with the opportunity to display further their language competence in terms of discourse management and interactive communication.)

In other speaking tests where candidates are involved in interactions with each other, not just the examiner, two candidates together may be asked to collaborate on a task, such as establishing the differences between two similar sets of photographs (see excerpt 4). With this test format there is even less control over the language produced: the examiner has no chance to influence candidate output by asking questions designed to elicit certain language forms.

Excerpt 4
(Taken from CAE Sample Materials)

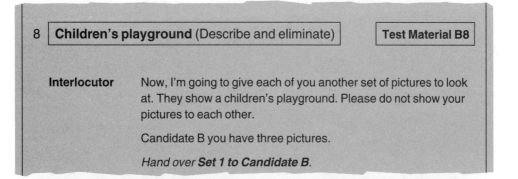

| 8 | **Children's playground** (Describe and eliminate) | **Test Material B8** |

Interlocutor   Now, I'm going to give each of you another set of pictures to look at. They show a children's playground. Please do not show your pictures to each other.

Candidate B you have three pictures.

*Hand over **Set 1 to Candidate B**.*

Candidate A, you have the same three pictures plus an extra one.

*Hand over **Set 2 to Candidate A**.*

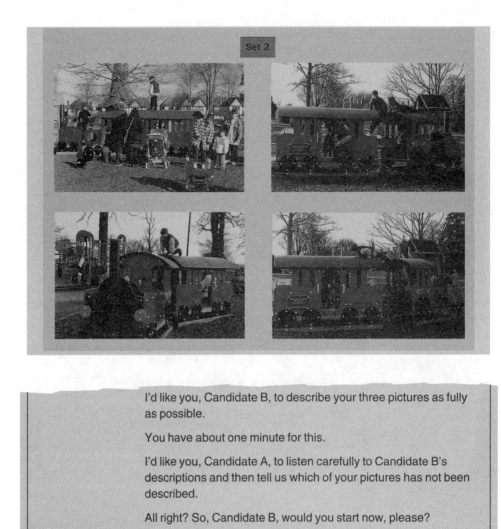

I'd like you, Candidate B, to describe your three pictures as fully as possible.

You have about one minute for this.

I'd like you, Candidate A, to listen carefully to Candidate B's descriptions and then tell us which of your pictures has not been described.

All right? So, Candidate B, would you start now, please?

Candidate B *Approximately one minute.*

Interlocutor Thank you. Now, Candidate A, can you tell us which picture has not been described?

Candidate A *Approximately twenty seconds.*

Interlocutor Thank you.

Such a test format clearly offers scope to assess many aspects of candidates' language, and this can be recognized in the marking criteria. The guidelines for CAE Speaking Test Part 2, for example, make it clear that the way in which candidates use language to structure their turns or to express agreement is just as important as the language they use to describe their prompt material (see excerpt 5). The parallel with approaches described in this book is clear.

Excerpt 5
(Taken from CAE Specifications, Speaking Test)

> **Part 3**
>
> Candidates will be presented with a problem-solving task, prompted by a written or visual stimulus. They will be given three minutes to reach agreement or to 'agree to disagree', having exchanged points of view. Tasks may include sequencing, ranking, comparing and contrasting, etc.
>
> This phase is designed to test negotiation and collaboration skills; the metalanguage of the exchange is as much part of the test as the utterances directly connected with the prompt material.

Any task with a focus on outcomes involves candidates in using language skills, both macro- and micro-skills, in an integrated way. Many writing tests now involve candidates in contextualized tasks with purpose and audience specified. The writing task is in response to reading input, and appropriate understanding of the input is necessary for completion of the task. For example, candidates may be placed in the situation of making a difficult claim on a travel insurance policy; they may be asked to refer to policy information and respond to a letter from the travel insurance company (see excerpt 6).

Excerpt 6
(Taken from CAE Sample Materials, Paper 2 Writing)

> 1. You have recently been on a trip to the USA and had problems with your baggage. On the flight to the United States (26 March 1990), your suitcase was lost and you didn't get it back for four days. On the flight home (16 April), the case was very badly damaged and now you need to replace it.
>
> You have made a claim on your travel insurance policy for £90 (suitcase) and £50 (delay), and have now received a letter and a cheque from the insurance company. You are dissatisfied with their treatment of your claim and want to do something about it.
>
> *Reply to their letter, explaining why you think the money they have offered is not enough and giving the additional information they need.*
>
> *Use the handwritten notes which you have made on the letter, the advertisement and the outline of your insurance cover to help you construct your letter.*
>
> *You may invent any necessary extra details to complete your answer (e.g. were you on holiday or on business?) provided that you do not change any of the information given. You are advised to write approximately 250 words.*

FREEDOM TRAVEL INSURANCE

MEDICAL EXPENSES	£1 million
PERSONAL ACCIDENT	£15,000
CANCELLATION/CURTAILMENT	£1,500
INTERRUPTION OF PUBLIC TRANSPORT SERVICES	£200
BAGGAGE	£1,000
BAGGAGE DELAY	£50
PERSONAL MONEY	£300
HOSPITAL INCONVENIENCE BENEFIT	£15 – £300
TRAVEL DELAY	£60 – £1,500
LOSS OF PASSPORT	£100
PUBLIC LIABILITY	£1 million

EXCESS The insured person has to pay the first £25 of each and every claim.

FREEDOM INSURANCE LTD.

Date: 18th May 1990

Dear Claimant,

Re: BAGGAGE/DELAYED BAGGAGE CLAIM

We acknowledge receipt of your recent correspondence, dated 13th May, the contents of which have been duly noted.

← ONLY £45 !

We attach our cheque in reference to your claim for the damage to your suitcase whilst in transit.

receipt lost

New !

Please note that in view of the <u>limited information and evidence</u> provided in respect of this part of your claim, our settlement has been reduced accordingly.

strap broken
side torn
wheels unusable

Bought specially for trip

We have also made deductions for wear, tear and depreciation and your claim has been subject to the usual £25 policy excess.

Turning now to your claim for delayed baggage, we respectfully remind you that the insured person must inform our representative if his or her baggage has been lost or misplaced for at least 24 hours on the outward journey. In such cases an amount of up to £50 for <u>replacement purchases</u> necessarily made at the time will be paid to the insured person.

Phoned rep. 26th and 27th

jacket, shoes (had to be smart for 28th) casual clothes and toiletries

As your correspondence makes no mention of any purchases we are unable to give any consideration to this part of your claim.

We hope you will appreciate the above comments.

Yours sincerely, for and on behalf of Freedom Insurance Ltd.

S. Watkins

S Watkins
Travel Claims

Methodology

We have already seen that certain test tasks involve candidates working together in pairs. There is therefore a good match between such tasks and the collaborative classroom interactions valued by many teachers today. Linked to the introduction of collaborative tasks is the fact that the exams described here are criterion-referenced, which means that candidates are assessed only in terms of their ability to meet certain performance criteria in the test, and are *not* judged against each other. There is no limit to the number of candidates who can pass each time the exam is administered. The knowledge that they are preparing for a criterion-referenced exam may help learners to maintain an atmosphere of co-operation, as opposed to competition, in the classroom.

Although reading and listening tend to be tested using a multiple choice format, we have seen above that writing and speaking are often tested by samples of performance that cannot in themselves be characterized as 'right' or 'wrong'. They need to be assessed in terms of the quality of the performance. When an exam task of this kind is practised in class, learners as well as teachers can become involved in the negotiation that is a prerequisite to a judgement about the quality of the performance. Learners can give feedback to their peers, and reflect on their own performance. The teacher is no longer the only person providing feedback on success of performance.

Even in the actual examination task-based tests do not penalize error as much as more traditional tests tended to. Candidates are usually marked on the task performance as a whole, and accuracy is just one factor. See for example CCSE skill criteria for test of oral interaction, which include five equally weighted factors (see excerpt 7 overleaf). Knowledge of the fact that tests are marked in this way will encourage candidates to continue experimenting with language in the classroom.

The review of tests and tasks in this section has of necessity been selective. We have nevertheless seen that in many senses tests are developing in line with the more genuinely 'communicative' approach which is increasingly valued in the English Language Teaching community.

In the following section, we will move away from the tests themselves and look at the vital contribution which teachers and learners are to make if the presence of tests in the classroom is to be a positive one.

Teachers, learners and tests

Test developers are aware of the influence of test backwash on teaching, and feel a responsibility both to base their work on, and try to encourage, what they see as good classroom practice (Morrow 1986, 1992).

However, it is not realistic to expect public examination bodies to do all, or even very much, of the work for development and change. Exam boards are conservative for very good reasons (Skehan 1991). Candidates and teachers need to be informed of change well in advance, which implies a considerable time lag in the implementation of change. Exam boards are also commercial operations, whose success depends on public familiarity with, and confidence in, their product. This is not a situation which is conducive to experiment for the sake of it.

Excerpt 7

(Taken from CCSE Teachers' Guide, Oral Test)

Degree of Skill

CERTIFICATES IN COMMUNICATIVE SKILLS IN ENGLISH: Oral Interaction

In order to achieve a pass at a given level, candidates must demonstrate the ability to complete the tasks set with the degree of skill specified by these criteria.

	Level 1	Level 2	Level 3	Level 4
ACCURACY	It is acceptable for pronunciation to be heavily influenced by L1 if it is generally intelligible. With support, the candidate must be able to clarify any confusions caused by lexical or grammatical errors.	Pronunciation must be clearly intelligible even if still obviously influenced by L1. Grammatical/lexical accuracy is generally high though some errors which do not destroy communication are acceptable.	Pronunciation must be clearly intelligible even if some influences from L1 remain. Grammatical/lexical accuracy is high though occasional errors which do not impede communication are acceptable.	Pronunciation must be easily intelligible though some residual accent is acceptable. Grammatical/lexical accuracy must be consistently high.
APPROPRIACY	Use of the language must be broadly appropriate to the function though it may not correspond to native-speaker expectations. The intention of the speaker can be perceived by a sympathetic listener.	The use of language must be generally appropriate to function. The overall intention of the speaker must be generally clear.	The use of language must be generally appropriate to function and to context. The intention of the speaker must be clear and unambiguous.	The use of language must be entirely appropriate to context, function and intention. There is nothing to cause confusion.
RANGE	It is acceptable for the candidate to have a severely limited range of expression and to have to search often for a way to express the desired meaning.	A fair range of language must be available to the candidate. Only in complex utterances is there a need to search for words.	A wide range of language must be available to the candidate. Any specific items which cause difficulties can be smoothly substituted or avoided.	There must be only occasional obvious limitations on the range of language. Few allowances have to be made for the fact that the candidate is not a native speaker.
FLEXIBILITY	The candidate is not expected to take the initiative in conversation, or to respond immediately to a change in topic. The interlocutor may have to make considerable allowances and often adopt a supportive role.	There must be some evidence of the ability to initiate and concede a conversation and to adapt to new topics or changes of direction.	There must be consistent evidence of the ability to "turn-take" in a conversation and adapt to new topics or changes of direction.	The candidate must be able to "turn-take" and "direct" an interaction appropriately and keep it flowing.
SIZE	Contributions limited to one or two simple utterances are acceptable.	Must be capable of responding with more than short-form answers where appropriate. Should be able to expand simple utterances with occasional prompting from the interlocutor.	Must be capable of making lengthy contributions where appropriate. Should be able to expand and develop ideas with minimal help from the interlocutor.	Must be capable of making lengthy and complex contributions as appropriate. The interlocutor does not need to support the candidate.

So, there are some practical factors which limit the role that test developers can play in innovation and change. But there is also a social/ educational factor which is far more important. A test developer can never guarantee the way that a test will be received by learners, teachers and examiners. We might say that no test is inherently communicative. Its validity and authenticity as a test of communicative language ability are a function of the interaction between the candidate, the test and the examiner. (For a detailed discussion of these issues, see Bachman 1990 Ch. 8.)

A test which aims to be 'communicative' might wish to avoid circumscribing the language of candidates and manipulating their responses in over-rigid situations. It may attempt instead to offer candidates situations where they can respond authentically and flexibly (Harrison 1991). But, its success in achieving this will depend primarily on the candidates themselves: on their willingness to suspend disbelief, to use language for meaning and to engage creatively in the task proposed.

Just as communicativeness and authenticity are not inherent properties of tests, neither is backwash. Backwash depends on the ways in which teachers interpret test requirements and bring them into the classroom. Teachers do, in fact, have considerable room for manoeuvre. The challenge, of course, is to respond to students' legitimate goal of passing the test while at the same time being true to our own principles and theoretical stances. The approaches to teaching articulated in this book represent one way of helping students to engage authentically with 'communicative' tests and hence perform to the best of their ability in the exam situation.

Exam practice in class is legitimate, since it is widely agreed that familiarity with the methods and formats of a particular language test tends to improve performance on it. But this does not have to be limiting for the teacher: Prodromou (1995) describes many ways of making the driest exam practice more genuinely educational. He emphasizes the use of personalization and humour, and the creative use of interaction patterns – all ideas which appear in this book too.

Creative exam practice in class has other benefits apart from just preparing for the exam. Many students express a desire for some sort of regular test, to help them perceive their own progress. Informal continuous assessment, though helpful to the teacher, may not always meet students' desire for *explicit* information about the stages they have reached.

The incorporation of creative exam practice into the classroom can help solve this problem. Pollitt (1991) points out that whereas summative assessment (as in the exam itself) necessarily provides a definitive judgement on the candidate's ability, formative assessment (throughout the course) does not only concern itself with whether a response meets certain criteria for correctness. Rather, it assesses the *quality* of the attempt in detail; there is always the possibility of doing better next time.

Therefore the incorporation of test-type activities into a task-based classroom (see Willis 1996) for formative assessment is particularly suitable. Students initially get exam practice by doing tasks in a private, non-threatening context. Their subsequent reflection on their performance, including peer and teacher feedback as appropriate, serves a dual purpose. It provides a point of comparison with their current level of achievement. It also contributes to the planning stage which is a prerequisite for the report phase of the task-based cycle. (See Willis, Paper 6.)

To give students extra information in their formative assessment, teachers can prepare written or taped examples of tasks as carried out by more competent speakers of the target language. These examples will both assist the students to judge their current level of achievement and also provide them with exposure which is equally helpful both for exam practice and for broader learning.

It would also be possible for teachers to repeat tasks. This repetition would help students to see that progress is not simply a matter of moving from easier to harder tasks, but also of performing the same task at a different level of skill. It could be very motivating for students to record themselves on the same or similar tasks at reasonable intervals in time, and then to analyse their progress.

In this section, then, we have seen that exams are not just something that 'happens to' teachers and learners. Teachers in particular have a great deal of influence on the backwash effect of tests. By engaging with test formats and adapting them in class to their own views of language, learning and methodological change and innovation, teachers contribute to a theoretical debate and achieve insights which may well work their way into public exams in time. 'Washforward' is not a term that seems to appear in the literature, but it happens in life and every exam class can be a part of it.

Appendix

List of examinations referred to in this paper
CAE: Certificate of Advanced English
CCSE: Certificate of Communicative Skills in English
FCE: First Certificate in English
KET: Key English Test
PET: Preliminary English Test

Sue Wharton teaches on the MSc in Teaching English/ English for Specific Purposes at Aston University, Birmingham, UK. Her previous post was with the University of London Examination and Assessment Council. Her current interests are language testing and descriptions of academic discourse.

Acknowledgements
I would like to thank staff at UCLES who kindly provided factual information about Cambridge EFL exams. Any inaccuracies or omissions are of course my own. The excerpts are reproduced by permission of the University of Cambridge Local Examinations Syndicate.

Curriculum innovation, teamwork and the management of change

16

Katie Jennings and Tom Doyle

Project background

This paper describes a curriculum development project carried out at the Language Centre of Ireland, a relatively small private EFL school situated in Dublin, Ireland. The project took place over a period of 15 months and involved all members of staff led by a core curriculum team of six members. The teaching staff all possess post-graduate TEFL qualifications, and their experience ranges from 1 to 25 years. No members of the staff lay claim to specific curriculum expertise. The project also involved some 260 learners from 28 different countries. Our existing curriculum was broadly based on a communicative approach.

The project was motivated by an on-going drive to maintain and improve the quality of the services we offered to our learners and was an integral part of our institutional agenda for managed change.

There was also a need to take into account new developments in teaching and learning. The rise and rise of discourse, socio-cultural awareness and language awareness were just some of the issues that we felt were not adequately addressed in our current curriculum, and that should be explicitly dealt with in our new curriculum framework.

Our then existing programme was based on the communicative approach, ie a functional syllabus with a methodological emphasis on creating communication gaps between learners, maximizing learner talking time, integrating the four skills, etc. However, there was a problem in that it was becoming harder and harder to define, as it was increasingly becoming all things to all people. There was a recognized need for a coherent, principled framework which would take into account some of the new developments described above. The experience of the teaching staff ranged from those who had taught through grammar translation and audio-lingualism and been trained into the communicative approach, and those for whom it was the established paradigm on entry to the profession. There was a danger of our programme being described as communicative, but in reality being an unprincipled eclecticism, varying from teacher to teacher. In addition, as the teaching staff had become more experienced and sophisticated over the years, there was a need to put in place a curriculum model which would allow for further teacher development to be directed as a team effort, and not as unrelated individual efforts.

Not all learners are enamoured of the communicative approach and we felt that we needed a curriculum framework which paid more than lip service to the notion of catering for a variety of learning styles.

Moreover, the teacher training team was frustrated by courses which were constructed around a PPP framework. This framework was not reflective of what actually happened in the classrooms that the trainees observed, nor was it a flexible and appropriate planning procedure for trainee teachers.

We needed a more coherent way to prioritize the needs of short stay learners, particularly on summer courses.

Lastly, there was a pedagogic and marketing need for a programme description for our learners which was closer in reality to what they actually encountered in our classes.

The need for a new management model of change

While there was a general recognition on the part of the academic staff that there was a need to reassess the curriculum area, it was considered to be such a daunting task that an explicit management model was required. The model, which we shall describe below, was one which we had successfully implemented on previous projects, such as teacher development and customer service, among others. However, we had never applied it on such a large scale, nor on such a central policy issue as curriculum design. We had come to this model through analysing previous false starts.

In the past, the approach most frequently adopted involved the assignment of a single 'expert' to a given project, reporting only upwards to the Director, and feeding back to the rest of the staff only on project completion. It is important to stress that previous disappointments did not stem from a lack of expertise or commitment on the part of staff members involved, but were rooted in the lack of a principled, coherent model for the management of change.

Firstly, as the Director was essentially a supervisor and not a participant, there was no real shared understanding of the need to set and review interim objectives, and the lack of measurement mechanisms resulted in unrealistic estimates of what resources to allocate to the project. This resulted in cost overruns, missed deadlines and frustration.

The lack of feedback loops to the rest of the staff resulted in an absence of understanding. While staff could identify the problem and indeed welcomed change, there were no mechanisms to involve them in the project. We would argue that genuine commitment can only be generated through an understanding of, and real participation in, the processes of change. Without such involvement, staff cannot be expected to offer real commitment derived from a shared understanding. Nor can they effectively implement the outcome when they have been alienated from the process that created it.

The lack of a coherent model for the management of innovation meant that all projects were discrete and unrelated efforts, contributing little or nothing to either institutional or personal development, in that there was no development of skills or abilities to carry into other projects.

It is indeed ironic that such a product-driven model of the management of change is almost inevitably bound to fail to produce an effective outcome, precisely because of its disregard for understanding and managing the process of any project, and its neglect of fundamental issues concerning people management. Drawing on reflection we developed a new set of assumptions and principles.

Some principles of the management of change

Stimulate participation

We believe that people support what they have helped to create and that shared participation utilizes all resources, mobilizes energy, and stimulates creative thinking and thus produces best results. However, we also took the view that participation does not simply happen, but that it needs to be facilitated. We set about equipping ourselves with the skills to do this. We first surveyed the available reading in this area and then established pilot teamwork development in which some members of staff were assisted in strengthening their team effectiveness. Based on this experience they could assess the likely impact of teamwork applied to the whole school. We then carried out a series of team building workshops for all staff, facilitated by external consultants. Such team work skills included time management, objective setting, conflict solving, candour, communication, critique and a commitment to quality. This process of team building was pivotal in developing the attitudes and skills required to tackle subsequent tasks. It provided us with a common language and shared understanding of process concepts to describe and evaluate the way in which we work together to achieve goals. It was also desirable that projects should result in the creation of skills and abilities of team members to carry into other projects.

Focus on real issues

We believe that real fulfilment comes from taking action which makes a difference to the immediate working environment, in that projects undertaken should be transparently relevant to daily tasks, and related to professional problems. Hence we formulated among all of our staff an action agenda. From this we established our priorities, which we were committed to follow through. Initially we focused on less complex issues which allowed participants to gain confidence in the process of change. For example, in the teacher development programme we drew up an action plan of issues to be addressed. From that, we chose to set up a scheme of training in computer skills, a high priority for teaching staff and management. This was an easy project in that it was non-contentious, easily measurable and was directly related to everyday tasks. Similarly we focused on communications within the school, working with all the staff in terms of who needed to communicate what to whom, when and how. Again, it was non-contentious and was directly related to everyday problems.

Focus on staffing

Change needs the understanding and commitment of all those affected by or involved in its implementation. But it is a practical impossibility to involve everybody in every task. In staffing each core project team, we opted for a small number of key staff in a position to support the whole effort. We chose staff on the basis of assessed skills (eg previous teaching), knowledge (academic record) and attitude in terms of openness to innovation. The latter was always the key element in staffing decisions. But we also allowed scope for members to 'volunteer' their participation. Once established the team took control and responsibility. Decision-making power concerning the setting of objectives, the allocation of resources, the division of tasks and other process decisions resided within the team itself, not outside it. Decisions on rewards, including pay, were also agreed at the outset.

Focus on objectives

It is often easy to identify the need for change – where practice has become ritualized or fossilized. Agreeing on the direction of change is another matter. Thus at the outset it is important to develop a model of the project from start to finish. While ultimate outcomes need to be challenging and set high standards to which staff can commit their energies, we also believe that a properly designed project needs clearly defined interim objectives and outcomes. The team's first task is to establish goals and timetables which can be regularly reviewed. The key to this common sense notion of planning lies in manageable, concrete goals in limited time frames. Defining intermediate and short-term goals allows for immediate feedback and correction.

Focus on performance appraisal

We believed it essential to have some concrete measures to evaluate performance in order to maintain control and direction in a project and to keep the project on schedule and budget. Appraisal was applied concurrently, that is the team monitored and assessed its own performance. Appraisal was reinforced through report back to general staff. And finally, for major work, such as the curriculum project, appraisal was carried out by an external academic assessor. By building in time for reflection on the process we could develop concrete measures for improvement and reinforce our skills.

The curriculum project

These were the background assumptions which the team had experience of putting into practice before they came together to begin work on the new curriculum. With these principles in mind, we would now like to describe our approach to the curriculum design project. It is important to stress that a large debt is owed to the AMEP programme as described by Nunan (1988, 1992). This constituted the core of our chosen academic model. Part of the challenge for us was to find ways of implementing this in a small, single institution, given all the limitations that this implies. However, the principal challenge lay in ensuring that all staff felt true ownership of it and that we applied and elaborated on the model in a way which was true to our own situation and learners. Our process is outlined in figure 1 below.

Figure 1

PHASES OF THE CURRICULUM PROJECT

PHASE 1: DATA GATHERING

- Detailed survey of client needs and preferred learning approaches
- Collation of previous student feedback
- Survey of teaching staff
- Evaluation of strengths and weaknesses of current programme

PHASE 2: DESIGN AND ELABORATION

- Choice of new curriculum model (a learner-centred, task-based approach)
- Presentation of model to all teaching and support staff
- Team development of curriculum goals, level descriptions, attainment scales, learning units
- Cascade meetings to share and evaluate on-going work of team with all teaching staff
- Evaluation by external academic consultant

PHASE 3: TRIAL AND TRAINING

- Teacher reading programme
- Case studies of new approach with several trial classes
- Materials development
- Staff training sessions and interactive poster display

PHASE 4: IMPLEMENTATION

- Implementation
- On-going observation and staff development sessions, combined with individual support
- On-going materials development
- Formal and informal elicitation of client feedback
- Evaluation by external academic consultant

Phase 1: Data gathering

Phase 1 consisted of team formation and data gathering. As all of the academic staff could not participate all of the time, it was necessary to establish a core team. Considerable thought went into the establishment of this team as it was crucial that its members were drawn from sub-teams in the academic staff so that its work would naturally 'cascade' or flow over in both formal and informal modes to the rest of the staff. This process of cascading involves participating staff keeping others informed on a small group basis. This is described in further detail below. In selecting team members, 'expertise' concerning curriculum design was not a prerequisite, given, as stated above, that attitude is considered to be the most important quality of effective team members. In this sense, attitude does not mean unquestioning acquiescence to management initiatives, but a positive willingness to commit to, and participate in, a process of change. In keeping with the principles laid out above, the team also had to contain decision-making powers within it. Thus, the team was made up of the academic director, the head of teacher support, members of the teacher training team and members of the teaching staff, whose experience ranged from twenty years to three, and across all proficiency levels and learning styles.

The team then set about data gathering. The head of teacher support researched the most current academic theory and practice, and prepared a composite bibliography spanning the area for the rest of the team. The director collated previous student feedback. The entire team designed a very detailed learning questionnaire covering learners' previous learning experience, reasons for learning English, and learning style preferences. This questionnaire was implemented by all of the teaching staff. The team also evaluated the strengths and weaknesses of the current programme. The findings of the learner survey were presented in a poster to both the teaching staff and the learners. The learners were remarkably interested in the results and were themselves surprised at the diversity of learning styles reported. In itself, this was a good exercise in raising learner awareness of the many different approaches to learning a new language. This phase was extremely important, as it satisfied many of the principles for an effective management of change outlined above. Firstly, the survey of learners involved those most central to the curriculum process – teachers and learners – and gave them a very strong input from the very beginning of the process, which determined the curriculum model chosen and implemented. The problem-solving approach gave all concerned greater confidence, as the task became one of solving issues of immediate concern, and internally generated, rather than attempting to impose an externally generated and prescriptive curriculum. The results of the survey threw up interesting findings, which also acted as a spur to development and informed our decision making concerning a new model considerably. As with other studies of learning styles (Willing 1988), we found that, contrary to staffroom folklore, biographical variables such as nationality, age, etc were not good predictors of learning style. While there were variations in learner preferences, all the learners consistently displayed the belief that interaction and feedback are central to language learning. They also place a high value on target-language rich sources of input such as newspapers, TV, etc. They also agreed that explicit attention needs to be paid to the language system itself. Some differences emerged in that higher proficiency level learners (intermediate+) were less enamoured of some of the more obviously classroom aspects of communicative methodology such as games and roleplay than lower proficiency level learners. Curiously, 20% more females than males were interested in learning about local culture. The most distinctive group was that of the Asian learners, whose previous learning experience was more traditional grammar-translation. They displayed a preference for highly structured activities with clear and tight role definitions and procedures, eg memorizing dialogues, games and pair/groupwork, while rejecting looser activities such as debates and projects. It appears that exposure to a different learning experience resulted in these learners selecting those aspects of a communicative methodology which are consonant with their culture and rejecting those which are not. These factors led us to believe that we needed to address these concerns through a more explicit exploration of cross-cultural issues and greater learner involvement in decision making concerning their learning.

Phase 2: Design and elaboration

Phase 2 consisted of the elaboration of the new curriculum model. The core team collated all the Phase 1 data and chose the new curriculum model: a learner-centred, task-based approach. This model consists of two strands. Firstly, that the curriculum is learner centred in that the learners' learning styles and objective and subjective needs must be central to each teacher's planning processes. This involves constant needs analysis in a broad sense, and consultation with the learners concerning the goals, activities and topics of the curriculum. The task-based approach allows for this in that it consists of sets of learning units for each proficiency level. Each learning unit consists of a real-life task, eg watching TV, applying for a job, and a specification of learning objectives and situations for each one. They also contain the structures, functions, notions/topics, lexis, phonology, learning strategies, socio-cultural awareness and pedagogic tasks (classroom learning activities such as roleplay, group writing, etc) associated with each. In the past, the curriculum centred around a set of language functions, structures and lexis and suggested activities which the teacher implemented. In the new model, learners' needs (classified in terms of real-life tasks and learning style preferences) form the centre of the teacher's planning process. This model was felt to provide the coherent framework which we were seeking, while at the same time containing an internal dynamic which would cater for changes in student base as well as advances in knowledge concerning language teaching and learning. The model was then presented to all of the staff, academic, administrative and marketing, as there was a need for a shared understanding of such a central policy. The team then together developed curriculum goals, level descriptors and attainment scales. Learning units for each proficiency level were developed by individual team members, some in conjunction with members of the teaching staff who were not members of the core team, in order to increase levels of participation. Each team member then held cascade meetings with teachers working at the same level of proficiency. At these meetings the core team member presented to the teachers at that level the draft learning units that he or she had prepared. The purpose of these cascade meetings was to share the work of the team, as well as to enable the general teaching staff to contribute to and evaluate the work completed so far. These meetings also fulfilled a further purpose, in that the teaching staff could share in the process of creation, and thus claim ownership of the final outcome, as well as participate in the process of change and hence alleviate the natural apprehension that some teaching staff may experience. At the end of this phase, an external academic consultant was invited in to evaluate the work in progress. His role was to ask questions to help us to clarify our thinking and reflect on our work. He was also asked to pinpoint any issues that we may have overlooked.

Phase 3: Trial and training

Phase 3 consisted of trial of the new approach and training. The trial involved case study classes of the new approach as implemented by core team members, team teaching with staff who were not members of the core team. This again was an opportunity to extend participation beyond the core team and to act as a predictor of the amount and type of training required for those who were not members of the core team. It also explicitly involved the learners in evaluating the new approach. The results of this were presented to the rest of the teaching staff. An intensive training programme took place over three months to allow teaching staff time to fully explore and assimilate the new approach. It consisted of a pre-reading programme followed by training sessions, which included issues such as formal and informal needs analysis, eliciting learner feedback, planning and task-based methodology among others.

Phase 4: Implementation

Phase 4 was the implementation phase. Each teacher was supported through individual help and observation by the head of teacher support. There was a marked increase in collaborative planning and materials pooling by teachers working at the same proficiency level, initiated by the teachers themselves. Initially, some teachers reported feeling 'in limbo' and admitted to feeling 'fear, apprehension and confusion' arising out of a concern that they may not be 'doing it right'. At least two development sessions have focused on articulating these doubts and fears. It is important that they are articulated and shared, because unless they are confronted collaboratively, solutions cannot begin to be found. In some areas there is no ready and pat solution, particularly with regard to task-based methodology, which is the major area of concern to us. However, in this model, the solution to these problems lies in collaborative problem solving, in the need for reassurance and support and in viewing the problems as a basis for further projects and opportunities for development. Encouragingly, four teachers this year have chosen to follow MA courses and some of these issues are at the heart of their research agendas. At the end of the first term of implementation, we invited our external academic consultant back to evaluate the implementation process, to fulfil the same role as on his previous visit.

Project outcome

The outcome of the project as regards the learners was, in general, favourable. The heavy emphasis on subjective and objective needs analysis on arrival and as the course develops is reassuring to learners, who enjoy and value 'being taken into the teacher's confidence'. There is a higher reported level of satisfaction with their class among learners. Learners are more aware that their needs are being taken into account and they are more realistic about what can be achieved. The greater group consultation in class leads to enhanced learner understanding of their own personal responsibilities in the learning process and they have displayed a greater increase in self-directedness, reflected in increased and different use of the learner self-access centre. They value the greater use of authentic materials.

The reaction of teachers has also been generally positive. They reported feeling more motivated and committed as they feel the new curriculum more accurately reflects what actually happens in classrooms and is more helpful in the planning process. They report that the learning units in particular help them focus on what may have been overlooked. They appreciate the freedom and increase in teacher responsibility and decision making that it entails. There has also been greater co-operation between teachers.

Problems that still remain concern the nature of real-life tasks, how to time and sequence them, as well as on what basis are larger tasks, eg watching TV, subdivided into more manageable units. Materials are also a problem, as learners insist that they want a textbook, but integrating this into the curriculum on a principled basis is difficult to achieve. There is also a need for a lot more authentic, real-life material than we currently have. Teachers also report that planning takes longer. Finally, there is the perennial problem of mismatches between teaching and learning styles. While this is not a problem inherent in a task-based curriculum, it is none the less a real one. We would argue that one of the primary benefits of this model is that such naturally occurring mismatches are not left to fester, but are explicitly articulated and explored in the classroom.

In order to maintain an internal dynamic, and to prevent the curriculum becoming set in stone, it is crucial that it is viewed as a framework, not a blueprint. In that the model itself sets heavy emphasis on constant needs analysis and learner consultation, there is an in-built re-evaluation mechanism. The problems highlighted above also provide the basis of further action agendas, particularly for the teacher development programme.

In summary, we believe that the management of student learning and the management of staff development are not independent but interdependent systems and we have tried to adopt a common set of principles to the management of both.

Katie Jennings is Head of Teacher Support at the Language Centre of Ireland in Dublin. Her areas of interest include teacher development, task-based learning and curriculum design. **Tom Doyle** has been Director of the Language Centre of Ireland in Dublin for the last twelve years. His main interests are EFL management, testing and evaluation.

Acknowledgements
We would like to take this opportunity to thank all of the participants in the project described in this paper. The core curriculum team consisted of Sarah Cleasby, David Doyle, Catherine Geraghty and Perla Moraghan. Without their commitment and enthusiasm, in addition to that of all of the teaching staff, this project would never have come to fruition. We would also like to acknowledge the debt we owe to our team-building consultants, Harry Conway, Jimmy Fischer and Páraic MacDonnchadha of PCS, Dublin. Finally we would like to thank Peter Maingay for the supportive and valuable role he played as our external consultant.

References and bibliography

1 Paradigm shift and the language teaching profession

Dufeu, B. 1994 *Teaching Myself* (OUP)

Grundy, P. 1989 A critique of accepted pre-service TT. Serialized in two issues of *The Teacher Trainer, vol. 3, nos. 2 and 3* (see also M. Parrott's reply in *vol. 4, no. 1, 1990*)

Kerr, P. 1993 Language training on pre-service courses for native speakers. In *Modern English Teacher, vol. 2, no. 4*

Kuhn, T. 1970 (2nd ed.) *The Structure of Scientific Revolutions* (Chicago University Press)

Lewis, M. 1993 *The Lexical Approach* (LTP)

Maley, A. 1993 Finding the centre. In *The Teacher Trainer, vol. 7, no. 3*

Morrow, A. 1993 From behind the barricades. In *The Teacher Trainer, vol. 7, no. 3*

Nattinger, J. and De Carrico, J. 1992 *Lexical Phrases in Language Teaching* (OUP)

Oller, J. W. Jnr. and Richard-Amato, P. A. (eds.) 1983 *Methods That Work* (Newbury House)

Prabhu, N. S. 1987 *Second Language Pedagogy* (OUP)

Sheen, R. 1994 A critical analysis of the advocacy of the task-based syllabus. In *TESOL Quarterly, vol. 28, no. 1*

Skehan, P. 1993 A framework for the implementation of task-based learning. In *IATEFL Conference Report: Plenaries*

Stevick, E. 1980 *Teaching Languages, a Way and Ways* (Newbury House)

Stevick, E. 1986 *Images and Options in the Language Classroom* (CUP)

Sweetman, J. 1993 Higher thoughts on teacher training. In *Guardian Education, Oct. 4 1993*

The Teacher Trainer, vol. 8, no. 1, 1994 'Conference Report'

UCLES/RSA 1993 *Consultation Document Proposal For Pre-Service Certificates*, Sept. 1993

Wilberg, P. 1987 *One To One* (LTP)

Willis, D. 1993 Syllabus, corpus and data-driven learning. In *IATEFL Conference Report: Plenaries*

Woodward, T. 1992 Training for medical general practice. In *TESOL France News, vol. 12, no. 1*

Woodward, T. 1991 *Models and Metaphors in Language Teacher Training* (CUP)

Wright, T. and Bolitho, R. 1993 Language awareness. In *ELT Journal, vol. 47, no. 4* (OUP)

2 Implications of a lexical view of the language

Lewis, M. 1993 *The Lexical Approach* (LTP)

Nattinger, J. and De Carrico, J. 1992 *Lexical Phrases in Language Teaching* (OUP)

Willis, D. 1990 *The Lexical Syllabus* (Collins COBUILD)

A seminal paper on lexical items was:

Pawley, A. and Syder, F. 1983 Two puzzles for linguistic theory: nativelike selection and nativelike fluency. In Richards, J. C. and Schmidt, R. (eds.) *Language and Communication* (Longman)

3 Second language acquisition research and task-based instruction

Anderson, A. and Lynch, T. 1987 *Listening* (OUP)

Bachman, L. and Palmer, A. S. (in press) *Language Testing in Practice* (OUP)

Bolinger, D. 1975 Meaning and memory. In *Forum Linguisticum, vol. 1, pp 2-14*

Brown, G., Anderson, A., Shilcock, R. and Yule, G. 1984 *Teaching the Spoken Language* (CUP)

Brumfit, C. and Johnson, K. 1979 *Communicative Methodology in Language Teaching* (CUP)

Bygate, M. 1988 Units of oral expression and language learning in small group interaction. In *Applied Linguistics, vol. 9, no. 1, pp 59-82*

Carroll, J. B. 1975 *The Teaching of French as a Foreign Language in Eight Countries* (John Wiley & Sons, New York)

Crookes, G. 1989 Planning and interlanguage variation. In *Studies in Second Language Acquisition, vol. 11, pp 367-83*

Doughty, C. and Pica, T. 1986 Information gap tasks: do they facilitate second language acquisition? In *TESOL Quarterly, vol. 20, pp 305-25*

Duff, P. 1986 Another look at interlanguage talk: taking task to task. In Day, R. (ed.) *Talking to Learn* (Newbury House)

Ellis, R. 1985 *Understanding Second Language Acquisition* (OUP)

Ellis, R. 1987 Interlanguage variability in narrative discourse. In *Studies in Second Language Acquisition, vol. 2, pp 12-20*

Ellis, R. 1994 *The Study of Second Language Acquisition* (OUP)

Fathman, A. 1976 Variables affecting the successful learning of English as a second language. In *TESOL Quarterly, vol. 10, pp 433-41*

Foster, P. and Skehan, P. 1994 *The influence of planning on performance in task-based learning.* Paper presented at the British Association of Applied Linguistics Conference, Leeds, Sept. 1994

Gregg, K. 1984 Krashen's Monitor and Occam's Razor. In *Applied Linguistics, vol. 5, pp 79-100*

Grellet, F. 1981 *Developing Reading Skills* (CUP)

Hilgard, E. R. and Bower, G. 1975 *Theories of Learning* (Prentice Hall)

Hubbard, P., Jones, H., Thornton, B. and Wheeler, R. 1983 *A Training Course for TEFL* (OUP)

Hulstijn, J. H. and De Graaf, R. 1994 Under what conditions does explicit knowledge of a second language facilitate the acquisition of implicit knowledge: a research proposal. In *AILA Review, vol. 11, pp 97-112*

Krashen, S. 1985 *The Input Hypothesis* (Longman)

Lightbown, P. 1985 Great expectations: second language acquisition research and classroom teaching. In *Applied Linguistics, vol. 6, pp 173-189*

Long, M. 1983 Does second language acquisition make a difference: a review of the research. In *TESOL Quarterly, vol. 17, pp 359-82*

Long, M. 1988 Instructed interlanguage development. In Beebe, L. (ed.) *Issues in Second Language Acquisition: Multiple Perspectives* (Newbury House)

Long, M. and Crookes, G. 1991 Three approaches to task-based syllabus design. In *TESOL Quarterly, vol. 26, pp 27-55*

Long, M. and Crookes, G. 1993 Units of analysis in syllabus design: the case for task. In Crookes, G. and

Gass, S. (eds.) *Tasks in Pedagogic Context: Integrating Theory and Practice* (Multilingual Matters)

Nunan, D. 1989 *Designing Tasks for the Communicative Classroom* (CUP)

O'Malley, J. M. and Chamot, A. 1990 *Learning Strategies and Second Language Acquisition* (CUP)

Pawley, A. and Syder, F. 1983 Two puzzles for linguistic theory: nativelike selection and nativelike fluency. In Richards, J. C. and Schmidt, R. (eds.) *Language and Communication* (Longman)

Prabhu, N. S. 1987 *Second Language Pedagogy* (OUP)

Rivers, W. 1968 *Teaching Foreign Language Skills* (University of Chicago Press)

Schmidt, R. 1990 The role of consciousness in second language learning. In *Applied Linguistics, vol. 11, pp 17-46*

Schmidt, R. 1994 Deconstructing consciousness: in search of useful definitions for Applied Linguistics. In *AILA Review, vol. 11, pp 11-26*

Skehan, P. 1986 Cluster analysis and the identification of learner types. In Cook, V. J. (ed.) *Experimental Approaches to Second Language Acquisition* (Pergamon Press)

Skehan, P. 1989 *Individual Differences in Second Language Learning* (Edward Arnold)

Skehan, P. 1992 Strategies in second language acquisition. In *Thames Valley University Working Papers in English Language Teaching, no. 1*

Skehan, P. 1994 A framework for the implementation of task-based learning. In *Thames Valley University Working Papers in English Language Teaching, no. 3*

Skehan, P. (in press) Analysability, accessibility, and ability for use. In Cook, G. and Seidlhofer, B. (eds.) *For Henry Widdowson: Principles and practice in the study of language and learning: A Festschrift on the occasion of his 60th birthday* (OUP)

Skehan, P. and Foster, P. (in preparation) The influence of planning and post-task activities on accuracy and complexity in task-based learning.

Stern, H. H. 1983 *Fundamental Concepts of Language Teaching* (OUP)

Swain, M. 1985 Communicative competence: some roles of comprehensible input and comprehensible output in its development. In Gass, S. and Madden, C. (eds.) *Input in Second Language Acquisition* (Newbury House)

Swain, M. (in press) Three functions of output in second language acquisition. In Cook, G. and Seidlhofer, B. (eds.) *For Henry Widdowson: Principles and practice in the study of language and learning: A Festschrift on the occasion of his 60th birthday* (OUP)

Van Patten, B. 1994 Evaluating the role of consciousness in SLA: terms, linguistic features, and research methodology. In *AILA Review, vol. 11, pp 27-36*

White, R. V. 1988 *The ELT Curriculum* (Blackwell)

Widdowson, H. G. 1989 Knowledge of language and ability for use. In *Applied Linguistics, vol. 10, p 2*

Willis, D. 1993 Syllabus, corpus, and data-driven learning. In *IATEFL Conference Report: Plenaries*

Willis, J. and Willis, D. 1988 *The Collins COBUILD English Course, Level 1 Teacher's Book* (Collins)

Wilson, D. 1994 Context and relevance. In Brown, G., Malkmjaer, K., Pollitt, A. and Williams, J. (eds.) *Language and Understanding* (OUP)

4 What learners know and what they need to learn

Brown, H. D. 1994 *Principles of Language Learning and Teaching* (Prentice Hall)

Chomsky, N. 1959 Review of Skinner, B. F. 1957 Verbal behaviour. In *Language, vol. 35, pp 26-58*

Chomsky, N. 1981 *Lectures on Government and Binding* (Foris, Dordrecht)

Chomsky, N. 1989 Some notes on economy of derivation and presentation. In *MIT Working Papers in Linguistics, vol. 10, pp 43-74*

Cook, V. 1988 *Chomsky's Universal Grammar: An Introduction* (Blackwell)

Eubank, L. 1991 *Point Counterpoint: Universal Grammar in the Second Language* (Benjamins, Amsterdam)

Fries, C. 1945 *Teaching and Learning English as a Foreign Language* (University of Michigan Press)

James, C. 1980 *Contrastive Analysis* (Longman)

Lado, R. 1957 *Linguistics across Cultures* (University of Michigan Press)

Larsen-Freeman, D. and Long, M. 1991 *An Introduction to Second Language Acquisition Research* (Longman)

Van Els, T., Bongaerts, T., Extra, G., van Os, C. and Janssen-van Dieten, A.-M. 1984 *Applied Linguistics and the Learning and Teaching of Foreign Languages* (Edward Arnold)

White, L. 1989 *Universal Grammar and Second Language Acquisition* (Benjamins, Amsterdam)

Willis, D. 1990 *The Lexical Syllabus* (Collins COBUILD)

5 Accuracy, fluency and conformity

Brumfit, C. 1984a *Theoretical Implications of Interlanguage Studies for Language Teaching*. In Davies et al (1984)

Brumfit, C. 1984b *Communicative Methodology in Language Teaching* (CUP)

Corder, S. P. 1967 The Significance of Learner's Errors. In *IRAL 5* (reproduced in Richards, J. C. (ed.) 1974 *Error Analysis: Perspectives on Second Language* (Longman))

Davies, A., Criper, C. and Howatt, A. B. R. 1984 *Interlanguage* (Edinburgh University Press)

Ellis, R. 1993 Second language acquisition research: how does it help teachers? An interview with Rod Ellis in *ELT Journal, vol. 47, no. 1* (OUP)

Long, M. and Crookes, G. 1992 Three approaches to task-based learning. In *TESOL Quarterly, vol. 26, no. 1*

Rutherford, W. E. 1987 *Second Language Grammar: Learning and Teaching* (Longman)

Sinclair, J. M. 1988 Collocation. In Steele, R. and Threadgold, T. (eds.) *Language Topics* (Benjamins, Amsterdam) (reproduced in Sinclair, J. M. 1991 *Corpus, Concordance, Collocation* (OUP))

Widdowson, H. G. 1989 Knowledge of language and ability for use. In *Applied Linguistics*, vol. 10, pp 128-37

Willis, J. R. 1992 Inner and outer: spoken discourse in the language classroom. In Coulthard, R. M. *Advances In Spoken Discourse Analysis* (Routledge)

6 A flexible framework for task-based learning

Ellis, R. 1993 Talking shop. In *ELT Journal, vol. 47, no. 1* (OUP)

Labov, W. 1972 *Language in the Inner City* (University of Pennsylvania Press)

Prabhu, N. S. 1987 *Second Language Pedagogy* (OUP)

Willis, D. and Willis, J. 1987 Varied activities for variable language. In *ELT Journal, vol. 41, no. 1* (OUP)

Willis, J. 1991 *First Lessons Teacher's Book,* Introduction (Collins COBUILD)

7 Consciousness-raising activities in the language classroom

Ellis, R. 1992 *Second Language Acquisition and Language Pedagogy* (Multilingual Matters)

Ellis, R. 1993 Second language acquisition research: how does it help teachers? An interview with Rod Ellis. In *ELT Journal, vol. 47, no. 1, pp 3-11*

Hoey, M. 1991 *Patterns of Lexis in Text* (OUP)

James, C. 1994 Explaining grammar to its learners. In Bygate, M., Tonkyn, A. and Williams, E. (eds.) *Grammar and the Language Teacher* (Prentice Hall)

Krashen, S. and Terell, T. 1983 *The Natural Approach* (Pergamon Press)

Lakoff, G. and Johnson, M. 1980 *Metaphors We Live By* (University of Chicago Press)

Pawley, A. and Syder, F. 1983 Two puzzles for linguistic theory: nativelike selection and nativelike fluency. In Richards, J. C. and Schmidt, R. (eds.) *Language and Communication* (Longman)

Rutherford, W. E. 1987 *Second Language Grammar: Learning and Teaching* (Longman)

Sharwood-Smith, M. 1981 Consciousness-raising and the second language learner. In *Applied Linguistics, vol. 2, no. 2*. (reprinted in Rutherford and Sharwood-Smith (eds.) 1988 *Grammar and Second Language Teaching* (Newbury House))

Sinclair, J. M. 1988 Collocation. In Steele, R. and Threadgold, T. *Language Topics* (Benjamins, Amsterdam) (re-published in Sinclair, J. M. 1991 *Corpus Concordance Collocation* (OUP))

Swales, J. 1990 *Genre Analysis* (CUP)

Willis, D. 1993 Syllabus, corpus and data-driven learning. In *IATEFL Conference Report: Plenaries*

8 ARC: a descriptive model for classroom work on language

Wajnryb, R. 1989 Is PPP passé? In *TEA News, Autumn 89*

The ARC analysis and some of the example lesson material in this article are used in Scrivener, J. 1994 *Learning Teaching* (Heinemann).

9 Grammar for trainee teachers

Andrews, S. 1994 The grammatical knowledge/awareness of native-speaker EFL teachers. In Bygate et al 1994, pp 69-89

Batstone, R. 1994a Product and process: grammar in the second language classroom. In Bygate et al 1994, pp 224-36

Batstone, R. 1994b *Grammar* (OUP)

Bell, J. and Gower, R. 1991 *Intermediate Matters* (Longman)

Bolitho, R. 1988 Language awareness on teacher training courses. In Duff 1988, pp 72-84

Bygate, M., Tonkyn, A. and Williams, E. (eds.) 1994 *Grammar and the Language Teacher* (Prentice Hall)

Chalker, S. 1994 Pedagogical grammar: principles and problems. In Bygate et al 1994, pp 31-44

Duff, T. (ed.) 1988 *Explorations in Teacher Training* (Longman)

Grundy, P. 1989 Gone to teachers every one: a critique of accepted pre-service teacher training. In *The Teacher Trainer, vol. 3, no. 2, pp 4-10*

Holden, S. (ed.) 1979 *Teacher Training* (MEP)

Kerr, P. 1993a Language training on pre-service courses for native speakers. In *Modern English Teacher, vol. 2, no. 4, pp 40-3*

Kerr, P. 1993b What makes an EFL teacher. In 1993 CTEFLA Conference Report (Birmingham) (UCLES)

Leech, G. 1994 Students' grammar – teachers' grammmar – learners' grammar. In Bygate et al 1994, pp 17-30

Lewis, M. 1993 *The Lexical Approach* (LTP)

Murphy, R. 1985 *English Grammar in Use* (CUP)

Odlin, T. (ed.) 1994 *Perspectives on Pedagogical Grammar* (CUP)

Pearce, K. 1991 The cost of failure. In *The Teacher Trainer vol. 5, no. 3, pp 17-18*

Rinvolucri, M. (ed.) 1991 RSA Cert. TEFL trainees speak out. In *The Teacher Trainer, vol. 5, no. 1, pp 26-9*

Rutherford, W. E. 1987 *Second Language Grammar: Learning and Teaching* (Longman)

Shaw, P. A. 1979 Handling a language component in a teacher training course. In Holden, S. 1979, pp 12-14

Skehan, P. 1994 Second language acquisition strategies, interlanguage development and task-based learning. In Bygate et al 1994, pp 175-99

Taylor, J. R. 1989 *Linguistic Categorization* (OUP)

Tomlin, R. S. 1994 Functional grammars, pedagogical grammars and communicative language teaching. In Odlin 1994, pp 140-78

UCLES 1994 *CTEFLA Pilot Syllabus* (UCLES)

Wright, T. and Bolitho, R. 1993 Language awareness: a missing link in language teacher education? In *ELT Journal, vol. 47, no. 4, pp 292-304*

10 Learning to learn how to teach: developing expertise through experience

Swan, M. 1985 A critical look at the communicative approach. In *ELT Journal, vol. 39, no. 1, pp 2-12 and vol. 39, no. 2, pp 76-87* (OUP)

Stevick, E. 1976 *Memory, Meaning and Method* (Newbury House)

University of Cambridge Local Examinations Syndicate/RSA Examinations Board *Certificate in the Teaching of English as a Foreign Language to Adults: Guidelines and Regulations for Centres, Course Tutors and Assessors* 1993/1994

University of Cambridge Local Examinations Syndicate *Cambridge Integrated Language Teaching Schemes: Certificate in the Teaching of English as a Foreign Language to Adults* (Pilot Syllabus) Aug. 1994

Wallace, M. 1991 *Training Foreign Language Teachers: a reflective approach* (CUP)

Willis, D. 1990 *The Lexical Syllabus* (Collins COBUILD)

Woodward, T. 1991 *Models and Metaphors in Language Teacher Training* (CUP)

11 Introducing innovations into your teaching

Allwright, R. and Bailey, K. 1991 *Focus on the Language Classroom* (CUP)

Allwright, R. 1993 Integrating 'research' and 'pedagogy' appropriate criteria and practical possibilities. In Edge, J. and Richards, K. (eds.) *Teachers Develop Teachers Research* (Heinemann)

Freeman, D. 1990 Intervening in practice teaching. In Richards, J. C. and Nunan, D. (eds.) *Second Language Teacher Education* (CUP)

Freeman, D. 1992 Language teacher education, emerging discourse, and change in classroom practice. In Flowerdew, Brock and Itsia (eds.) *Perspectives on Second Language Teacher Education* (Hongkong City Polytechnic)

Nunan, D. 1992 *Research Methods in Language Learning* (CUP)

Orem, R. 1981 TESOL entering the eighties: some professional perspectives. In *TESOL Newsletter 15*

Parrott, M. 1993 *Tasks for Language Teachers* (CUP)

Wajnryb, R. 1992 *Classroom Observation Tasks* (CUP)

12 Doing the task better: how planning time influences students' performance

Crookes, G. 1989 Planning and interlanguage variation. In *Studies in Second Language Acquisition, vol. 11, pp 367-83*

Doughty, C. and Pica, T. 1986 Information gap tasks: do they facilitate second language acquisition? In *TESOL Quarterly, vol. 20, no. 2, pp 305-25*

Ellis, R. 1987 Interlanguage variability in narrative discourse: style-shifting in the use of the past tense. In *Studies in Second Language Acquisition, vol. 9, pp 12-20*

Krashen, S. 1981 *Second Language Acquisition and Second Language Learning* (Pergamon Press)

Krashen, S. 1982 *Principles and Practice in Second Language Acquisition* (Pergamon Press)

Long, M. 1983 Native-speaker/non native-speaker conversation and the negotiation of meaning. In *Applied Linguistics, vol. 4, pp 126-41*

Varonis, E and Gass, S. 1985 Non-native/non-native conversation: a modal for the negotiation of meaning. In *Applied Linguistics, vol. 6, pp 71-90*

13 Effects of task repetition: appraising the developing language of learners

Anderson, A. and Lynch, T. 1988 *Listening* (OUP)

Brown, G. and Yule, G. 1983 *Discourse Analysis* (CUP)

Bygate, M. 1994 Adjusting the focus: teacher roles in task-based learning of grammar. In Bygate, M., Tonkyn, A. and Williams, E. (eds.) 1994

Bygate, M. and Porter, D. 1991 Dimensions in the acquisition of oral language. In Sadtono, E. (ed.) *Language Acquisition and the Second/Foreign Language Classroom* Anthology Series 28 (Singapore: SEAMEO, RELC)

Bygate, M., Tonkyn, A. and Williams, E. (eds.) 1994 *Grammar and the Language Teacher* (Prentice Hall)

Bygate, M. 1987 *Speaking* (OUP)

Chafe, W. L. (ed.) 1980 *The Pear Stories: Cognitive, Cultural and Linguistic Aspects of Narrative* (Ablex, Norwood, N.J.)

Crookes, G. 1989 Planning and interlanguage variation. In *Studies in Second Language Acquisition, vol. 11, no. 4, pp 267-83*

Crookes, G. and Gass, S. M. (eds.) 1993a *Tasks and Language Learning* (Multilingual Matters)

Crookes, G. and Gass, S. M. (eds.) 1993b *Tasks in a Pedagogical Context* (Multilingual Matters)

Doughty, C. and Pica, T. 1986 Information gap tasks: do they facilitate second language acquisition? In *TESOL Quarterly, vol. 20, no. 2, pp 305-25*

Duff, P. A. 1993 Tasks and interlanguage performance: an SLA perspective. In Crookes, G. and Gass, S. M. (eds.) 1993a

Ellis, R. 1987 Interlanguage variability in narrative discourse: style shifting in the use of the past tense. In *Studies in Second Language Acquisition, vol. 9, pp 12-20*

Færch, C. and Kasper, G. 1983 Plans and strategies in foreign language communication. In Færch, C. and Kasper, G. (eds.) *Strategies in Interlanguage Communication* (Longman)

Garman, M. 1990 *Psycholinguistics* (CUP)

Gass, S. M. and Varonis, E. M. 1985 Task variation and non-native/non-native negotiation of meaning. In Gass, S. M. and Madden, C. G. (eds.) *Input in Second Language Acquisition* (Newbury House)

Levelt, W. J. M. 1978 Skill theory and language learning. In *Studies in Second Language Acquisition, vol. 1, no. 1*

Levelt, W. J. M. 1989 *Speaking: From Intention to Articulation* (Cambridge: MIT Press)

Littlewood, W. 1992 *Teaching Oral Communication: A Methodological Framework* (Blackwell)

Long, M. H. and Crookes, G. 1993 Units of analysis in syllabus design: the case for task. In Crookes, G. and Gass, S. M. (eds.) 1993b

Long, M. H. and Porter, P. A. 1985 Groupwork, interlanguage talk and second language acquisition. In *TESOL Quarterly, vol. 19, no. 2, pp 207-27*

Morrison, D. H. M. and Low, G. 1983 Monitoring and the second language learner. In Richards, J. C. and Schmidt, R. (eds.) *Language and Communication* (Longman)

Nunan, D. 1993 Task-based syllabus design: selecting, grading and sequencing tasks. In Crookes, G. and Gass, S. M. (eds.) 1993b

Pawley, A. and Syder, F. H. 1976 The one clause at a time hypothesis. Unpublished paper read to first congress of the New Zealand Linguistic Society, Auckland

Pica, T. 1987 Second language acquisition, social interaction, and the classroom. In *Applied Linguistics, vol. 8, no. 1, pp 1-25*

Pica, T., Kanagy, R. and Faludon, J. 1993 Choosing and using communication tasks for second language instruction and research. In Crookes, G. and Gass, S. M. (eds.) *Tasks in Language Learning: Integrating Theory and Practice* (Multilingual Matters)

Skehan, P. 1993 A framework for the implementation of task-based learning. In *IATEFL Conference Report: Plenaries*

Skehan, P. 1994 Second language acquisition strategies, interlanguage development and task-based learning. In Bygate, M., Tonkyn, A. and Williams, E. (eds.) 1994

White, L. 1987 Against comprehensible input: the input hypothesis and the development of second language competence. In *Applied Linguistics, vol. 8, pp 95-110*

Widdowson, H. G. 1983 *Learning Purpose and Language Use* (OUP)

15 Testing innovations

A-Angeles, S. 1993 *A concordanced comparison of frequency and collocations of some FCE test items against corpus evidence of actual language use.* Unpublished MSc dissertation, Language Studies Unit, Aston University, Birmingham, UK

Bachman, L. 1990 *Fundamental Considerations of Language Testing* (OUP)

Harrison, A. 1991 Language assessment as theatre. In Alderson and North (eds.) *Language Testing in the 1990s* (Modern English Publications)

Morrow, K. 1986 Evaluating tests of communicative performance. In Portal, M. (ed.) *Innovations in Language Testing* (UK NFER: Nelson)

Morrow, K. 1992 Evaluating communicative tests. In *IATEFL Testing SIG Newsletter*

Pollitt, A. 1991 Giving students a sporting chance: assessment by counting and by judging. In Alderson and North (eds.) *Language Testing in the 1990s* (Modern English Publications)

Prodromou, L. 1995 The backwash effect: from testing to teaching. In *ELT Journal, vol. 49, no. 1, pp 13-25*

Skehan, P. 1991 Progress in language testing: the 1990s. In Alderson and North (eds.) *Language Testing in the 1990s* (Modern English Publications)

University of Cambridge Local Examinations Syndicate *Specifications and handbooks for CAE, CCSE, FCE, KET, PET* (UCLES)

Willis, D. 1990 *The Lexical Syllabus* (Collins COBUILD)

Willis, J. 1996 *Task-based Language Learning* (Longman)

16 Curriculum innovation, teamwork and the management of change

Blake, R., Mounton, S. and Allan 1987 *Spectacular Teamwork* (John Wiley & Sons, New York)

Blake, R. and Mounton, S. 1985 *The Managerial Grid II* (Houston Gulf)

Council of Europe 1991 *The Threshold Level* (Council of Europe, Strasbourg)

Johnson, R. K. 1989 *The Second Language Curriculum* (CUP)

Long, M. H. and Crookes, G. 1991 Three approaches to task-based syllabus design. In *University of Hawaii Working Papers in ESL, vol. 10, no. 1, pp 1-36*

Nunan, D. 1992 *Collaborative Language Learning and Teaching* (CUP)

Nunan, D. 1988a *Syllabus Design* (OUP)

Nunan, D. 1988b *The Learner-Centred Curriculum* (CUP)

Willing, K. 1988 *Learning Styles in Adult Migrant Education* (NCELTR)

Abbreviations

CUP: Cambridge University Press
LTP: Language Teaching Publications
MEP: Modern English Publications
OUP: Oxford University Press
UCLES: University of Cambridge Local Examinations Syndicate

Index